More praise for

SuccessAbilities!

1,003 Practical Ways to Keep Up, Stand Out, and Move Ahead at Work

"Paula Ancona knows that busy working people want precise answers to their job and career problems, without sifting through a lot of mumbo jumbo. *SuccessAbilities!* will help them zero in on relevant topics they're interested in today, but also address issues they'll face tomorrow. It's easy to scan the well-organized lists of solutions to find the ones that work for you. This is the kind of helpful book I'll keep handy for years to come."

— Chris Kuselias, Author
The Career Coach audiocassette program

"Paula Ancona's *SuccessAbilities!* is an extremely well-researched guide for any working person who needs practical information. And there are hundreds of useful resources listed to help readers find extra assistance."

— D. Larry Moore, President
Honeywell, Inc.

"Paula Ancona has nailed the critical, relevant concerns of today's working people. Her book stands out because it is written for a wide range of work styles, rather than assuming we should conform to one. It's fun just to flip at random and find something to read about and improve on. The extra resources at the end of each topic are fantastic. Many I have heard of but didn't know how to find. Now I know."

— Ann McGee Cooper, Author
Time Management for Unmanageable People
and *You Don't Have to Go Home From Work Exhausted*

"I was impressed with the numerous ideas and solutions employees, business owners and managers can utilize. Anyone interested in advancing or changing their career will use *SuccessAbilities!* as a resource. It is a useful guide for the crossroads in their careers."

— Laurel Caprio, President, Laurel Personnel
and VP, Connecticut Association of Personnel Services

"SuccessAbilities! is a thought-provoking, well-researched compendium of valuable information on careers, communication, work and self-improvement. It is easy but powerful reading in the tradition of Tom Peters' *Thriving on Chaos.* Current resources and cross-referencing to other sections make the book especially useful.

— Doug Benton, Professor of Management
Colorado State University

"Ms. Ancona strikes the call for action right up front with her statement that 'It's up to you to do good work and build your career.' Then, chapter by chapter, in clear, concise language and with good sense, she proceeds to point the way on exactly how to do that. *SuccessAbilities!* is a good guide for success as America goes to a more self-motivated and self-directed workforce concept."

— Jack Miller, President
Quill Corp.

"Paula Ancona's book is thoroughly useful. I recommend it to anyone interested in career advancement."

— Debra Benton, Author
Lions Don't Need To Roar

"*SuccessAbilities!* is necessary reading and a terrific reference guide for every business professional."

— Elizabeth L. Craig, Author
Don't Slurp Your Soup: A Basic Guide to Business Etiquette

"This book is a great tool for helping individuals achieve career success. For those who are seeking a career, not just a job, I highly recommend reading this book!"

— Tee Houston-Aldridge, V.P., U.S. Marketing
Priority Management Systems, Inc.

SuccessAbilities!™

1,003 Practical Ways to Keep Up, Stand Out, and Move Ahead at Work

By Paula Ancona

SuccessAbilities!™
1,003 Practical Ways to Keep Up, Stand Out, and Move Ahead at Work
©1998 by Paula Ancona

Published by JIST Works, Inc.
720 N. Park Avenue
Indianapolis, IN 46202-3490
Phone: 317-264-3720 Fax: 317-264-3709 E-mail: jistworks@aol.com
World Wide Web Address: http://www.jist.com
Revised edition — previously published by Chamisa Press.

See the back of this book for additional JIST titles and ordering information.

Interior Design by Michael Hudson, Ltd.
Interior Layout by Debbie Berman
Cover Design by Honeymoon Image & Design, Inc.

Printed in the United States of America

02 01 00 99 98 97   9 8 7 6 5 4 3 2 1

Library of Congress Cataloging-in-Publication Data
Ancona, Paula.
    SuccessAbilities! : 1,003 practical ways to keep up, stand out,
and move ahead at work / by Paula Ancona.
        p.   cm.
    Previously publised: Minneapolis, MN : Chamisa Press. c 1995.
    Includes bibliographical references and index.
    ISBN 1-56370-444-7
    1. Vocational guidance. 2. Career development. I. Title.
    HF5381.A773 1997
    650. 1--dc21   97-36833
                                                CIP

We have been careful to provide accurate information throughout this book, but it is possible that errors and omissions have been introduced. Please consider this in making any career plans or other important decisions. Trust your own judgment above all else and in all things.
ISBN 1-56370-444-7

This book is dedicated to my husband, Don, whose love, support, and honest feedback never waiver.

— PMA

Contents

Section I: Working Smart

Chapter 1: Productivity

Chapter 2: Relationships

Chapter 3: Technology

Chapter 4: Conflicts at Work

Section II: Communication Skills

Chapter 5: Clear Messages

Chapter 6: Speaking

Chapter 7: Writing

Chapter 8: Communicating with a Purpose

Section III: Self-Improvement

Chapter 9: Sharp Thinking

Chapter 10: Coping with Work

Chapter 11: Family Issues

Chapter 12: Details

Section IV: Career Moves

Chapter 13: The Job Search

Chapter 14: Career Reinforcement

Acknowledgments

Hundreds of people helped write *SuccessAbilities! 1,003 Practical Ways to Keep Up, Stand Out, and Move Ahead at Work.* Without their advice, ideas, inspiration, and encouragement I could not have completed this book.

Thanks to the dozens of experts in career development, management, organizational development, psychology, law, and other fields who generously shared their valuable knowledge and insights with me. Those people and their books and articles are credited in the **Notes** and **Bibliography** sections. Many of the experts' books and products also are listed in the **Resources** listings at the end of each topic.

Thanks to the many working people who have written me and talked with me, helping me understand the problems they face.

Thanks to *The Albuquerque Tribune* and Scripps Howard News Service for their support for my "Working Smarter" newspaper column. The hundreds of columns I've written provided the framework for this book.

Others who deserve to be mentioned by name are Pat Bell, Laurel Caprio, Elizabeth Craig, Joanne Frank, Joan Guiducci, Michael Hudson, Barb Page, Steve Pikala, and Robert Riskin. Also, many thanks to the Midwest Independent Publishers Association for its resources and guidance.

And thanks to my family, who consistently supported me throughout this project, gave me their feedback, and put up with my depleted energy stores and fractured attention spans.

— PMA

How to Use This Book

This book is designed to be one of the easiest workplace advice books you can use.

It's a quick reference for busy people who need practical information and solutions now. But if you do want more details on a subject, this book will tell you where to find them.

SuccessAbilities! is divided into four sections:

■ **Section I: Working Smart** contains ideas for being more efficient and effective on the job.

■ **Section II: Communication Skills** has hundreds of tips to help you get your messages across better.

■ **Section III: Self-Improvement** shows you how to sharpen personal skills and handle other facets of your life that overlap with your work.

■ **Section IV: Career Moves** is about getting and keeping good jobs and charting your own career paths.

You can find help with specific workplace or career situations by scanning the **Contents** or **Index** or simply by flipping through any of the four sections.

After the tips you'll see a list of **Resources**. These books, materials, and organizations can provide more information. Many of them provided information used in that segment. You'll even find ordering information for items you may not find easily in stores.

Next is the **See Also** section. It guides you to related topics throughout the book.

Also check out the **Notes** and **Bibliography** segments. In **Notes** you'll find the experts, articles, and other resources that helped shape the tips for each topic. You may wish to contact or obtain some of those resources for further assistance.

— PMA

Introduction

Work is a huge part of our lives. Many of us spend at least 50 percent of our waking hours at our jobs. What we do at work and how we do it affect us in countless ways.

And so it is smart self-management to develop and nurture what I call *SuccessAbilities.*

SuccessAbilities are essential skills that will help working people thrive in the 1990s and beyond. They're the kind of practical approaches successful people use to solve problems, set direction, and stay ahead of work and career challenges.

One way to develop those essential skills is to use this book, *SuccessAbilities! 1,003 Practical Ways to Keep Up, Stand Out, and Move Ahead at Work.* It's a treasury of easy-to-use suggestions culled from a wide variety of expertise and experience. Flip through the chapters; read up on issues affecting your job and career; pick and choose the ideas that make sense for you.

Some of the tips here may seem deceptively simple—but worthwhile lessons often are. We even may have to relearn them several times before they become standard tools in our work kits. *SuccessAbilities!* will help you begin to turn these practical ideas into new skills.

You'll detect several recurring philosophies about people, work, and success throughout this book. They outline a positive, self-directed view of work and its role in our lives. The principles apply to all kinds of people: young and experienced, technicians and generalists, clerical workers and managers, and blue-collar and white-collar workers.

The principles are these:

Take responsibility for doing good work and building your career. It's not your boss' responsibility, nor your coworkers', nor your company's. It's part of your job, and you have the power to do it. You have access to internal strengths and external resources that can help you get what you want and need out of your job.

Don't settle for being miserable at work. It's not worth it. In almost every case, there are reasonable changes you can make to improve your job–or at least change your attitude about it. They're worth doing.

If you see something that's not working right, do something about it. You'll earn respect from others and yourself if you can redirect your energy from constant complaining to positive action steps.

Remember, it's only a job. Don't give it supreme power over you. Yes, what happens there is important and may have significant effects on your life. But don't take it too seriously too often. Use the ultimate worst-case scenario test on your work-related problems: Will this kill you?

Work smarter. That means think, think, think. Analyze, plan, shift, anticipate, prepare, focus. Working harder is not always the key to success.

Expect that you will have several jobs and careers in your lifetime. Prepare for them. Various experts say that most Americans will have three to eight careers in their lifetime. Look at your career and life as a series of stages, each with its own special focus and goals. Don't try to do and be everything at once.

Create your own definition of success. Steer your work and career in the direction that fulfills you most and serves your needs best. Success doesn't have to be rooted in money and status. It can include flexibility, independence, being respected, doing meaningful and purposeful work, and affecting others in positive ways. And success can have different meanings at different times of your life.

Give it time. Changing your skills, job, attitude, or workplace takes time and patience. Don't expect immediate results every time. Stick to your plan and watch the improvements blossom.

Learn constantly. It's the only way to be effective in your job and successful at your career. And you can do it in many ways. Learn from the millions of publications, workshops, videos, television programs, professional groups, and experienced people within your reach. Use your public library and its knowledgeable staff frequently. Learn from your mistakes. Expose yourself to new ideas that can make big differences in your life.

Always set goals for yourself. Visualize where you want to be in your life and career in one year, three years, five years. Without goals your life will just happen to you. You can define your future, starting today. And you can make progress by taking small steps. Your goals don't have to be grandiose, but they do have to be specific.

Enjoy your journey to greater success at work! Good luck!

—PMA

To laugh often and much;

to win the respect of intelligent people and affection of children;

to earn the appreciation of honest critics and endure the betrayal
of false friends;

to appreciate beauty, to find the best in others;

to leave the world a bit better, whether by a healthy child,
a garden patch or a redeemed social condition;

to know even one life has breathed easier because you have lived.

This is to have succeeded.

— Ralph Waldo Emerson

SECTION I

Working Smart

CHAPTER

1

Chapter 1

Productivity

Finding More Time in Your Day

Despite the many "time-saving" devices available, many of us still are hunting for spare minutes to get our work done. Our employers are giving us more duties and responsibilities but no extra time or resources to do them. Our calendars are jammed with meetings, appointments, and long to-do lists.

There always will be only 1,440 minutes in a day. But we can make them count more by being more effective and efficient in our jobs.

- Be honest about your time. Tell visitors that you can't meet with them right now but could at a specific time later. Tell people on the phone that you only have a few minutes to complete this call. Don't promise more than you know you can complete in the time allotted.

- List what you need to cover during your phone conversations before you make the calls.

- Try to conclude almost every phone call in five minutes or less, no matter to whom you're talking.

- If you use an answering machine, don't promise on your recording that you'll return every call.

- Find a single daily planning system that works for you. You might use a simple yellow legal pad on which you write daily lists of tasks to do, jobs to delegate, and people to call—all on one page. Check out various calendar planning systems available in office supply stores catalogs or those advertised in business magazines; or look at compact electronic organizers that keep schedules and maintain phone numbers and addresses.

- Don't keep multiple lists or schedules in different places.

- Build in success as you tackle your prioritized to-do list. Start with one or two easy—but important—tasks you know you can complete. Enjoy your achievement and the boost it gives you.

- Drop low-priority tasks from your list; you'll probably never get to them anyway.

- Develop a system to help you keep track of communication—who called or wrote, asking for what, by when, how you responded, and what happens next. You might use a large desk or wall calendar, Post-It notes, notes on your phone message slips, your daily planner notebook, project scorecards on which you can keep track of developments, or an electronic organizer or contact management software. Keep your system readily accessible and updated.

- As you go through your mail and in-basket, decide immediately whether to deal with an item now, throw it away, delegate it, add it to your to-do list, or put it in a holding file for another day.

- Take reenergizing mini-breaks during your day. Read a cartoon book, enjoy a brief conversation, soak up some different scenery, or have a snack.

- Organize your desk and files logically and consistently so you won't waste time searching for misplaced materials.

- Keep your desk clear except for materials you need for the project you're working on now. Put other files and items like photos, purses, books, and mementos on a shelf or credenza, or in a drawer.

- Don't work too hard at trying to be neat if it goes against your nature. Your system, messy as it is, may be OK if you can find what you need in a couple of minutes and regularly accomplish your high-priority goals.

- If you hate being organized make it easier on yourself by using nonstandard office supplies (fun calendars, bright folders, decorative labels, clear or fancy storage boxes, unusual cabinets).

Resources
➡ *What They Still Don't Teach You at Harvard Business School* (audiotape), Mark McCormack, Bantam Audio Publishing, 1989.
➡ *The Organized Executive*, Stephanie Winston, W.W. Norton, 1994.
➡ *Ready, Set, Organize!* Pipi Campbell Peterson, Park Avenue Productions, 1996.
➡ *Time Management for Unmanageable People*, Ann McGee-Cooper, Bantam, 1994.
➡ *Office on the Go: Tools, Tips, and Techniques for Every Business Traveler*, Kim Baker and Sunny Baker, Prentice Hall, 1993.

See Also
⇨ **Improving Your Filing System,** *page 10.*
⇨ **Controlling Paperwork,** *page 12.*
⇨ **Boosting Efficiency with Your Calendar,** *page 16.*
⇨ **Making Better Decisions,** *page 122.*

Improving Your Filing System

Filing is not a popular job. You may regularly put it off or do it haphazardly just to get it out of the way. Then you curse your filing system because you can't find what you need; or your coworkers and supervisors become upset because they can't find what they need.

Keeping orderly files requires a little planning and time. But it yields big benefits.

- Before you file anything ask yourself: Do I really need it? Will I ever use it? When? (If you can't answer that, toss it.) Is this information available elsewhere (in a computer file, on microfiche, in a company or public library)? Is the information current? (If it's out-of-date, get rid of it.) What would I be unable to do if I get rid of this?

- If your files are a mess, resolve to devote five to 15 minutes a day gradually straightening them out. Don't plan to spend an entire afternoon or day doing it. After a couple hours it will become unbearable.

- Don't save meeting notes unless you were in charge of the meeting; you need to take action as a result of the meeting; you will need to answer questions about the meeting later; or you were assigned to record minutes.

- Don't save information sent to you "For Your Information." Read it, become informed, and discard it.

- Get rid of internal memoranda announcing an event or action after the event has taken place.

- Don't save copies of documents if you have the original, unless you expect to receive several requests for copies in the near future.

- Don't save early drafts of contracts, agreements, and other legal documents once the final version has been signed. Preliminary versions can cause trouble in court.

- Use a simple, color-coding system to help you find and file items more readily. Designate certain colors to mark categories such as high priority, frequently used, internal office matters, or future business ideas. Use colored folders, colored sticker dots, or colored file labels, all available at office supply stores. Post your color key on your file cabinet.

- Set aside a few minutes at the end of each working day for filing.

- To prevent lost files ask others who routinely use your files to sign a simple log sheet to note which file was taken, by whom, and when. Post a borrowing time limit.

■ Make refiling easier with out-guides (large pieces of colored paper or card stock that you slide into the place where a file had been). File users even could use the out-guide as a log by writing the name of the file, their name, and the date on the guide.

■ Create lots of subdivision files under major headings so you can find information quickly.

■ Allow three to four inches of working space in your file drawers. If a folder becomes crammed with more than 3/4-inch of material, subdivide it or clean it out.

Resources
➡ *How to File and Find It,* booklet from Quill Corp., 100 Schelter Rd., Lincolnshire, IL 60069-3621, 847-634-4850. Web address: http://www. quillcorp.com, $2.95.

See Also
⇨ **Finding More Time in Your Day,** *page 8.*
⇨ **Controlling Paperwork,** *page 12.*

Bonus Tip!

Review and clean out file folders each time you use them.

Controlling Paperwork

Almost two trillion pieces of paper are generated in American offices annually, according to BIS Strategic, a Massachusetts research company. One survey of 200 top U.S. executives found that they waste about six weeks a year trying to find misfiled, misplaced, or mislabeled paperwork.

How many of those trillion pieces of paper lurk on, in, or under your desk? How much time do you waste shuffling and sifting through them? What would someone conclude about your competence if they saw your disorganized heap?

- Immediately sort incoming paper into files labeled To Do, To Pay, To Read, To File, and To Pass On.

- Get rid of junk drawers and pending files. They keep you from handling paperwork decisively the first time.

- Handle simple matters with a phone call or discussion instead of a memorandum, especially if the tone of your voice could be an important part of your message.

- Don't routinely distribute reports, data, or memoranda unless you know others need or want them.

- Write comments to others right on the documents they send you instead of composing a memorandum on another sheet of paper. Eliminate routine cover letters that contain no new information or state the obvious. Post notices instead of distributing copies to everyone.

- Don't respond to paperwork rashly; instructions might change. Make sure your client's or supervisor's wishes are solid and clear before you act. Don't read material for an upcoming event too early. You'll have to reread it later.

- Don't assume that all paperwork deserves your time. Scan it first to see if you need it or if someone else is controlling your time by asking for your involvement. Get off unnecessary distribution lists. Send unnecessary material back with a polite note. ("Thanks, but I don't need to receive this.")

- Make notes on business cards about where you met the person and why you need to know that person. File by event or future need.

- Automate. Develop model letters or word-processor templates for specific purposes and keep copies readily accessible. Use short, preprinted forms, rubber stamps, or preprinted postcards for standard correspondence ("Your expense report is incomplete"). Put sections marked "Approval/Comments" on memoranda and reports so recipients can mark OKs or concerns right on the document instead of generating more paper.

■ Reward yourself for good paper management. Put a quarter or dollar in a box every time you deal with a piece of paper promptly. At the end of the week use the money to buy yourself a treat.

■ Organize small notes and papers with a compact bulletin board or message center for your work area. Look in computer supply stores and catalogs for compact boards or file pockets that attach to the sides of your monitor.

Resources
➡ *Clean Up Your Act: Effective Ways to Organize Paperwork and Get It Out of Your Life*, Dianna Booher, Warner, 1992.
➡ *How to File and Find It*, booklet from Quill Corp., 100 Schelter Rd., Lincolnshire, IL 60069-3621, 847-634-4850. Web address: http:// www. quillcorp.com, $2.95.

See Also
⇨ **Improving Your Filing System**, *page 10.*
⇨ **Managing Your Reading Material**, *page 14.*
⇨ **Boosting Efficiency with Your Calendar**, *page 16.*

Bonus Tip!

Write meeting notes on your copy of the agenda instead of using more paper.

Managing Your Reading Material

Reading can be a source of pleasure and pain. You might love to read for fun and relaxation and you also may be haunted by a persistent pile of ponderous, must-read reports, articles and books related to your work.

A few simple changes can make big improvements in your ability to read more quickly and efficiently.

- Don't look at reading as goofing off. Reading helps you keep current in your field and you get ideas for doing your job better. If your reading doesn't do that you must be reading unnecessary material.

- Prioritize your reading. Priority A is urgent and important. B is important, but not urgent. C is neither important nor urgent. Throw Cs away; you'll never get to them anyway.

- Read with a purpose. Know what information you need to meet your goals before you start.

- Preview material so you don't waste time reading unnecessary information. For newspaper and magazine articles read headlines, the first and last paragraphs, and material that is bold or italicized. Look for words, phrases, names, dates, and graphics that tell you if the material meets your needs. With a book, scan the jacket cover, table of contents, introduction, conclusion, index, and glossary. If pressed for time, read just those parts.

- Don't skip tables, charts, maps, illustrations, or photos. They're packed with important, condensed information.

- Don't be a passive reader. Strip away clutter and try to uncover the author's main points or outline. Ask questions as you read. Search for sections that explain the topic or state the main problem and solution. Look for the topic sentence—usually the first couple of lines in a paragraph. Try to uncover the who, what, when, where, why, and how.

- Improve comprehension by mapping the text. Draw a picture of the main idea. Then use other pictures, arrows, lines, or other symbols that help you relate other concepts in the article to the main concept. Jot down brief questions you have, and then write the answers as you discover them. Note ways you could use the information.

- If you must know everything in an article or book, read it as if you are editing it. Review it for organization, simplicity, and word choice.

- Use different senses as you read. Form a picture in your mind. Imagine smells, tastes, or textures. These can help you comprehend and retain information better.

- Move your fingers along the lines of text as you read to increase your speed. Use your left hand to follow the words, your right hand to turn pages.

- Don't slow yourself by mouthing the words as you read. Don't use your inner voice to repeat the words, either; use it to form short, meaningful phrases that condense information and make it easier to recall.

- Devote one or two lunch hours a week to reading. Minimize distractions by sitting somewhere other than at your desk; or keep up by vowing to read one piece of reading material every day.

- Consider a speed-reading course. But realize that you're unlikely to keep up that rapid pace unless you use the speed technique for all your reading—business and pleasure.

Resources

➡ *The PhotoReading Whole Mind System*, Paul Scheele, Learning Strategies Corp., Wayzata, MN, 1997, 800-735-8273, $14.95 + shipping and handling. Web address http://www.learningstrategies.com or Web address http://www.photoreading.com.

➡ *Super Reading Secrets*, Howard Stephen Berg, Warner, 1992.

See Also

➩ **Finding More Time in Your Day**, *page 8.*

➩ **Controlling Paperwork**, *page 12.*

➩ **Boosting Efficiency with Your Calendar**, *page 16.*

Bonus Tip!

Have a separate folder or table just for reading material.

Boosting Efficiency with Your Calendar

In its simplest form a calendar helps you keep track of your days. With a little embellishment your calendar can do more. It can help you pace your work, meet deadlines, eliminate excess paper, and get more accomplished than if you just stumbled through the day without a plan.

Just a few simple changes can produce big results, even if you hate lists and other standard organization techniques.

■ Don't assume that you must buy a fancy, expensive calendar system. Depending on how many activities you juggle, a simple daily planner from a discount store may be fine. Choose a calendar that will cover both your personal and professional needs so you don't have to maintain two calendars. Make sure you can carry it around easily.

■ Write daily goals on your calendar. Know what you want to accomplish by the end of the day so you can determine how to spend your time. Otherwise you'll do whatever comes up first instead of what's most important.

■ If you tend to be spontaneous and less organized, make maintaining a calendar easier by using one that is funny, colorful, inspiring, or roomy enough for doodling or colorful stickers. Use brightly colored pens and novelty notepads.

■ Reward yourself when you follow your calendar system, save time, or complete a goal.

■ If you hate conformity, invent your own customized calendar. Copy the blanks and keep them in a binder; or keep a simple action list in your computer. Update and print it daily; or make your to-do list and schedule for the day by writing tasks on small Post-It notes. Arrange the notes in categories on a clear, legal-sized, self-standing clipboard at your work area, as leadership development coach Ann McGee-Cooper recommends (see **Resources** below). She rearranges the notes and her schedule as priorities change.

■ When you mark appointments on your calendar, also note what you need to accomplish at that event. Remember to mark off travel time before and after the appointment.

■ When you set up your next meeting or deadline, record it immediately in your calendar. Make calendar notes one and two weeks before a big deadline to help you set and meet intermediate goals.

- Use Post-It notes to create extra space on a crowded calendar page.

- Include these mini-lists on your calendar: action steps for goals (break your big goals into smaller pieces); imperative (urgent, deadline matters that you cannot put off); and important (items that you can put off but are high priority). Anything else probably doesn't deserve your time.

- Before you go home for the day, review your lists to see what you accomplished. Then spend five to 10 minutes planning your next work day. This can reduce your worries about work while you're off duty, and position you for a quick start the next day.

- Have your calendar handy when you open your mail. When you receive a meeting notice, jot down the date in your calendar along with details about costs, location, and reservations. Discard the notice; or cut out the important part of the notice and clip it to the appropriate page in your calendar.

- Use index cards to create a running log for big goals. Record what has been accomplished, the date, and what's next. Keep the cards in a pocket in your calendar notebook.

Resources
➡ *Ready, Set, Organize!* Pipi Campbell Peterson, Park Avenue Productions, 1996.
➡ *Time Management for Unmanageable People*, Ann McGee-Cooper, Bantam, 1994.

See Also
➪ **Finding More Time in Your Day**, *page 8.*
➪ **Improving Your Filing System**, *page 10.*
➪ **Controlling Paperwork**, *page 12.*
➪ **Setting Goals**, *page 116.*

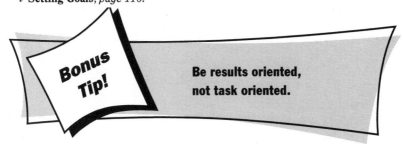

Bonus Tip!

Be results oriented, not task oriented.

Getting More Out of Meetings

Meetings take up many hours of work time, whether you're an employee, manager, or executive. Add the time spent preparing for and following up on meetings, and you've got a sizable chunk of time and energy.

Although they might be frustrating, meetings are important platforms for launching careers, solving problems, and building successful organizations.

- Know what you want to get out of every meeting you attend.

- Use meetings as tools to demonstrate your self-respect, organization, confidence, and competence. Know that others use them to judge your skills.

- If you're invited to a meeting, ask for an agenda ahead of time. You'll be sending the message that you don't want to waste your time in a meandering meeting.

- Schedule meetings at unusual starting times (9:12 a.m. or 1:39 p.m.) to encourage participants' prompt arrival.

- Set some meetings right before lunch or quitting time to discourage long, drawn-out discussions. People more likely will be prompt, focused, and decisive because they'll want to leave soon.

- Ask yourself: Will this meeting help me achieve my main goals? What would happen if I didn't attend (or hold) it?

- Take responsibility for helping to make the meeting a success. Prepare ahead of time, participate in the discussion, provide complete information, share the workload, and avoid disruptive behavior.

- Avoid flare-ups by asking, "how would you do that?" instead of "why do you think that?" Why puts people on the defensive. How helps them focus on action.

- To look good in a meeting—even if you don't have much to contribute—ask questions. It's safe participation.

- If you expect opposition at a meeting, line up support for your ideas ahead of time. Anticipate your opponent's arguments and plan stronger counter arguments. Have your facts ready and available to share.

- Don't offer a proposal in a meeting without answering these questions: How much will it cost? Why should we do it? What is the goal?

- If you disagree with someone's idea, listen carefully for one aspect that you like and on which you can build. Then say "I liked the part about setting deadlines. What if we started there and …" Other keys for disagreeing effectively: be respectful; listen first; ask questions to clarify; be specific and constructive; don't be judgmental; and offer alternatives.

- If humor is welcome in your workplace, try a goofy game like "Drag in the Word" once in a while. Gather before the meeting with other participants and give each other unlikely words to use during the meeting (elephant, asparagus, laundry). See who can work in their weird words first.

Resources

➡ *How to Talk So People Listen: The Real Key to Business Success*, Sonya Hamlin, HarperCollins, 1989.

➡ *The Strategy of Meetings*, George Kieffer, Simon & Schuster, 1988.

➡ *Manage Your Time, Your Work, Yourself*, Merrill Douglass and Donna Douglass, AMACOM, 1993.

➡ *We've Got to Start Meeting Like This!*, Roger K. Mosvik and Robert B. Nelson, Park Avenue Productions, 1996.

See Also

⇨ **Communicating for Success**, *page 66.*
⇨ **Listen Up**, *page 70.*
⇨ **Tuning Up Informal Speech**, *page 76.*
⇨ **Giving Clear Instructions**, *page 100.*

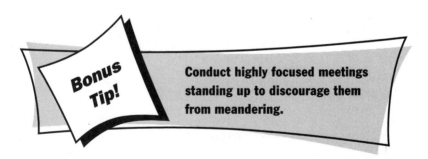

Bonus Tip!

Conduct highly focused meetings standing up to discourage them from meandering.

Cubicle Survival Tips

One of the realities of working in modern workplaces is that many employees no longer have doors to their offices. In fact, they may not even have offices. They have cubicles—small work areas without doors or walls that may or may not reach the ceiling.

Working in a cubicle presents big challenges when you want to keep interruptions down and productivity up.

- If possible, move your desk so your back faces the entrance to your cubicle. You'll be distracted less often.

- Establish visiting hours for your cube—times when it's OK for people to stop in with comments or questions. Post them at the entrance.

- Use signs that announce whether people can come in now or if they should come back later. There even are ready-made cubicle signs available (see **Resources** below); or string a small chain across the entrance to your cube to signal that your "door" is closed. Hang a sign on the chain to say when you'll be available.

- Don't just barge into other's doorless cubicles. Wait at the entrance and ask if you may come in.

- Be assertive when people drop in. Don't let them draw you into a conversation that you don't have time for. Stand up and say something like, "I'd love to talk to you about this but I'm in the middle of this project. Can I come talk with you at about 4:30?"

- Make calls, complete reports, or do other work that requires uninterrupted concentration during lunch hour when colleagues are out; come in earlier; or stay later to take advantage of the quiet time.

- Ask your supervisor if you could take your work home or to a public library for an afternoon so you could concentrate better.

- Find out if your building has a conference room with real doors. Ask if you could reserve it occasionally for special meetings or projects.

- If conversations and noise from outside your cube bothers you, try wearing earplugs, a Walkman, or other headphones that could help you block out noise—if your supervisor permits.

- Be considerate about decorating your cube. Personalize it but don't include photos or posters that might offend coworkers, customers, or visitors.

- Create a warmer atmosphere with plants, a small accent lamp that softens harsh office light, and a small radio you keep tuned to a mellow station—if your company permits.

- Keep your cubicle clear and free of distractions. Piles of clutter can become big problems in small cubicles.

- Use your walls or bulletin board to enhance your professional image. Display framed articles or diagrams of your successful projects. Post charts and graphs that show your accomplishments. Show off awards, certificates from training courses, and letters of appreciation from customers, colleagues, or supervisors.

Resources
➡ CubicleCues, four 5x8 signs that help you announce whether you're available, from CubicleCues, 343-E Asbury Commons, Dunwoody, GA 30338, 800-322-7724, $5.95 + shipping and handling.

See Also
⇨ **Finding More Time in Your Day,** *page 8.*
⇨ **Controlling Paperwork,** *page 12.*
⇨ **Working with Difficult People,** *page 30.*

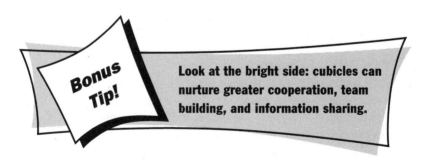

Bonus Tip!

Look at the bright side: cubicles can nurture greater cooperation, team building, and information sharing.

Working at Home Successfully

Phenomenal advances in computers, fax machines, telephone communications, and other technologies have nurtured the growth of telecommuting, which allows employees to work from their homes or satellite offices.

It's a good option for people who want more flexibility and independence and less commuting. Working at home, however, requires special techniques to maximize productivity.

- Get your supervisor's support before you try telecommuting. Even if your company favors home work, you won't get far if your immediate boss opposes it.

- Make sure your job is well-suited for telecommuting. You should produce results that are easily measured, require little unscheduled face-to-face contact with supervisors, and not require frequent access to resources in the main office.

- Evaluate whether you have the right personality for working at home. Are you self-motivated and trustworthy? Can you set deadlines for yourself and stick to them? Do you mind isolation? Can you visualize a project from beginning to end? Can you juggle many different work roles?

- Set aside a place exclusively for home work. Avoid using a room with another primary purpose, such as a bedroom or family room. Working in those areas makes it tough to draw the line between work and personal time.

- Choose chairs, keyboard surfaces, computer monitors, and writing surfaces that are appropriate for your work. Don't expect to be comfortable or efficient using a laptop computer on your kitchen table.

- Explicitly define your work arrangement for your family and others. Establish rules about where and when you'll work and when you'll be unavailable to family, friends, and neighbors. Let clients, colleagues, and supervisors know when you're available to them.

- Don't expect telecommuting to eliminate your need for child care unless your job requires very little concentration or solitude.

- Set up a buffer period between your personal time at home and your working time. This would replace the thinking or relaxing time you might have had while commuting. Read a newspaper or trade publication, take a brief walk, or call a coworker to catch up on office news.

- Sharpen your communication skills; they become even more important because you're not in the same office as coworkers and supervisors.

- Don't become a hermit. Use the phone, fax, or electronic mail to cover the day's progress and problems with your supervisor. Set up a buddy system by asking a colleague to regularly tell you about news at work. Make sure you receive company newsletters and memos. Maintain a mailbox in the main office.

- Watch that you're not being exploited in terms of hours, assignments, or wages. This is another good reason to keep in touch with the office.

- Make sure that influential people recognize the work you've done and the obstacles you overcame to complete it.

- Look for social or professional opportunities to meet with supervisors and other "higher-ups" you would normally see around the office.

Resources

- *Best Jobs in America for Parents Who Want Careers and Time for Children, Too*, Susan Dynerman and Lynn Hayes, Ballantine, 1991.
- *Home but Not Alone: The Parents' Work-at-Home Handbook,* Katherine Murray, Park Avenue Productions, 1997.
- *Telecommute! Go to Work Without Leaving Home,* Lisa Shaw, John Wiley & Sons, 1996.
- Mothers' Home Business Network, P.O. Box 423, East Meadow, NY 11554, 516-997-7394. Membership: $19.95–$59.95.
- *How to Raise a Family and a Career Under One Roof,* Lisa M. Roberts, Bookhaven Press, 1997.
- *Telecommuting: How to Make It Work for You and Your Company*, Gil Gordon and Marcia Kelly, Prentice Hall, 1986.
- *Working From Home*, Paul Edwards and Sarah Edwards, Putnam, 1993.
- *The Work-at-Home Sourcebook*, Lynie Arden, Live Oak, 1992.
- *Women and Home-Based Work*, Kathleen Christensen, Henry Holt & Co., 1988.

See Also

⇨ **Shifting to Part-Time Work**, *page 224.*
⇨ **Arranging Your Parental Leave**, *page 244.*
⇨ **Negotiating for What You Want**, *page 98.*

CHAPTER

2

Chapter 2

Relationships

2-1 Making Your Boss Your Partner

2-2 Understanding Your Bothersome Boss

2-3 Working with Difficult People

2-4 Communicating with the Opposite Sex

2-5 Handling Customer Problems

Making Your Boss Your Partner

Bosses are the folks many people love to hate. Whether you think your boss is a saint or a villain, establishing a good working relationship is crucial to your success and job satisfaction. And it's just as much your responsibility as it is your boss' responsibility.

You know you need to work on your relationship with your boss if that relationship keeps you from reaching your work or personal goals.

- Try to understand your conflicts with your boss by looking at where you differ in values, roles, backgrounds, goals, and styles. The problem may be that you approach work differently, not that your boss is a bad person.

- Explore each other's expectations about your job. Ask your boss to write down the overall purposes and key elements of your job. You do the same. Talk about your lists and how they differ.

- Don't expect your boss to change until you're willing to change too. Try to pinpoint certain areas that always cause tension. How could you approach those situations differently to avoid a conflict?

- Praise your boss when you get the kind of supervision you want. You'll be more likely to get that kind of treatment again.

- Don't complain about your boss to higher-level supervisors unless you've tried to work out your problems directly with your boss. Also make sure you've got a good relationship with your boss' supervisor and that you will appear objective, helpful, and concerned about the organization as a whole.

- Politely tell your boss about behaviors that prevent you from doing your job well. Yes, this works best if you have a boss who is caring, willing to accept criticism, and wants to improve. But even if you're not so lucky, voicing your concerns may bring about eventual improvement.

- If you do talk to your boss about your working relationship, protect your boss' ego. Don't come off as threatening by appearing to want your boss' job. Don't be accusatory or judgmental; speak in terms of "I feel …" instead of "You did …" Negotiate. And don't get upset if your first attempt to bring about change fails.

- Make it easy for your boss to give you negative feedback. Show that you welcome it by reacting objectively and professionally.

- Don't waste your boss' time with petty details. Only bring up items that need your boss' approval or input, directly affect your boss' job, or could help your boss make future decisions.

- Help your boss out sometimes. You're more likely to get support if your boss knows you're there in a crunch.

- Don't expect your boss to be infallible.

- Observe which actions, projects, or situations please your boss. Does your boss prefer casual or formal meetings? Daily progress reports or monthly updates? Do more of what pleases your boss and less of what doesn't. You might have to grit your teeth sometimes, but you'll probably have a better working relationship and less stress.

- Get to know your boss better. Ask general questions about life away from the job. Ask open-ended questions that could draw out opinions on business, management, and other issues. This builds your relationship and helps you understand your boss better.

- If you want your boss to give you more responsibility and important work, look for opportunities to demonstrate your sharp skills. Ask to do some of your boss' work. Demonstrate that you can work well on your own and save your boss time too.

- Don't suffer if you just can't make this relationship work. Look for a transfer or a new job. It's acceptable and common to change jobs because of personality or style differences.

Resources
➡ *How to Fire Your Boss*, Chris Malburg, Berkley, 1991.
➡ *Job Savvy: How to Be a Success at Work,* LaVerne L. Ludden, JIST Works, Inc., 1998.
➡ *1,000 Things You Never Learned in Business School: How to Get Ahead of the Pack and Stay There*, William Yeomans, Signet, 1985.

See Also
➪ **Understanding Your Bothersome Boss**, *page 28.*
➪ **Communicating for Success**, *page 66.*
➪ **Negotiating for What You Want**, *page 98.*

2-2 Understanding Your Bothersome Boss

Figuring out how to work with a difficult boss is puzzling and maddening. But it's imperative when you hope to be effective and successful—unless you're willing to leave your job.

One tactic is to learn what makes your boss tick. Then you can change your approach so you can be more effective. Another, longer lasting solution is to get and maintain control of your own job. Become less dependent on your boss and demonstrate that your boss' overbearing ways are unnecessary.

- **A bullying, angry, or sarcastic boss:** Firmly show what kind of treatment you will accept. Don't let the boss use you to vent anger. Say that you can see your boss is upset and you would like to continue the discussion later. Don't show agitation or fear. Consider honestly and calmly telling your boss how difficult it is to work when an explosion could occur at any time. Try to spot and solve problems before they become severe.

- **A vague boss or a procrastinator:** Ask for clarifications often and settle only for specifics. Help your boss help you with projects and decisions. List several alternatives, rank them, and ask what your boss thinks you should do next.

- **A people pleaser boss:** Praise behavior that you like; your boss will try to please you by giving you more. Mention what you dislike; your boss won't want to upset you again. Help your boss give you accurate, constructive criticism. ("I'm sure there are things I could improve.") Don't get too close to a pleaser boss; higher-ups usually don't respect them.

- **An unhappy pessimist boss:** Don't reinforce negativism or allow your boss to draw you into arguments. Listen to your boss' concerns. Acknowledge those that are constructive and inject a dose of reality where necessary. Discuss the worst-case scenario and how you could handle it to show how the problem is not really that bad.

- **A know-it-all boss:** Challenge the boss to form a problem-solving team with you instead of dictating a plan. Ask for input early. Give positive feedback on the ideas you like. Then suggest alternatives for the weak ideas. ("I like the part about... What would you think of...?")

- **An introvert boss or poor communicator:** Be patient. Draw your boss out with open-ended questions. Don't interrupt. Polish your own communication skills so you can get important messages across to others instead of hoping your boss will do it.

- **An incompetent boss:** Don't waste time pointing out shortcomings; it's improper, and this boss may not care anyway. Keep communication brief and to the point; this boss is likely to lose the details. Don't wait for your boss' tardy or weak directions; clarify what your boss wants and develop a plan for getting there. Solve your own problems; don't wait for your boss to put out the fire. Make sure other influential people at work know about your successes and good ideas.

- **A boss who won't share information:** Carefully build arguments for why you need (not want) the information. Fortify your network so you can get important information from other sources.

- **A boss who doesn't give feedback:** Ask for it. Ask what your boss liked about your latest project and how you could have improved. ("Everyone can improve something. What areas do you think I could work on?")

- **A workaholic boss who demands you work long hours:** Help your boss measure your work by results, not hours worked. Become a superb manager of your own time. Talk about your life away from work occasionally to show that it is important to you.

Resources

➡ *1,000 Things You Never Learned in Business School: How to Manage Your Fast Track Career*, William Yeomans, NAL-Dutton, 1990.

➡ *How to Work for a Jerk: Your Success Is the Best Revenge,* Robert Hochheiser, Vintage, 1987.

➡ *How to Fire Your Boss,* Chris Malburg, Berkley, 1991.

➡ *Never Work for a Jerk!* Patricia King, Franklin Watts, 1987.

See Also

⇨ **Quitting**, *page 234.*
⇨ **Making Your Boss Your Partner**, *page 26*
⇨ **Unethical or Unlawful Employers**, *page 52.*
⇨ **Handling Sexual Harassment**, *page 56.*

Working with Difficult People

We all know a few jerks, boneheads, and pains-in-the-neck. They are the coworkers, clients, supervisors, and others who make it so difficult for the rest of us to accomplish anything. They make unreasonable demands or ridiculous decisions. They drain our energy. It's difficult just to be around them.

You may not be able to change those impossible people, but you can use strategic thinking to deal with them more effectively.

- Try to bring the difficult person over to your side by pinpointing an adversary you both share (a competitor, an uncooperative coworker, outdated equipment). The difficult person will think of you as an ally if you fight the same foe.

- If you're dealing with a power maniac who ranks higher than you, present an overwhelming argument in favor of your approach. Provide a scapegoat so the higher-up can shift gears and go with your idea. ("If accounting had released these figures earlier, you could have seen that.")

- Don't assume that a difficult person is an idiot, especially if it's your boss. That person must have some smarts to have reached this level. Maybe your boss knows more than you think but sees the world differently.

- Don't discount anyone's potential importance to you and your goals. Anyone could help or hurt you, so don't treat anyone like dirt.

- Give troublemakers some of what they want. If one loves a crisis, ask for help with yours. If one is a bureaucrat, find a rule that's important to that person and show how your idea will uphold it.

- Remember that your job is a path to your personal and professional goals. Don't devote your career to conquering the bonehead. Learn to work with or around that person so you can meet your true goals.

- Don't confront jerks about what jerks they are unless: you really can't take anymore; you'll lose something valuable if you don't speak up; you can win the argument; you can control your emotions; or you're ready to face the consequences.

- Score points with egomaniacs by asking for their help.

- Don't downplay turf battles. They're serious to the people involved. Don't enter others' territory until you've talked with them about what you need to do. Show that you understand that this is their turf and ask for help.

- If a complainer starts whining and wants you to play savior, don't take the bait. Say "Oh, that's too bad. What are you going to do about it?"

- When a difficult person confronts you angrily, catching you off guard, ask for time to stop and think. ("You've hit me cold with this. I just can't respond right now. Let's meet after lunch.") If you give an immediate response it probably will be a nonproductive counterattack, anyway.

- If someone yells at you, don't say anything until the yelling stops. Then ask, "Could you run that by me again more slowly?" Who can yell and speak slowly at the same time?

- Change the way you react to difficult people. So what if they act like jerks? Don't give them control over you.

Resources

➡ *Dinosaur Brains: Dealing with All Those Impossible People at Work*, Albert Bernstein and Sydney Rozen, John Wiley & Sons, 1989.

➡ *How to Work for a Jerk: Your Success Is the Best Revenge*, Robert Hochheiser, Random House, 1987.

➡ *Job Savvy: How to Be a Success at Work*, LaVerne L. Ludden, JIST Works, Inc., 1998.

See Also

⇨ **Understanding Your Bothersome Boss**, *page 28.*
⇨ **Handling Customer Problems**, *page 34.*
⇨ **Preparing for a Conflict**, *page 50.*
⇨ **Dealing with Verbal Abuse**, *page 58.*

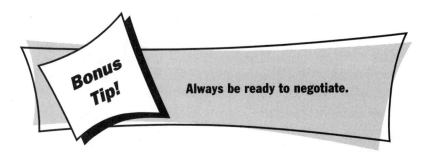

Bonus Tip! Always be ready to negotiate.

Communicating with the Opposite Sex

Have you ever talked about a conflict with someone of the opposite sex and found that each of you had sharply opposing views of what happened? You're not imagining these gender-talk glitches. Researchers have shown that, in general, men and women communicate differently.

"For most women, the language of conversation is primarily a language of rapport, a way of establishing connections and negotiating relationships," Deborah Tannen writes in *You Just Don't Understand* (see **Resources** below). "For most men, talk is primarily a means to preserve independence and negotiate and maintain status in a hierarchical social order."

Don't waste time, energy, and good ideas because you and your colleagues are talking to each other with different goals.

- Don't assume that one person's way of communicating is better than the other. They're just different. Respect the strengths and weaknesses of each style and use parts of each to communicate better. (Some men might be more effective if they built consensus more often. Women might be more effective if they trusted themselves to make quicker decisions.)

- Temporarily adopt some of the communication styles of the opposite sex to fit your audience and goals. (A woman might use a sports analogy with a mostly male group, or a man might discuss a sense of community when addressing a female audience.)

- If you're seen as someone who asks too many questions (many women are), modify your information gathering techniques. Spread your questions around to a variety of people instead of just one or two. Do more research on your own.

- If your coworkers or subordinates ask few questions (like many men) find out if they really understand what you're saying. Don't just ask "Does everyone understand?" after discussing a new project. Ask "What do you think I just said?" or "How do you think you'll approach this?"

- When working with a get-to-the-point communicator (as many men are) give clarifications and elaboration only if asked. Keep them brief.

- If you don't usually gather a lot of information but operate more on intuition (as many women do), pull your information together ahead of time so detail-oriented workers will see that you've done your homework.

- If you tend to use language primarily to compete instead of connect (as many men do), give yourself a break from that pressure. Take a few deep breaths and listen instead of planning your comeback. Ask some sharp clarifying questions.

- If you like to know how others are feeling (many women do) but your coworkers resist sharing their feelings (many men do), try accepting less information about the feelings. Realize that your coworkers' emotions may not be related to you. Men could provide a little information about their feelings or reactions in a brief sentence.

- If you tend to use soft language with vague descriptions or disclaimers (many women do), practice using direct, specific, and forceful words that convey action and confidence.

- Frequently paraphrase what you believe the other person has said and ask if you share the same understanding.

- Use humor to boost rapport. Women can show that they're not too serious about work by telling funny stories, sharing cartoons, or making wry observations. They should avoid self-deprecating humor, which may appear to signal low self-confidence. Men, who tend to enjoy one-liners and put-down humor, could tell lighter, humorous stories more often. Everyone should avoid sex-related jokes—there's too much room for offense.

- Avoid bashing the opposite sex at work. It doesn't nourish good working relationships or effectiveness.

Resources

➡ *You Just Don't Understand: Women and Men in Conversation*, Deborah Tannen, Ballantine, 1991.
➡ *Genderflex: Men and Women Speaking Each Other's Language at Work*, Judith C. Tingley, AMACOM, 1994.
➡ *Talking from 9 to 5: Women and Men in the Workplace*, Deborah Tannen, Avon, 1995.

See Also

➪ **Communicating for Success**, *page 66.*
➪ **Listen Up**, *page 70.*
➪ **Making Gossip Work for You**, *page 102.*
➪ **Using Humor at Work**, *page 114.*

Handling Customer Problems

You may deal with customers or potential customers every day, even if it's not your primary job responsibility.

Office visits, misdirected phone calls, and unexpected problems put you in touch with the people who buy and use your organization's products and services. If you're not interacting with those folks you're probably working with an internal customer—someone within your organization to whom you provide goods or services.

Serving both kinds of customers better will keep your career and your organization healthy.

- Never be rude, insensitive, or sarcastic with customers, even if you think they deserve it.

- If you're new to the customer-relations game, look for someone in your organization with more experience who can be your mentor. Observe how that person handles customers and ask that person to critique your methods.

- Let the customers talk. Don't interrupt. Don't finish their sentences. Upset customers often will be satisfied simply by having someone listen to their complaints.

- Pay attention to your body language. Are you smiling? Are your arms crossed defiantly? Are you watching the clock? Are you doing anything else other than looking at the customer and listening?

- Write down the customer's name as soon as the customer mentions it. Use it in the conversation.

- Repeat what you think are the customer's main points to make sure that you understand them.

- Be true to your word. If you say you'll pass a comment along to a supervisor, do it. If you say you'll check into the problem and keep the customer informed, do it. If you say you'll expedite an order, do it. Customers are turned off by empty promises.

- Do whatever you can to understand your customers. Ask lots of questions to find out what's important to them.

- Resist the temptation to blurt out "No" when a customer makes a request. Instead, think "How could I make that work?" before saying anything.

- Increase your customer service awareness by keeping track of how you're treated when you are a customer. How do the clerks or receptionists make you feel? What do you expect as a customer? What irritates you about doing business where customer service is a low priority?

■ Whenever possible give the customer options instead of a single take-it-or-leave-it solution.

■ Discuss what you'll do about the situation instead of what the customer ought to do. ("I'll talk to the XYZ department about that for you, Ms. Woolsey," instead of "You'll have to call the XYZ department about that.")

■ Use humor with your coworkers to help you cope with stressful customer-related duties. But avoid joking about customers or making fun of them. Those comments could get back to customers and harm important relationships.

Resources

➡ *Service America: Doing Business in the New Economy*, Karl Albrecht and Ron Zemke, Warner, 1990.

➡ *Don't Slurp Your Soup: A Basic Guide to Business Etiquette*, Betty Craig, Brighton Publications, Inc., 1991.

➡ *The Customer Is Usually Wrong!* Fred Jandt, Park Avenue Productions, 1995.

See Also

➪ **Working with Difficult People**, *page 30.*
➪ **Preparing for a Conflict**, *page 50.*
➪ **Listen Up**, *page 70.*
➪ **Cooling Your Anger**, *page 138.*

Bonus Tip!

Thank the customer for bringing the matter to your attention.

CHAPTER

3

Chapter 3

Technology

Using Your Fax Machine Wisely

Comfortable Computer Tips

Voice Mail and Answering Machine Savvy

Maximizing Your Electronic Mail

Using Your Fax Machine Wisely

Fax machines can make work more efficient and save money. But used unwisely they can waste staff time and interrupt your work flow.

In fact, Dan Stamp, chair of Priority Management Systems, Inc., Bellevue, Wash., says fax machines have doubled the interruptions the average manager faces from one every eight minutes to one every four minutes.

- Don't assume that it's important just because it was faxed. Don't let incoming faxes needlessly change your priorities.

- Use standard forms for sending faxes. Include names of sender and recipient; fax and voice phone numbers for each person; total number of pages being sent; other people who should get copies; and deadline for response. Also include room for additional comments. Most word-processing software includes fax transmission-sheet templates; or use small, adhesive-backed fax transmission notes that you stick onto documents, eliminating the need for a separate cover sheet.

- Avoid faxing personal or confidential information. If you can't avoid it, call ahead so the recipient can be waiting at the fax machine for the document.

- If you're environmentally conscious, note that thermal-sensing fax paper (the rolled type) cannot be recycled. You can recycle faxes produced by plain-paper fax machines. They use regular, uncoated paper.

- Ask yourself if this material absolutely positively has to be there in the next two minutes; or would it be equally efficient and more economical to walk the papers over to another department, or use interoffice or electronic mail, or use two-part carbon-copy forms instead of faxing copies to others?

- Know how much faxing costs you. Have someone in your office calculate the costs of sending small and large documents to key cities by fax, regular mail, overnight delivery, or two-day delivery. (Your long-distance phone company can help with rates.) Post the chart on your fax machine so everyone can decide whether speed is worth the cost.

- Don't let faxes weaken business relationships by replacing face-to-face communication. The personal touch is more important than ever in a high-tech environment. Continue to call or visit important clients or business partners.

- Make your faxes short and concise.

- Be cautious about giving out your office fax number. You may be overloaded with unwanted faxes—and you'll pay for the paper. Be cautious about tying your fax to your organization's toll-free phone number—unscrupulous callers could use it to solicit business at your expense or fax material that could be delivered in less expensive ways.

■ Know that federal law prohibits companies from sending "junk faxes" that solicit business unless you have a previous business relationship. If you receive unwanted faxes and the sender ignores your requests to stop, report the matter to the Federal Communications Commission (check government listings in your phone book).

■ If you don't fax very often, consider sharing a fax machine with other nearby offices; or it may be cheaper to use a neighborhood mail or copy center's fax service (typical charges: $1 to $3 per page to send a fax, $1-$1.50 per page to receive).

Resources

➡ *Fax This Book* (a collection of clever, humorous fax cover sheets you can copy), John Caldwell, Workman, 1990.

➡ *Fax for Home and Office: The Guide to Buying and Maintaining Facsimile Machines*, Casey Dworkin, Chilton, 1989.

➡ "Home Fax Machines" section in *1994 Buying Guide*, Consumers Union, or "Home Office Products" section in *Consumer Guide Best Buys 1994*, Publications International, 1993 (check public library reference section).

See Also

⇨ **Finding More Time in Your Day**, *page 8.*
⇨ **Controlling Paperwork**, *page 12.*
⇨ **Communicate for Success**, *page 66.*
⇨ **Writing Effective Memos**, *page 86.*

Comfortable Computer Tips

Many of us spend long hours working at our computers but we give little serious thought to how we set up our work areas. We use any old chair that's nearby, settle for existing lighting, and hold cramped positions for long stretches of time.

As a result we strain—and possibly injure—our eyes, necks, backs, wrists, arms, and shoulders. We can avoid that discomfort if we set up our computer workstations properly.

- Place your keyboard at the level of your thumb joints when your elbows are at 90 degrees and your arms and hands are parallel to the floor. If your desk is too high, raise the level of your chair or lower the keyboard by adding a sliding keyboard rack (available at computer and office supply stores) to the underside of the desk.

- Place a soft, smooth wrist rest in front of your keyboard to keep wrists straight (check office supply stores) or use a rolled up towel.

- Use a lighter touch on the keyboard. Strengthen wrists and fingers by squeezing a rubber ball or toy five to 10 minutes a day.

- Position your computer screen at least 20-28 inches away from your face. The sharper the image on your screen, the farther away you can position the monitor, which may relieve more eye strain.

- Put the computer screen at eye level or just slightly below. Some experts say eye level is best because it keeps your head and neck in the most neutral positions. Others prefer slightly below eye level, saying that people feel most comfortable reading that way.

- When you're doing only computer work dim the lights in your work area so your monitor is the brightest light there. Turn off overhead lights and use a desk light or remove or turn off about half the bulbs in overhead fluorescent lights, or use bulbs of smaller wattages. However, if you'll be mixing computer work with other tasks use brighter lights.

- Use a high-quality glare screen to prevent reflections and sharpen the screen image. Don't use cheap ones that make your screen appear fuzzier; they'll increase eye strain. If you don't have a glare screen make a glare hood by taping cardboard or paper above the monitor to keep light from hitting the screen from above.

- Move away from your workstation frequently. Frequent, short breaks—one to three minutes long every 30 minutes—seem to be better than longer breaks every hour or two. During breaks look away from the screen. Focus your eyes elsewhere and roll them around. Stretch and move shoulders, neck, back, fingers, and wrists. Stand up. Take a short walk.

- Alternate computer work with tasks like filing or phone calls.

- Use a document holder that attaches to the side of your monitor at eye level (check office supply stores).

- Keep your back straight and your legs bent at 90- to 100-degree angles most of the time you're at your computer. Avoid leaning forward when you use your mouse.

- Clear out the area under your desk. Allow your legs and feet to stretch and move as you work.

- Make sure your desk or workstation is the right height. For most people, that's 27-29 inches. If your desk is too high, raise your chair seat and use a foot rest so your feet can rest flat on the floor. If your desk is too low, raise your computer and/or the desk by placing objects (wood blocks, phone books) beneath them.

- Use a good quality chair that's the right size for you. You should be able to easily adjust the arms, seat, back rest height, and back rest angle. Ideally, you could fit two fingers between the back of your knees and the edge of the seat when your legs are bent at 90-degree angles and your feet are flat on the floor. If you can't and the chair is not adjustable, place a pillow behind your back.

Resources
➡ *How to Survive Your Computer Work Station*, Julia Lacey, CRT Services, Inc., Kerrville, TX, 1997, 800-256-4379, $17.95 + shipping and handling.
➡ *Sitting on the Job*, Scott Donkin, Houghton Mifflin, 1986, 800-552-6347, $11.95 + shipping and handling.

See Also
⇨ **Cubicle Survival Tips**, *page 20.*
⇨ **Working at Home Successfully**, *page 22.*

3-3 Voice Mail and Answering Machine Savvy

They may annoy you at times, but it's clear that answering machines and voice mail are here to stay. Learn to use them effectively to enhance your professional image and improve your efficiency.

- Plan and write down your outgoing message (the one callers hear when they reach your number) before you record it so you'll sound smooth and professional.

- Keep your outgoing message short—say, 15 seconds or less. Don't let callers become frustrated waiting for the end of your message.

- Make sure your outgoing message tells callers what information you want (name, phone number, time and day of call, brief message) or else you may not get it.

- Avoid making humorous or cute outgoing messages on a business line. Some callers won't know how to react. They may not leave a message or may not leave the information you need.

- Change your outgoing message frequently to give updates on your availability. Don't let outdated messages remain on your machine or in your voice mail system.

- Give callers an opportunity to speak with a real person if possible. Avoid referring them to another extension with another voice mail message.

- If your speaking voice is unpleasant, a monotone, or jittery ask a coworker or friend with a smooth voice to record your outgoing message for you.

- Always be prepared to leave a message when you make a call. Think ahead about what you need to say if you don't reach the other party.

- When leaving a message give your name and phone number first. Next, briefly say why you called or what you want from the other party. Repeat your phone number slowly and clearly before you hang up. Also repeat your name if it's unusual.

- Leave brief and simple messages. Save long explanations for a two-way conversation. The one exception is if it's crucial that the other person get the information now and you won't be available for a while.

- Specify in your message when you'll be available to receive calls; you'll avoid playing phone tag this way, or set up a phone appointment on the recording. ("I'd like to call you at 2 p.m. Wednesday about this report. If you're not available then please call me to suggest another time.")

- Speak clearly and at a reasonable pace. Strive to sound conversational. Maintain eye contact with someone or something as you record your message so you'll sound friendly and attentive rather than robotic.

- Pay attention to your mood. If you're grouchy, rushed, or angry your tone will be heard in the tape and may obscure your intent. Take a few deep breaths and smile before speaking.

- Check your outgoing message periodically to make sure it sounds good and your system is operating correctly. Change answering machine tapes frequently to ensure good sound quality.

- Leave messages for yourself on your machine or in your voice mail box to remind yourself to do something, or even to congratulate yourself for good work.

Resources
➡ *Great Customer Service on the Telephone*, Kristin Anderson, AMACOM, 1992.
➡ *The How To of Great Speaking: Stage Techniques to Tame Those Butterflies*, Hal Persons, Black and Taylor, 1992.

See Also
⇨ **Finding More Time in Your Day**, *page 8.*
⇨ **Tuning Up Informal Speech**, *page 76.*

Bonus Tip!

Keep messages you leave short and to the point.

Maximizing Your Electronic Mail

Is electronic mail a blessing or a curse for you?

Does it save you time or flood you with hassles? Does it cut interruptions or make work too impersonal? Does it help you meet your goals quicker or make you drop your priorities more?

E-mail is a cross between a phone call and a letter. It lets you send and receive messages at your convenience, but with some sense of urgency. It's good for reaching people who are hard to catch or in different time zones. It promotes a quick exchange of ideas.

But like any high-tech tool, e-mail can waste time and cause problems when it's not used wisely.

- Keep e-mail short. A one-word answer may seem terse but sometimes that's all that's necessary. Can't keep it short? Have a personal conversation instead.

- Get to the point quickly. Make it easy for recipients to see why they should read this message now instead of filing or deleting it. Your message may be one of dozens they will see that day.

- Use your return key often to avoid creating dense blocks of type and long lines that don't fit on the screen.

- Don't use fancy font treatments (bold, italic, underline). They may show up as confusing control characters.

- Don't use e-mail for personal or sensitive messages. It's not private. Others may easily see it on purpose or by accident. Also, e-mail at work may be the property of your employer. Your employer may have the right to retrieve e-mail messages in cases of litigation. Don't expect that adding "Erase this immediately!" will cover you.

- Check your mailbox once a day or more. Otherwise, what good is speedy delivery?

- Avoid anger, sarcasm, harassment, or phrases that could easily be misinter-preted. Resist the urge to be more nervy or negative than you would in a personal conversation.

- Only send e-mail copies to people who really need them. Oversending routine and irrelevant copies could cause people to ignore your mail.

- Use e-mail to supplement, but not replace, communication with staff members or coworkers. Continue to have personal conversations to build strong relationships. Also, give personal feedback in private and in person.

- Don't let e-mail eat up your time by involving you in unnecessary work. You might reply, "Thanks but I don't need to be involved at this level." Or, "I'll stay out of this one unless you really need me for a specific job."

- Check spelling, grammar, and accuracy. E-mail may be informal but it still reflects on you.

- Stop and reread your message before sending it. Does it say what you want? Could it be misinterpreted? Have you written too much? How will you know whether it succeeded in its purpose? What do you expect the recipient to do upon receiving it? Does the recipient know that? Will you regret it if it becomes public knowledge?

Resources
➡ *Smileys (a collection of symbols to jazz up your e-mail)*, David Sanderson, O'Reilly & Assoc., 1993.
➡ *The Whole Internet: User's Guide and Catalog*, Ed Krol, O'Reilly & Associates, 1992.
➡ *Pocket Guide to the Internet: Vol. 4, the Internet E-Mail System*, Mark Veljkov and George Hartnell, Mecklermedia, 1994.

See Also
⇨ **Controlling Paperwork**, *page 12.*
⇨ **Comfortable Computer Tips**, *page 40.*
⇨ **Writing Effective Memos**, *page 86.*

Bonus Tip!

Don't waste time and money making paper copies of most e-mail messages.

CHAPTER

4

Chapter 4

Conflicts at Work

Creative Problem Solving

Problem solving can be as dull or as enjoyable as you make it. But in most cases the more fun and creative the process the better your ideas will be.

Next time you look for a solution to a dilemma, go beyond making lists of pros and cons and prioritizing your options. Try some creative techniques to be more effective.

- Turn the situation upside down to get some new ideas. For example, if your goal is to improve quality ask, "What could we do to worsen quality?"

- Describe the problem with feeling words that trigger emotions and creativity. (Don't define meetings as unproductive. Call them boring or mind-numbing.)

- Apply manipulation or action verbs to your problem. (If you're trying to improve a product or service, ask, "What would happen if I twist it? Raise it? Reduce, eliminate, complicate, or simplify it? Animate it, electrify it, speed it up, make it fly, or purify it?")

- Ask these problem-solving questions, "How can I improve on what has worked before? What is the ideal solution over the long term? What elements can I combine to develop a new idea? What basic assumptions can I challenge and what new ideas would result?"

- Look at what makes this problem different from other situations. Don't automatically try to solve it the same way you have similar problems.

- Try looking at the problem from your customer's point of view which could be your boss, a consumer, a coworker, or yourself). The big issues for most customers are how long it takes to get it right, how much it costs, and how many defects it has. Which issue ties in to your current problem?

- If you're faced with several problems at once, concentrate first on the one that causes the most trouble in the most important area.

- Do collect relevant data, but don't get so bogged down in it that you miss good alternatives. Stay focused on solutions, not facts and figures.

- Try mind mapping. Write the problem in the center of a large sheet of paper. Using colored markers, jot down the ideas that spring from yourself or your work group. Write all over the paper. Link related ideas with colored lines. Watch creative solutions pop out.

- Don't work too hard at being creative. If you're stuck, just start somewhere, even with the easiest part to get your ideas flowing; or get away from the problem for a while. When you return you may see new solutions.

■ Don't avoid creative problem solving out of concern that your ideas may be too wacky to work. After your creative side comes up with a good solution, run it through the analytical side of your brain to check out the consequences and fine-tune it.

■ Turn your creative ideas into action plans. What will you and others do, and when, to make your idea a reality?

■ Make one change at a time so you can see which action yields which result.

Resources

➡ *A Kick in the Seat of the Pants*, Roger Von Oech, HarperCollins, 1986.

➡ *A Whack on the Side of the Head*, Roger Von Oech, Warner, 1993.

➡ Creative Whack Pack (64 cards featuring creativity strategies), U.S. Games Systems, Inc.

➡ *99 Percent Inspiration: Tips, Tales and Techniques for Liberating Your Business Creativity*, Bryan Mattimore, AMACOM, 1993.

➡ *Quantum Improvement Coloring Book: Problem-Solving Made Easy*, Lowell Jay Arthur, LifeStar, 2244 S. Olive St., Denver, CO 80224, 303-757-2039, $12.95. E-mail: lifestar@rmii.com. Web address: http://www.rmi.net/~lifestar.

See Also

⇨ **Nurturing Your Creativity**, *page 118.*
⇨ **Making Better Decisions**, *page 122.*

Bonus Tip!

Celebrate even your smallest creative ideas.

4-2 Preparing for a Conflict

When preparing for a confrontation we often think only about steeling ourselves so the other person won't walk all over us. But most conflicts—everything from working with a harshly critical boss to dealing with an irate colleague—would go more smoothly if we think about the other person's style and needs.

- Know your goal. You'll be most successful if your purpose is professional (I want to get support for this project) instead of personal (I want this designer to think I'm brilliant).

- Know who you'll be dealing with so you can anticipate that person's responses. How does this person make decisions, handle problems, or react to surprises? What are this person's values, experiences, and concerns?

- Think about everything that could go wrong when you meet to discuss a problem. Plan responses to defuse each argument you expect from the other person. Think about the impulsive comments you don't want to make and the professional, calm ones you'd prefer to say.

- As you discuss the conflict clearly define what each of you thinks is the problem and state your goals so you both can address the same issue.

- Talk about what you did and felt instead of what you think the other person did or felt. Explain what you believe happened, how you feel about it, how it affects you or your work, and what you'd like to see happen. Describe behavior instead of labeling it or the person performing it. Avoid making destructive remarks. ("You were rude and incompetent.")

- Acknowledge the other person's feelings. ("I can see that you're angry about...") This reduces defensiveness and encourages the person to open up more.

- Tell the other person about the positive consequences ahead if you get what you want and the negative consequences if you don't. Try to sound reasonable, not threatening.

- Remain professional no matter what. Let your appearance, actions, and words show that you're cool and objective.

- Don't look for compromises; everyone has to give up something for them. Try instead to combine solutions and meet everyone's critical needs.

- Try to resolve conflicts by influencing others, not forcing them to do it your way.

- Suggest that you try a solution for a while, see what happens and then re-evaluate if necessary.

- When discussing a problem try saying that you believe the other person had good intentions. You may encourage that person to open up about what happened.

- End the meeting with a commitment to action: what happens next, who will do what, and by when.

- Avoid future conflicts by getting to know your colleagues, bosses, and clients and their values and experiences better. Routinely explore others' expectations; don't assume you know what they mean. Ask clarifying questions.

- Handle small conflicts promptly so they don't become big ones.

Resources

→ *Conflict Resolution*, Donald Weiss, AMACOM, 1993.
→ *Job Savvy: How to Be a Success at Work*, LaVerne L. Ludden, JIST Works, Inc., 1998.
→ *Resolving Conflicts on the Job*, Jerry Wisinski, AMACOM, 1993.
→ *The Seven Habits of Highly Effective People*, Stephen Covey, Simon & Schuster, 1989.

See Also

⇨ **Understanding Your Bothersome Boss**, *page 28.*
⇨ **Working with Difficult People**, *page 30.*
⇨ **Handling Customer Problems**, *page 34.*
⇨ **Cooling Your Anger**, *page 138.*

Bonus Tip!

Look for a solution that is better than either person's proposal standing alone.

Unethical or Unlawful Employers

If you discover that your employer is behaving illegally or unethically you basically have three choices: you can keep quiet and keep working; you can decide not to be part of the situation and leave; or you can report it to authorities in hopes that it will change.

The latter option—blowing the whistle on your employer—is risky and requires careful thought.

- If you bring a serious problem into the open be prepared to experience a wide range of emotions, lose friends, see increased tension in your family life, and possibly lose your job and lifestyle.

- Consult your family and close friends before you disclose any information. You'll need their support.

- Make sure your motives are to help others, not just yourself.

- Watch that you're not so closely aligned with this boss that you could be tied to the unethical or illegal behavior.

- Document the activity. The best records are self-explanatory and are generated by the organization instead of you (financial records, time logs). If you are to remain anonymous, make sure the documents can't be traced to you.

- Identify and copy pertinent records before anyone knows you may blow the whistle.

- Keep a diary of events. Date and initial each entry. Write and sign "memoranda for the record" whenever you need to record a conversation or event. Have someone witness and sign them, if possible.

- Discreetly look for others who are upset about the problem. They can provide information and help you determine if your suspicions are well founded.

- Consider carefully whether to go public or remain anonymous. If you go public you'll be in the middle of the controversy and may be harassed. If you're anonymous you can watch the improper actions quietly from the inside. But your documentation will have to stand alone and you may be less effective.

- If the improper behavior is an isolated case (not an entrenched practice), you may have some success constructively discussing it with the supervisor involved. Talk about the issue in a low-key, nonaccusatory way. Explain your concern about how this could affect the company (lawsuits, large fines, lost business).

- Discuss the problem with a sympathetic manager who may be willing to help. You might start with one of the more minor infractions to see how the manager reacts.

- Another tactic may be to mention the problem to nonprofit watchdog groups, elected officials, professional organizations, or community leaders who might investigate, or to notify company shareholders or the board of directors. They want to see the company succeed.

- Reveal only what you know for sure. Don't speculate. Don't exaggerate. In fact, you'll probably have more credibility if you understate the problem.

- Don't expect too much from company-sponsored hotlines and oversight agencies. They often fail at investigation and follow-up and may be biased.

- Get support from coworkers and company officials by speaking up for the ethics and values of the company.

- Plan for possible legal expenses.

Resources
➡ *Courage Without Martyrdom*, Government Accountability Project, Washington, D.C., 202-408-0034, free.
➡ *The Whistleblowers: Exposing Corruption in Government and Industry*, Myron Glazer and Penina Glazer, Basic Books, 1991.
➡ *Never Work for a Jerk!* Patricia King, Franklin Watts, 1987.

See Also
⇨ **Understanding Your Bothersome Boss**, *page 28.*
⇨ **Working with Difficult People**, *page 30.*
⇨ **Working with a Drug or Alcohol Abuser**, *page 54.*
⇨ **Handling Sexual Harassment**, *page 56.*

Bonus Tip!

Reveal only facts about questionable behavior. Don't speculate.

Working with a Drug or Alcohol Abuser

You've seen commercials urging families to get help when a loved one has a drinking, drug, or severe emotional problem. But what if it's your boss or coworker who has the problem and it keeps you from doing your job properly?

If it truly is affecting your work you have a right to do something. But think through your options carefully—this is a minefield.

- Before deciding how to react analyze how much you are willing to get involved. Also look at what kind of relationship you have with your boss or coworker; what kind of relationship you have with your organization; and how much support you will have from your family, coworkers, and counseling professionals.

- Maintain your own sense of integrity. Honor your own principles. What can you live with? Groups like Al-Anon (see **Resources** below) can help with this, as can books on dealing with someone's drug or alcohol problem.

- Before you do anything talk with others. Ask coworkers how they see the problem. If you can't risk speaking out about it use your employee assistance office or a reputable counseling organization

- Don't throw around words like alcoholic, drug addict, or mentally ill when you discuss the problem with others. Avoid making conclusions about the extent of the problem or its root causes. You may not be qualified to make those judgments, and you could wind up on the wrong end of a defamation lawsuit.

- If you do discuss the problem with anyone (including the person you're concerned about), stick to observable behavior and its consequences. Note what your boss or coworker does and when, such as taking long lunches, staggering, sleeping in the office, or missing meetings. You may want to document it.

- If supervisors regularly ask you to cover for them at meetings or take on their responsibilities refer to your job description. Say that you're not prepared to do those tasks and that doing them prevents you from completing your work.

- Be cautious about telling your boss' supervisor about your boss' drug or alcohol problem. Think about how the supervisor is likely to react. Consider the type of organization, the chain of command, and your relationship with that supervisor. However, if the level of impairment is serious, you may have a moral obligation to report it to prevent accidents and injuries.

- Consider referring your boss or coworker to your company's employee assistance program, if you and that person have a reasonably close relationship.

- Be cautious about using your organization's human resources office. Some officials may be more interested in enforcing policies about chemical abuse on the job than helping your boss or coworker deal with the problem.

- Join forces with others in your workplace if they also are affected by this problem and can document inappropriate behavior. As a group, and with the help of a chemical abuse counselor, you could confront your boss or coworker and strongly recommend help.

- Remember that you can't change someone with a drug or alcohol problem unless that person wants to change.

Resources

→ *What Can I Say to Get You to Stop?* (free pamphlet), Hazelden, PO Box 11, Center City, MN 55012-0011, 800-257-7800. Web address: http://www.hazelden.org.

→ Al-Anon, listed in your local telephone book, or Al-Anon Family Group Headquarters, Inc., PO Box 862, Midtown Station, New York, NY 10018-0862.

→ *Drugs and Alcohol in the Workplace: A Guide for Managers*, Drusilla Campbell and Marilyn Graham, Facts on File, 1988.

See Also

⇨ **Understanding Your Bothersome Boss**, *page 28.*
⇨ **Working with Difficult People**, *page 30.*
⇨ **Unethical or Unlawful Employers**, *page 52.*

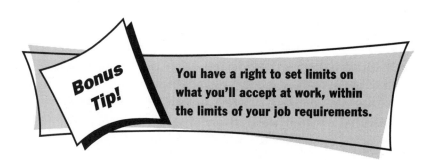

Bonus Tip!

You have a right to set limits on what you'll accept at work, within the limits of your job requirements.

Handling Sexual Harassment

Sexual harassment in the workplace has received a lot of attention in the past several years. And it's still a big problem. Women and men filed almost 15,350 sexual harassment charges with the U.S. Equal Employment Opportunity Commission and state and local agencies in 1996. Experts say there are many more cases that never are reported.

Some basics about sexual harassment:

- Sexual harassment is unwelcome behavior of a sexual nature. It includes dirty jokes, pornography, gestures, propositions, or repeated requests for a date, touching, repeated personal questions, and comments about a person's appearance.

- It may involve a supervisor harassing an employee, a coworker harassing a peer, or a nonemployee (subcontractor or client) harassing an employee.

- It's harassment when a boss tells an employee to accept sexual behavior to keep a job or get promoted. It's also harassment when an employee's job performance is compromised because of persistent, unwelcome, offensive sexual behavior directed at only one gender at work (which creates a "hostile working environment").

- An employee who knows about harassment in the workplace and is adversely affected by it also could be a victim of that harassment, even if that person was not the target.

There are many steps you can take if you are being sexually harassed at work. You are not powerless.

If you are being harassed, take these steps:

- Act immediately. Don't wait for it to go away.

- Plainly tell the harasser to stop. Say that you don't like, don't want, and don't appreciate those actions; or deliver a sealed letter to the harasser explicitly describing the harassment and how you felt, and demanding that it stop.

- Take action even if you consented to sexual behavior in the past. You may have felt forced into those actions. Plus, past behavior does not mean you welcome other sexual advances.

- Keep a diary of the harassment, noting time, date, place, events, witnesses, your feelings, and effects on your work.

- Document your work performance and quality. Otherwise, when you complain about the harassment the harasser may try to weaken your case by claiming that your work has been poor.

- Learn about your organization's sexual harassment policy.

- If a colleague is harassing you, tell a trusted supervisor or human resources official.

- If a supervisor is harassing you and ignores your direct request to stop, contact your human resources office, affirmative action officer, or your supervisor's boss. If you feel you won't get a fair hearing from an in-house authority, go directly to outside authorities.

- To get outside help check the government listings in your phone book for your local human rights office, state human rights commission, state women's commission, or U.S. Equal Employment Opportunity Commission (see **Resources** below).

- When you make a complaint specify when you expect the problem to be resolved and how (job transfer, monetary award, discipline).

- Remember that retaliation by your employer is illegal and should be reported to the company or outside authorities.

Resources

➡ U.S. Equal Employment Opportunity Commission, 800-669-4000, (connects you with nearest regional office) or the local EEOC office listed in the government section of your phone book.

➡ *Sexual Harassment in the Workplace: How to Prevent, Investigate, and Resolve Problems in Your Organization*, Ellen Wagner, AMACOM, 1992.

➡ *Sexual Harassment on the Job*, William Petrocelli and Barbara Kate Repa, Nolo Press, 1992.

➡ 9 to 5, National Association of Working Women, 231 Wisconsin Ave., Suite 900, Milwaukee, WI 53203, 414-274-0925. Membership: $25/year. Job Survival Hotline (open to all): 800-522-0925, 10 a.m.-3:50 p.m. EST, Monday-Friday.

See Also

⇨ **Quitting**, *page 234.*
⇨ **Unethical or Unlawful Employers**, *page 52.*

Dealing with Verbal Abuse

Some bosses and coworkers don't just give feedback. They hurl blistering criticism or mean comments.

"Even PAT could have typed this report better." Or, "It's OBVIOUS that you don't CARE about your work; you NEVER get to a meeting on time."

The problem may be more than rudeness, aggressiveness, or poor communication skills. If the verbal jabs are part of a regular pattern they may be verbal abuse—language that intentionally hurts people, says Alan Lovejoy, principle of Lovejoy & Lovejoy, human and organization consultants, Denver, Colo. It can rob you of productive work time and chip away at your self-esteem.

Use your own language power to diffuse verbal abuse with dignity.

■ Learn to recognize verbal abuse. Pay attention to the tone of voice and the words the speaker uses. Watch body language.

■ Respond to abusive comments immediately, calmly, and evenly so the abuser won't conclude that you're an easy mark. Show that you demand respect for yourself. Refuse to accept such unnecessary and harmful language. Ask the abuser to stop.

■ Resist the urge to become defensive ("I am NOT always late!") or to respond in kind ("YOU're the inCOMpetent one!"). These strategies tend to fuel the abuser's fire, and they show that the abuser successfully manipulated you into becoming upset.

■ Don't get into a debate over insults or name-calling. You'll just escalate the confrontation. It's better to walk away without comment or ignore the remark and move on to another subject.

■ Answer attacks on your performance with the word "when" instead of taking the accuser's bait. (If the abuser says "EVen SUZANNE could have done a better job on this SIMple report than YOU!", don't reply with "Why do you think SHE could have done a better job?" Instead ask, "When did you start feeling that my work didn't measure up to standards?") This forces the abuser to give you information that you can respond to rationally. Steer the conversation to a more positive path by asking probing questions. ("What was it about the work that needs to be changed? How would you like me to do it next time?")

■ Keep your tone of voice cool and flat, the volume low, and your words evenly spaced. Keep your body language neutral too. Avoid sharp gestures, rushing to your feet, pounding on a desk, or clenching your teeth.

Section I: Working Smart

- If someone throws an indisputable fact at you in the middle of a nasty comment ("You only met 80 PERCENT of the quota when everyone ELSE had 100 PERCENT!"), cool the confrontation by acknowledging the fact (Answer with "You're right."). Then move into problem solving. ("I think this territory is too spread out. What would you think if I... ")

- If you face verbal abuse often, keep a log. Record the words the abuser uses and emphasizes. Note common words and phrases, the timing of the abuse and other circumstances. Look for patterns that will help you know how to respond.

Resources
➡ *Success with the Gentle Art of Verbal Self-Defense*, Suzette Elgin, Prentice Hall, 1989.

See Also
➪ **Understanding Your Bothersome Boss**, *page 28.*
➪ **Working with Difficult People**, *page 30.*
➪ **Handling Sexual Harassment**, *page 56.*
➪ **Boosting Your Self-Esteem**, *page 112.*

Bonus Tip!

Don't throw insults back at a verbal abuser.

Avoiding Excessive Overtime Work

Many people see overtime work as part of their hectic jobs or a welcome fringe benefit.

But some workers dread their supervisors asking them to stay late or work weekends. These employees may have young children waiting for them at home or staying with child-care providers who close at a strict time; they may care for an elderly parent; or they may have important personal commitments like a college class. They usually can't work overtime at a moment's notice.

Getting out of the overtime straitjacket requires strategic thinking.

- Give your boss advance notice that working late will be difficult for you. Explain why. Ask for one to three days advance notice.

- If overtime requests still are a problem, talk with your boss. Many people won't do this, fearing that their boss will think they're not dedicated. But if you don't discuss it, your boss may just assume you're unwilling to work and may ask you to leave or change jobs. Tell your boss that you are serious about your job, but that overtime creates big problems in your personal life.

- Offer your boss alternatives. You could come in early tomorrow instead of working late today; go home for a few hours and return after you've arranged alternate child or elder care; work occasional Saturday mornings when your partner or friend could help at home; or swap duties with a coworker.

- Prove your commitment. Work steadily when you're on duty. Work through lunch sometimes. Take work home when absolutely necessary.

- Know how much notice your child's or relative's caregiver needs to work late. Are there extra charges? Tell your caregiver how often you expect to work late. Find out if a neighbor or friend occasionally would take your child home for a few hours when you get stuck.

- Know your rights. If you're in a union, check your contract about advance notice for overtime and whether you can refuse it. If you don't have a contract your employer may be able to fire you for refusing overtime, saying that you couldn't or wouldn't do what was necessary in your job. Check into your company grievance policy.

- Suggest ways to eliminate costly overtime (change deadlines, redistribute the workload, plan better, use temporary workers or interns.)

- Find coworkers who also feel overtime pressures and arrange for the group to meet with managers about the problem. Managers are more likely to deal with an issue that affects many employees—including highly valued ones.

- Ask managers to survey employees on family issues related to work. You may find that many managers share your concerns and would like to institute changes to benefit everyone.

- Argue that more flexible overtime policies and schedules can cut employee turnover, increase productivity, improve morale, and attract good job candidates.

- Use outside resources to help your employer create a flexible workplace. Try social service agencies, women's organizations, and consulting firms (see **Resources** below).

Resources

➡ Women's Bureau Clearinghouse, a national information center on women's workplace issues, 200 Constitution Ave. NW, Washington, D.C. 20210, 800-827-5335 or 800-347-3741, 11 a.m.-4 p.m. EST, Monday-Friday. Web address: http://www.dol.gov/dol/wb.

➡ 9 to 5, National Association of Working Women, 231 W. Wisconsin Ave., Suite 900, Milwaukee, WI 53203, 414-274-0925. Membership: $25/year. Job Survival Hotline (open to all): 800-522-0925, 10 a.m.-3:50 p.m. EST, Monday-Friday.

➡ *The Working Parents' Handbook,* Katherine Murray, Park Avenue Productions, 1996.

See Also

⇨ **Finding More Time in Your Day,** *page 8.*
⇨ **Negotiating for What You Want,** *page 98.*

Bonus Tip!

Help managers compile a list of late-hour child-care providers to help parents who must work late.

SECTION II

Communication Skills

CHAPTER

5

Chapter 5

Clear Messages

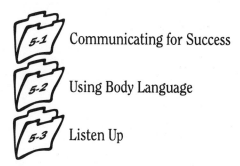
Section II: Communication Skills

Communicating for Success

When you're having problems at work it's easy to blame the difficulties on your boss, coworkers, or job description. But many on-the-job problems are rooted in poor communication.

Your work performance could soar if you improve the way you get your messages across, pick up on others' messages, or communicate with difficult people.

These are warning signs that you're having communications problems at work, author Carol Cox Smith says:

- You dread going to work. It's unpleasant, tiring, stressful.

- People don't want to work with you. You're isolated.

- You're engulfed in an ongoing argument with a coworker or supervisor. Your energy goes toward perpetuating the disagreement instead of seeking a solution.

- People routinely don't understand you when you speak or write a memo.

- You rarely think ahead before you communicate. You're usually in a crisis mode when you speak or write a memo.

- You have good technical skills but regularly receive poor performance reviews.

- You keep changing jobs because they all turn sour on you. The common factor in each of those jobs: you.

Here are ways to polish your communication skills:

- Strive to make your communications clear, direct, honest, planned, realistic, consistent, concise, problem solving, respectful, sharing, open minded, and considerate.

- Don't just blurt out important comments or instructions to people in passing. Make sure the other person has time to listen, can concentrate on your message, and can hear you. Give the other person time to question you. Make sure that person has enough background information to make sense of your comments and gestures.

- Face up to conflicts with others at work. Try to meet with them to discuss the problem and how it prevents both of you from doing your jobs effectively. Don't finger-point or focus on what you think the other person is doing wrong or what you think you're doing right.

- Share some of your feelings and thoughts with others. People will be more likely to communicate honestly with you (describe how a change at work makes you feel, tell a personal story).

- Only send out memoranda or written communication when you can't get your message out in person. Written words often can be misinterpreted because of readers' different perspectives. Get your message across verbally first. Then follow up with a written note to confirm the details.

- Accept responsibility for your own communication. When others don't grasp what you're saying look at how you could have communicated it better instead of how they should have listened better.

- Take responsibility for having clear communication with your boss. Initiate discussions about uncomfortable situations. Invite positive and negative feedback. Let your supervisor know where you stand. Repeat what you think your supervisor said. Ask for clarification often.

- Ask your coworkers for feedback often. Were your instructions and comments clear? What could have been better? What problems do they see in your communications?

Resources

➡ International Association of Business Communicators, One Hallidie Plaza, Suite 600, San Francisco, Calif. 94102, 415-433-3400, membership dues vary. Web address: http://www.iabc.com.

➡ *A Guide to Open Communications* (audiotape), Susan Campbell, Psychology Today Tapes, 800-444-7792, $11.95 + shipping and handling.

➡ *Effective Communication Skills,* Marsha Ludden, JIST Works, Inc., 1992.

See Also

⇨ **Making Your Boss your Partner,** *page 26.*
⇨ **Understanding Your Bothersome Boss,** *page 28.*
⇨ **Composing Better Letters,** *page 84.*
⇨ **Giving Clear Instructions,** *page 100.*

Section II: Communication Skills

5-2 Using Body Language

Using the right body language to convey your message is just as important as choosing precise words. It even may be more important. Various studies have shown that from 65 to 90 percent of all communication comes from nonverbal sources such as appearance, facial expressions, gestures, posture, use of silence, use of touch, space between speaker and listener, vocal tone, and rhythm of speech.

Using nonverbal cues wisely can help you communicate more clearly, accurately, vibrantly, and credibly. Reading those cues accurately tells you what people really are feeling and thinking.

- Make sure your body language matches your verbal message. If you're not speaking sincerely your body language probably will reveal your true feelings. (You say you're not upset or angry, but your jaw is tight.) Astute listeners and observers will pick up on the inconsistency.

- Become a student of body language. Observe others' body language. Watch TV without the sound to see if you can read nonverbal cues. Practice signaling an emotion nonverbally in front of a mirror. Try to describe your own body language. What do you reveal about yourself without speaking? Can you describe the body language of your spouse or close friend?

- Remember one of the simplest and most effective forms of body language: a smile. A sincere, relaxed smile exudes confidence and helps people react positively to you and your message.

- Be careful when using and interpreting body language across cultural lines. Some body language is universal, such as a smile. But some gestures and movements (prolonged eye contact, touching another's arm) can have different meanings to different people. Nonverbal cues also can vary with a person's gender and social or economic class.

- Tune in to negative body language you may use without knowing it (wearing an insincere smile, speaking too aggressively, touching people too much, slumping in your chair, holding your body tightly and tensely). Identify these undesirable cues in yourself by observing how others react to you, asking close friends for input, or even asking someone to videotape you at a meeting. Then practice substituting other more acceptable types of body language.

- Use eye contact. Don't stare, but maintain a steady gaze aimed at the other person's eyes and face. Good eye contact signals that you think the other person is important and that you want to cooperate. It also can signal dominance and assertiveness.

- Keep three to eight feet between you and your audience. If you're closer you might invade others' personal space. If you're farther away, conversation may be awkward, unclear, and inaudible.

- When at a table, sit around a corner from the other person. That signals cooperation and active listening. Sitting straight across from another tends to be confrontational. Sitting side-by-side can make conversation awkward.

- Beware of body language that sends an aggressive message, such as pointing with a finger or pen, wagging your index finger back and forth, or standing with your feet astride and your hands on your hips.

- Eliminate irrelevant, distracting gestures such as fidgeting, picking at your fingernails, or doodling. They'll weaken your verbal message.

- Use your posture to send messages. Walking tall and straight shows confidence. If you're stiff the message is formality. If you face someone directly you show deep attention. Turning the body or face away while you talk says you don't want to get involved.

Resources
➡ *How to Talk So People Listen: The Real Key to Business Success*, Sonya Hamlin, HarperCollins, 1989.
➡ *More on the Gentle Art of Verbal Self-Defense*, Suzette Elgin, Prentice Hall, 1991.
➡ *Subtext: Making Body Language Work in the Workplace*, Julius Fast, Viking, 1991.

See Also
➪ **Communicating for Success**, *page 66.*
➪ **Projecting a Successful Image**, *page 110.*

Section II: Communication Skills

Listen Up

Many of us have been trained to believe that the burden for good communication is on the person speaking or writing. But that ignores the importance of skilled, active listening

Proficient listeners send and receive messages effectively, remember more of what they hear, discover and probe hidden problems quickly, and build better relationships with supervisors, coworkers, and customers.

- Think about your listening style. When do you listen well, to whom, where, and under what circumstances? Do you tend to listen for concepts or facts? Do you listen best to superiors or equals? Which way do you absorb information best: audio (hearing), visual (seeing), or kinesthetic (hands-on experience)? Try to get the speaker to communicate in the way that's most effective for you. (If you prefer visual communication ask, "So just what would this new product look like?")

- Listen with a goal in mind. Think about how the information relates to you and your job, what you need to get out of this, or how you might need this information in the future.

- Keep your interest up by listening for the speaker's central idea. Evaluate all other information against that concept.

- Be as active as you can, especially when complicated issues are being covered. Ask questions to clarify terms. Paraphrase the speaker periodically. Ask for examples. Use open body language to convey that you're interested (lean forward, don't cross your arms). At the end, summarize what you think are the speaker's main points.

- When your mind races ahead of the speaker don't waste that time daydreaming, planning your response, or picking apart the speaker's word choice. Instead, concentrate on content and intent.

- Fight the urge to interrupt by repeating to yourself, "I will not interrupt" or by jotting it down in your notes as a reminder.

- If you take notes keep them brief and focused on the main points. Taking excessively detailed notes means you're spending more time writing than listening.

- Cultivate the attitude that all topics can be interesting and that you can learn from anyone. Any other approach tells your brain not to listen even before the speaker speaks.

- Move into the speaker's head when you need help focusing. Think about why the speaker chose that phrasing, tone, and style. What is the speaker's true intent?

- Don't try to do other tasks while you're listening.

- Always be prepared to listen closely, even when you think the message isn't very important. Look for clues in body language, tone of voice, and word choice that help you know when you'd better listen up.

- Prompt the speaker to repeat the message so you'll be able to grasp it better. Ask questions and paraphrase often so the speaker will restate and clarify the main message.

- Beware of assumptions that block good listening. Are you hearing only what you want to hear? Are you assuming that everyone sees the world as you do?

Resources
➡ *How to Speak and Listen Effectively*, Harvey Robbins, AMACOM, 1992.
➡ *Effective Communication Skills*, Marsha Ludden, JIST Works, Inc., 1992.

See Also
⇨ **Working with Difficult People**, *page 30.*
⇨ **Handling Customer Problems**, *page 34.*
⇨ **Using Body Language**, *page 68.*

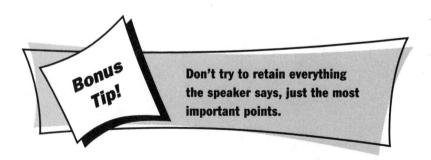

Bonus Tip!

Don't try to retain everything the speaker says, just the most important points.

CHAPTER **6**

Chapter 6

Speaking

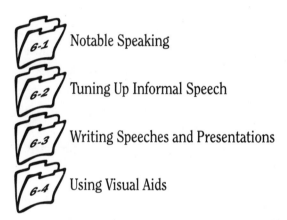
Section II: Communication Skills

Notable Speaking

Speaking is a basic skill that most of us have but few of us hone to an art. One reason is that the thought of speaking to groups, strangers, or authority figures horrifies many of us.

But sharp speaking skills—in formal and informal settings—clearly separate successful people from others.

- Plan all your speeches and talks, even casual discussions you think you may have in the hallway or cafeteria. You will sound more professional and thoughtful.

- Learn about your listeners. They'll pay attention if you show that you've bothered to find out what matters to them.

- Be able to sum up your talk in one short, focused sentence or phrase.

- Rehearse, even if it's in the shower or while commuting.

- Greet people as they enter the room. It tells them you want their attention.

- Provide the moderator with a brief, written introduction about yourself, including proper pronunciation of your name.

- Don't tell your listeners that you're nervous. They probably won't notice unless you bring it up. Just plunge into a story or topic.

- Use specific, plain language. Avoid unfamiliar acronyms. Use contractions (can't, don't) to maintain an easy-going tone.

- Avoid trendy, imprecise language (cool, neat, like) in most professional settings. It's especially harmful when you're speaking to older people who may see you as immature or inexperienced.

- Use anecdotes or stories that are short, to the point, and relevant to your purpose and subject.

- Give lots of examples, even if they're hypothetical. Signal that one is coming by saying "For example…"

- Use statistics to convince, not bedazzle. Round off large numbers and underline important numbers on overheads.

- Don't use visual aids (flip charts, overheads, slides) unless you have practiced with them. If you fumble, that's what your audience will remember about you.

- Don't slap your listeners with anger, sarcasm, or fighting words. They'll be more receptive without those negatives.

- If you must use notes make them simple and easy to follow. Don't read straight from them; use them as a guide. Double or triple space them. Don't use staples or arrange your papers in such a way that they'll make noise as you use them during your talk.

- Maintain effective eye contact by dividing your audience into several sections. Address each section for a while before moving to the next. If you flounder, look back to the section that seemed to offer the most positive feedback.

- Avoid pacing, leaning, scratching, fiddling, covering your mouth, gripping the podium, standing frozen, and looking away from the audience.

- When you take questions after your talk, maintain eye contact with the questioner as you begin to respond. Quickly give your answer as a succinct headline that defines the heart of your response. Then move your eyes away so the questioner won't try to take the floor.

- Let your concluding remarks sink in for a moment before saying thank you; or don't say thank you at all—some experts say it dilutes your final message.

Resources

➡ *The Persuasive Edge: The Executive's Guide to Speaking and Presenting*, Myles Martel, Fawcett, 1989.

➡ *Persuasive Business Speaking*, Elayne Snyder, AMACOM, 1990.

➡ *How to Speak and Listen Effectively*, Harvey Robbins, AMACOM, 1992.

➡ Toastmasters International, PO Box 9052, Mission Viejo, CA 92690-9052, 714-858-8255, new member fee $16. Web address: http://www.toastmasters.org.

➡ *The Working Communicator* (newsletter) includes an eight-page insert, *The Winner's Circle*, filled with facts, humor, quotes, and lists that would be helpful in writing or speaking. From Ragan Communications, 212 W. Superior, Suite 200, Chicago, IL 60610, 800-878-5331, $89/year for new subscribers. Web address: http://www.ragan.com.

See Also

⇨ **Tuning Up Informal Speech**, *page 76*.
⇨ **Writing Speeches and Presentations**, *page 78*.
⇨ **Using Visual Aids**, *page 80*.
⇨ **Projecting a Successful Image**, *page 110*.

Section II: Communication Skills

Tuning Up Informal Speech

When we think of good speaking skills we may picture formal speeches or presentations before large or important groups of people. But most of us do the bulk of our public speaking in informal settings: meetings, workshops, impromptu gatherings at the water cooler, or social events.

Learning how to speak clearly and confidently in those more relaxed settings is just as important for your career as doing polished formal public speaking.

- Have something relevant to say before you speak. Extensive preparation and smooth speaking techniques won't make mush sound like wisdom.

- Take a deep breath or a mental pause before you respond to a question or comment. It gives you time to collect your thoughts and encourages people to listen.

- When asked to give your opinion before a group, first restate the topic. Others might have missed the question. Then clearly and succinctly state your position. Next, give your rationale. Try to begin and end with your strongest reasons; people tend to forget what was in the middle. Conclude by repeating your position.

- Practice relaxation techniques described in books or audiotapes. Relaxing can help lower the pitch of your voice so you won't sound squeaky or shrill. And it can keep you from speaking too loudly.

- Work on your listening skills. Concentrate on the substance of the speaker's comments, the words used to express it, and nonverbal cues like tone of voice and body language. Think about what the speaker is saying, not what you want to say next.

- Watch for overbearing body language. If you're nervous or feel strongly about the topic you may lean forward too much and appear to crowd your audience; or you might use a loud, imposing tone of voice.

- Breathe evenly so you speak slowly and carefully. Don't run words together or talk so fast that you make glaring pronunciation and grammatical errors.

- If you have an accent try to soften it just a little so others won't spend all of their energy deciphering your speech. But don't try to erase it; that would sound false and stifle an interesting quality that may set you apart from others.

- Wipe out the verbal fluff that weakens your message (ah, er, um, you know, really).

- Eliminate distracting nervous physical habits—twirling your hair, tapping your fingers, jiggling change, bouncing your knees or feet, drumming pencils, or rocking back on your chair. Relaxation techniques and smooth breathing can help.

- Spend extra time and effort when communicating by phone. When two speakers can't see each other they miss out on the many nonverbal cues that help increase understanding. Talk more slowly and summarize the conversation more often to make up for it.

Resources

➡ *Never Be Nervous Again: Time-Tested Techniques for the Foolproof Control*, Dorothy Sarnoff, Ivy, 1989.

➡ *Change Your Voice and Change Your Life*, Morton Cooper, Macmillan, 1984.

➡ *How to Get Your Point Across in 30 Seconds—or Less*, Milo Frank, Simon & Schuster, 1986.

➡ Communication Briefings (monthly newsletter), PO Box 25467, Alexandria, VA 22314. 800-888-2084, $79/year. Web address: http://www.combriefings.com.

See Also

➪ **Getting More Out of Meetings**, *page 18.*
➪ **Using Body Language**, *page 68.*
➪ **Notable Speaking**, *page 74.*
➪ **Powerful Persuasion**, *page 96.*

Bonus Tip!

Take the hint: slow down if listeners often ask you to repeat yourself.

Section II: Communication Skills

Writing Speeches and Presentations

Writing a speech or presentation requires a strong blend of skills. Good research and writing will build a better presentation, and knowing the basics of good speaking will make the writing easier.

- Don't try to cover everything in one speech. Focus on one main message.

- Know your objective. What end result do you want?

- If you think you have nothing to say ask yourself who, what, when, where, why, what if, and how? Who got us in this mess? What is our greatest strength? Why didn't we do that?

- Jot down everything you already know about the topic: facts, opinions, examples, experiences, stories, and ideas for graphics. Keep this list with you for a while so you can easily add ideas that pop into your head at odd times.

- Next, determine which specifics you need. What will your audience need to know so you can reach your objective: anecdotes, statistics, quotes, studies, definitions, and comparisons?

- Start looking for those specifics in nearby places: your files, books, magazines, friends, and colleagues. Call a specialist and ask for a comment. Gather a variety of specifics.

- If you speak frequently establish a good working relationship with your local reference librarian.

- Use statistics wisely and sparingly. Relate them to something important or well understood. Break them into smaller units (cost per taxpayer instead of total cost). Use them to paint a picture.

- Follow this successful advertising formula when you write, says speaking expert Hal Persons (see **Resources** below): grab the audience's attention, make your recommendation, support it with information the audience can grasp, and summarize briefly. Conclude by asking the audience to take some action.

- Begin with the unexpected. Steer clear of dull, "I'm delighted to be here tonight" openings.

- Look for a closing that will trigger applause. Especially memorable are quotes and anecdotes (see **Resources** below). Avoid ending with "Thank you." It draws attention away from your final words.

- Never settle for your first draft.

- Cut all that is boring, irrelevant, unverifiable, and trite. Drop what you wouldn't want to see linked to your name in the local newspaper.

- Use vivid, everyday language in brief sentences. Eliminate jargon, abbreviations, acronyms, euphemisms, foreign terms, sexist language, and wordy phrases.

- Before you use humor, ask yourself if it would be effective with your audience. Also, does it help make a point or is it just a good joke? Look for brief stories or comments that let the humor in your audience, subject, self, or situation come out naturally.

Section II: Communication Skills

Resources
➡ *How to Write and Give a Speech*, Joan Detz , St. Martin's Press, 1992.
➡ *The How To of Great Speaking: Stage Techniques to Tame Those Butterflies*, Hal Persons, Black & Taylor, 1992.
➡ *The Business Speaker's Humor Handbook*, Michael Iapoce, John Wiley & Sons, 1988.
➡ *Braude's Treasury of Wit and Humor*, Jacob Braude, Prentice Hall, 1986.
➡ *Familiar Quotations*, John Bartlett, Carol Publishing Group, 1983.
➡ *The Speaker's Lifetime Library*, Leonard Spinrad and Thelma Spinrad, Prentice Hall, 1987.
➡ *The Little, Brown Book of Anecdotes*, Clifton Fadiman, Little, 1991.

See Also
➪ **Notable Speaking**, *page 74.*
➪ **Tuning Up Informal speech**, *page 76.*
➪ **Choosing the Right Words**, *page 88.*
➪ **Using Humor at Work**, *page 114.*

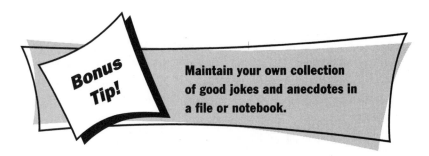

Bonus Tip!

Maintain your own collection of good jokes and anecdotes in a file or notebook.

Using Visual Aids

Have you ever sat through a presentation where the speaker's confusing use of slides and charts kept you too distracted to listen? Or technical problems made grasping the main points all but impossible?

Visual aids—slides, overhead projections, handouts, and props—can give oomph to your speech, meeting, workshop, or sales pitch. But if they're used sloppily, carelessly, or without enough preparation, they can sabotage the sharpest presenter.

- Scrutinize each visual aid you're considering. Will it add depth to your message or obscure it? Don't rely on visuals to save a weak presentation.

- Make sure your visuals have a clear message and aren't just a lot of flash. Keep them simple and consistent.

- Don't start a presentation with visuals. Speak for at least two or three minutes to establish your identity and credibility and build a rapport with the audience.

- Add pictures and designs to your visuals when possible.

- Use color to improve and brighten visuals. Color can provide continuity between charts or slides. It also can make a particular figure or word stand out (yellow or orange on dark blue is especially effective).

- Don't crowd too much on a single slide, overhead transparency, or flip-chart page. Limit the number of lines per page, slide, or transparency to seven. Limit words per line to six. Don't photocopy a full page of text and display it on an overhead.

- When using graphs, be sure you understand what your data means so you can choose the right type of graph—vertical bar charts, bar graphs, pie charts, or line graphs.

- Make your text legible from about 30 feet away. Don't use all uppercase letters; mix upper- and lowercases. Stick to only one or two type sizes and styles.

- Occasionally use colored, grease pencils and hand lettering on overheads to add interest.

- Use presentation graphics software and your computer for a professional look; or use a graphics service bureau that will produce color visuals for you based on the data you provide (check under graphics designers or graphics services in your phone book).

- Don't use flip charts for large groups or large rooms. They're most effective and readable in meetings with small groups.

- If you like to write on flip charts while you speak, make them look neater by lightly writing the words in pencil ahead of time. Darken them with a marker during the presentation (try out the markers beforehand to make sure they make easy-to-read marks). Make letters about four inches high.

- Minimize the time you spend with your back or side facing the audience while you attend to your visuals. Have photocopies of your visuals for yourself so you won't have to look at the screen; or ask someone else to operate the slide projector while you speak so you won't be distracted.

- Talk while you change slides or transparencies to maintain momentum.

- Don't leave visuals up too long—it's distracting. Also, don't leave the projector on without a transparency; people will be waiting for the next visual instead of listening to you.

- Don't read your visuals to the audience. It's dull. Let the visuals be a bonus filled with extra details.

- Rehearse. Ask a colleague to critique your visuals.

- Have a technical expert on standby to handle glitches.

Resources

➡ *How to Create High-Impact Business Presentations*, Joyce Kupsh and Pat Graves, NTC Business Books, 1993.
➡ *The Presentation Design Book: Projecting a Good Image with Your Desktop Computer*, Margaret Rabb, ed., Ventana Press, 1990.
➡ *Never Be Nervous Again: Time-Tested Techniques for the Foolproof Control*, Dorothy Sarnoff, Ivy, 1989.

See Also

⇨ **Notable Speaking**, *page 74.*
⇨ **Writing Speeches and Presentations**, *page 78.*
⇨ **Powerful Persuasion**, *page 96.*

CHAPTER

7

Chapter 7

Writing

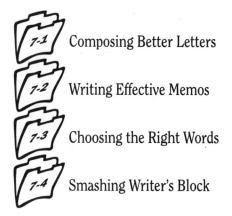

7-1 Composing Better Letters

7-2 Writing Effective Memos

7-3 Choosing the Right Words

7-4 Smashing Writer's Block

Composing Better Letters

Clear, concise business writing does not require special talent or a more rigid form of English than what you speak.

It does require good planning and judicious revision, and the payoffs are great. Writing effective letters helps you establish good relationships and boost productivity. And it saves time and money because the recipients of your writing will be able to quickly absorb your messages.

- Pinpoint your true purpose before you write. (Do you want to simply report a problem or do you want someone to fix it?)

- Jot down everything you want to cover, without worrying about the order. Next, write the entire letter at once, based on the list of issues you just made. Use strong, ordinary words and short sentences. At this point don't worry about spelling, names, dates and other details.

- As you read your piece, check your organization by jotting down what each paragraph is about. You'll have a chronological list of all your points. Do they take the reader to the right place in the most effective way?

- Limit most business letters to a page. One trick is to write as if it were a telegram and you had to pay for every word.

- Be flexible with letter formats. There is no single correct style. You may want to use old-fashioned, formal models if you're writing to a conservative person. Otherwise, try new formats in current business writing books or your word-processing program. One style replaces the greeting ("Dear Sir") with a line summarizing the subject of the letter ("Request for final report").

- Be careful with traditional salutations such as "Dear Madam" or "Gentlemen," which may not fit your audience. Use the person's name or title instead. If you don't know either, use a subject line, as described above.

- Write what your readers need and want to know, not what you want to say. (Write, "You'll be interested to know…" instead of "I want to tell you…")

- Be conversational but also be respectful and restrained. If you're old pals with the person you're writing to, it's OK to write jokes or use slang. Otherwise, write as if you were having a polite conversation.

- Don't try to sound cute, well educated, or flippant. Simply strive for clarity and brevity.

- Don't write your anger. It could harm your reputation. And it usually isn't necessary for getting your message across.

- Replace antiquated business phrases with more direct language. (Instead of "Enclosed please find…" write "I have enclosed the…" Instead of "Received yours of the 15th" write "Thank you for sending me the information on XYZ.")

- Make your document look easy-to-read by using ample margins, shorter paragraphs, subheadings, and lists.

- Don't try to write a perfect letter on your first try. Instead, revise, correct, and shorten.

Resources
➡ *Business Writing the Modular Way*, Harley Bjelland, AMACOM, 1992.
➡ *The Basics of Business Writing*, Marty Stuckey, AMACOM, 1992.

See Also
⇨ **Writing Effective Memos**, *page 86.*
⇨ **Choosing the Right Words**, *page 88.*
⇨ **Smashing Writer's Block**, *page 90.*
⇨ **Business Etiquette for the '90s**, *page 158.*

Bonus Tip!

Write in a way that saves time for your reader, not yourself.

Section II: Communication Skills

Writing Effective Memos

Memos are a dreaded reality of working life. People hate them because they're so often dull, accusing, obtuse, or unbearably long.

Not only are poorly written memos annoying, they also can cause misdirection, inaccurate orders, soured relationships, and bad decisions. They waste the time of the author who isn't organized, and the reader who must figure them out.

- First ask, "Is a memo really necessary? Can I give this message in person? Would my target audience receive it more readily that way?"

- Next ask, "What am I trying to accomplish? How will I know if I succeeded?" If you don't know, don't write it.

- Know your audience. Consider the number of people who will read your memo, how they'll use the information, and their knowledge of the subject.

- Outline your message before you start writing, or at least jot down your main points.

- Limit most memos to three brief but complete sentences, says Debra Benton, author of *Lions Don't Need to Roar*. Make the first sentence reader oriented, starting with the word "you." ("You've done a lot of work with the Barker account.") The second sentence is writer oriented, telling why you're writing. ("I need some help with a new, similar account.") The third sentence is action oriented, explaining the next step. ("Could you share some ideas with me at 2 p.m. Friday?")

- Try the compact writing formula Harley Bjelland describes in *Business Writing the Modular Way* (see **Resources** below). It's the "Hey! You! See? So!" method. Hey! is the opening attention getter. You! involves the reader and gives a good reason to read this. See? is your main point. So! leaves a closing thought or call to action. It convinces the reader that it was worthwhile reading the memo.

- Whatever format you use, get to the point quickly. Don't start with a dull introduction, heavy details, or background information. Summarize your message, then give the details.

- Avoid snide sarcasm, profanity, and condescending demands. Words written in moments of anger or frustration usually are counterproductive.

- If you feel you must write a long memo, break it into several paragraphs or sections. Mark sections with small headlines that summarize that portion.

- Don't be arbitrary. Explain your reasons.
- Anticipate the reactions your writing might cause. Think about how people might receive bad news or criticism in your memo and address that as you write.
- Choose the most specific words possible. Avoid exaggeration.
- If possible, wait a few hours or a day before you edit for clarity, details, and tone. Read the memo aloud to yourself as you edit. Look for anything that readers could misinterpret.
- Ask someone else to read your memo to be sure it's understandable and sends the right message.

Resources
→ *Writing at Work*, Ernst Jacobi, Ten Speed Press, 1985.
→ *Business Writing the Modular Way*, Harley Bjelland, AMACOM, 1992.
→ *The Perfect Memo!* Patricia Westheimer, Park Avenue Productions, 1995.
→ *How to Write Complaint Letters that Work!* Patricia Westheimer and Jim Mastro, Park Avenue Productions, 1994.

See Also
⇨ **Composing Better Letters**, *page 84.*
⇨ **Choosing the Right Words**, *page 88.*
⇨ **Giving Clear Instructions**, *page 100.*
⇨ **Cooling Your Anger**, *page 138.*

Bonus Tip!   **Write in a conversational tone.**

Choosing the Right Words

Precision is doubly important in business writing. You want to convey your exact meaning so there won't be any confusion. And you don't want to look bad. Or is it badly?

Learn about commonly misused words that could spoil your business communications.

- **Affect/effect:** Affect is a verb that means to produce an effect on something. (That will affect my decision.) Effect can be a noun that is a change produced by an action. (The weather will have an effect on my plan.) Effect also can be a verb that means to bring about. (The research will effect a cure.)

- **Among/between:** Use among when referring to more than two people or objects. Use between when referring to two people, groups, or objects.

- **Bad/badly:** Bad is an adjective, which describes a noun. (He was a bad piano player; I feel bad; that smells bad.) Badly is an adverb, which modifies a verb, adjective, or other adverb and describes how, when, or where. (He played the piano badly.) Don't use badly to describe how you feel. (I feel badly.)

- **Compliment/complement:** To give someone a compliment is to express admiration or praise. But to complement a report is to make it complete, possibly by adding to it.

- **Disinterested/uninterested:** A disinterested person is unbiased. An uninterested one doesn't care about the topic.

- **Farther/further:** Farther refers to actual distances (...two miles farther down the road). Further is intangible; it means to a greater extent. ("I won't discuss this further.")

- **Finalize:** Avoid this. It's jargon that means to finish or put in final form. Use finish or complete.

- **Fortuitous/fortunate:** An event is fortuitous if it happened by chance: it could be good or bad. A fortunate occurrence brings about or is brought by good fortune.

- **Imply/infer:** A listener infers by reading a hidden message into what someone else says. A speaker or writer implies by hinting at something indirectly.

- **Judgment:** Don't insert an extra e after the g.

- **Lead/led:** Lead is the present tense; led is past. (She led the meeting.)

- **Lie/lay:** To lie is to be on a horizontal surface and generally refers to people. (I'll lie down.) To lay is to place an object on a horizontal surface. (I'll lay this book here.)

- **Manageable:** You need an e after the g here.

- **Personally:** It's usually unnecessary. Of course you, personally, believe whatever you're writing. You're the one doing the writing.

- **Presently/soon:** Presently often is used to mean now, but it actually means soon.

- **Regardless/irregardless:** Regardless is the correct choice.

- **Requirement/requisite/perquisite/prerequisite:** A requirement is needed, desired, or demanded. A requisite is a necessity. A perquisite, or perk, is a fringe benefit such as a company car. A prerequisite is a required advanced condition, as algebra is a prerequisite for geometry.

- **Stationary/stationery:** Stationary means not moving. Stationery is writing paper and envelopes.

- **-wise:** Another piece of jargon that gums up your writing. (Productivity-wise, she's a terrible worker.) Rewrite the sentence to avoid -wise.

Resources
➡ *The Dictionary of Confusable Words*, Laurence Urdang, Facts on File, 1988.

See Also
➪ **Composing Better Letters**, *page 84.*
➪ **Writing Effective Memos**, *page 86.*

Section II: Communication Skills

7-4 Smashing Writer's Block

There's a tapping going on in thousands of workplaces. It's the tapping of pencils on desks and feet on floors. It's the sound of nervous people who are trying to write a report, letter, or memorandum, but can't get started. It's the sound of wasted time and unnecessary frustration.

Don't despair if you are a stalled, would-be writer. Use these ideas to pry yourself loose and produce clear, focused, and concise writing.

- Relax. Writing doesn't have to be complicated. It's best to keep it simple and straightforward, like conversation.

- Don't let grammar or punctuation paralyze you. You do need to follow basic rules that let your readers understand your message the first time around without tripping on construction. Don't worry about obscure edicts.

- Don't insist that you write perfectly the first time.

- Plan first. Maybe you're stuck because you don't know what you're writing. Outline why you're writing this and to whom you're writing; the format, tone and results you want; the best points you can make; and in which order you should make them.

- Start on each main point by filling in the blanks of this sentence: the main thing about…is…, writer Marty Stuckey suggests in his book (see **Resources** below). Next, fill in this sentence: this is important because….

- Make sure you're writing at your most productive, creative time of day.

- Don't put off writing so that you wind up doing it when you're tired.

- Do something completely different and absorbing—preferably an activity that will engage the creative side of your brain (see a movie, view an art display, listen to music). When you return to your writing task you're likely to have a new perspective.

- Try writing in a different place: the cafeteria, a park, another department, the lobby, or your car.

- "Write a letter to someone about what you would say if you could only get started," suggests Boston-based creativity consultant Marcia Yudkin (see **Resources** below).

- Pretend you have 10 seconds to make your case before your boss fires you. Limber up by writing nonstop—about anything—for five minutes. Then throw it away.

- Set a timer for 15 or 30 minutes. Write until the timer goes off. Take a break. Repeat.

- Make a list. Write down everything about this writing project that scares you, no matter how goofy. List the benefits you get from stalling, or list all the events you're waiting for before you write. Make one of those events happen so you eliminate an excuse.

- Find someone else who has writing to do too. Give each other deadlines. Check up on each other and offer encouragement.

- Start at the middle or end instead of the beginning.

- Write the opposite of what you really want to say.

- If guilt motivates you, figure out how much you've been paid so far for not writing.

- Talk it out. Pretend you're explaining your topic to your mother or dictate your memorandum or report into a tape recorder. Transcribe it and use it as a rough draft.

Resources
➥ *Exploding Writer's Block* (audiotape), Marcia Yudkin, PO Box 1310, Boston, MA 02117, 800-898-3546, $14.95 + shipping and handling. E-mail: marcia@yudkin.com.
➥ *Become a More Productive Writer* (audiotape), Marcia Yudkin (address above), $14.95 + shipping and handling.
➥ *The Basics of Business Writing*, Marty Stuckey, AMACOM, 1992.

See Also
⇨ **Finding More Time in Your Day**, *page 8.*
⇨ **Creative Problem Solving**, *page 48.*
⇨ **Composing Better Letters**, *page 84.*
⇨ **Writing Effective Memos**, *page 86.*

Chapter 8

Communicating with a Purpose

8-1   Arguing Productively

8-2   Powerful Persuasion

8-3   Negotiating for What You Want

8-4   Giving Clear Instructions

8-5   Making Gossip Work for You

Arguing Productively

In the work world disagreements with others are common. Often, they degenerate into counterproductive and damaging arguments.

Others may have taught you that it's not nice to argue. But a well-conducted argument can be polite and even helpful.

- Don't automatically try to avoid arguments. They can be positive if you govern yourself with self-control and confidence rather than emotions. Arguments can bring difficult issues out into the open, which usually is better than letting them ferment. And arguments can strengthen working relationships by teaching colleagues how to respect differences and survive criticism.

- Think of arguments or disagreements as communication breakdowns. Focus on how to clarify the communication. Try to figure out what caused the breakdown. Among the possibilities are a personality clash, misinterpreted words or body language, poor timing, and inappropriate tone of voice.

- Avoid using the words I, me, and my in arguments. They pit people against people instead of ideas against ideas. They indicate that emotions and ego are getting in the way of objectivity.

- Remember that the more emotional you and your opponent get during a communication breakdown, the less likely you are to reach agreement.

- Rely on facts, figures, and experts to make your points. This will encourage your opponent to accept your ideas, and can keep the discussion from becoming inflammatory.

- Treat others' opinions with respect, even if you disagree. People tend to see their opinions as part of themselves; it's tough to give them up.

- Be specific, constructive, and empathetic when disagreeing with another person. Don't be judgmental or arrogant.

- Hear the other person first. Then talk about where you agree and disagree. Acknowledge your opponent's good points before you begin mentioning the faulty ones.

- When your opponent makes a weak conclusion, use it to your advantage. Press for explanations of the reasoning. Question the soundness of data. If you can shoot holes in the reasoning, then you have a good chance of winning the argument.

- Concentrate on issues instead of personalities. If your opponent throws negative comments at you about your background insist that everyone stick with the issues.

- Avoid taking an all or nothing position. You're most likely to reach agreement if you can accept middle ground.

- Yield to whatever is in the best interest of your company or organization, unless it's an important personal issue.

Resources
➡ *How to Talk So People Listen: The Real Key to Business Success*, Sonya Hamlin, HarperCollins, 1989.

See Also
⇨ **Handling Customer Problems**, *page 34.*
⇨ **Preparing for a Conflict**, *page 50.*
⇨ **Listen Up**, *page 70.*
⇨ **Powerful Persuasion**, *page 96.*

Section II: Communication Skills

Bonus Tip!

Eliminate disagreements by setting clear expectations often.

Powerful Persuasion

Convincing people to change their minds or accept your ideas is a routine part of working life. We do it when proposing projects to a supervisor, seeking support from a coworker, and convincing a customer to buy our service or product.

Learning about how people change their attitudes can help make you a more effective communicator and persuader.

- Know your listeners' attitudes, beliefs, and values before you make your pitch. You must cause a shift in those factors before they'll change their behavior. Find out why they're here, what they already know about your subject, how they feel about it, and how they feel about you.

- Build your arguments according to what you want to accomplish. (Do you want praise or monetary support?) Present those arguments in terms of what your listeners want, not what you want.

- Use the first few moments of your talk to establish positive feelings. Smile. Offer sincere praise. Tell a warm story. Say thanks for the opportunity to speak. Establish common ground. ("I'm concerned about this, too.")

- Create in your audience a need or desire for your idea, goods, or services. How? Use the three classical modes of proof in your pitch: ethical (why they should believe you), emotional (appealing to their sympathies), and logical (facts). Stress the approach that will appeal most to your audience (accountants will want facts and figures).

- Use strong words, well-timed pauses, and a steady tone.

- Don't announce, "I will convince you that…" You'll make your listeners defensive and invite them to challenge you.

- Never call the opposition foolish, ignorant, or uninformed. Insults won't win support.

- Present both sides of the argument when you know your audience opposes your side, or will hear about opposing arguments in the future. Present the opposing side fairly and logically; don't let people conclude that you're twisting the opposition's arguments to make your own look better.

- Give only your side of the argument if your audience is predisposed to supporting you anyway.

- Use your two strongest arguments at the beginning and end of your talk. People remember best what came first and last.

- If you're addressing someone who is uninterested in your topic, showcase peripheral factors like your credibility, appearance, expertise, likability, and trustworthiness.

- Stress the positive. Discuss what you'll do about a problem, not how pessimistic you are about it.

- Be absolutely truthful. Lying will harm your cause more than it will help you.

- Time your debate carefully. Don't try it when the other person can't or won't be able to concentrate.

- If possible, let the other person experience your argument personally. Let the person try your method to see how it works.

- Stay cool and unflappable at all costs.

- Conclude by asking for what you want (support, a raise, the job) with confidence and conviction. Don't leave it unspoken.

Resources

➡ *The Persuasive Edge: The Executive's Guide to Speaking and Presenting*, Myles Martel, Fawcett, 1989.
➡ *Persuasive Business Speaking*, Elayne Snyder, AMACOM, 1990.
➡ *Business Communication Skills: Principles and Practice*, John Makay and Ronald Fetzer, Prentice Hall, 1984.
➡ *Face-to-Face Selling*, Bart Breighner, Park Avenue Productions, 1995.

See Also

⇨ **Asking for a Raise,** *page 202.*
⇨ **Notable Speaking**, *page 74.*
⇨ **Tuning Up Informal Speech**, *page 76.*
⇨ **Negotiating for What You Want**, *page 98.*

Section II: Communication Skills

Negotiating for What You Want

You may not think of yourself as a negotiator, but you probably negotiate all the time. You negotiated when you asked for a raise or job change, sought a coworker's cooperation, or arranged child care for your toddler.

You don't have to be tough and mean to negotiate successfully, but you don't want to be too conciliatory either.

- Before you negotiate know your needs, wants, assumptions and beliefs—and your opponent's. Know what you're willing to give up and what you'll settle for. Anticipate the other person's objections. Know the issues.

- Build a friendly base before negotiations. Chat informally with people from the other side when they're off guard. Mention the issue at hand. Give a little information. Be likable, sincere, friendly, and fair.

- Use strong language like we need, must, and require instead of we would like, hope, or prefer.

- Be prepared to stick to your demands and possibly walk away empty-handed if you like to negotiate hard. Softening your approach at the last minute will cost you credibility and respect.

- Listen to the other side's proposal completely and without immediate negative judgment. Don't interrupt. You might miss out on a concession they planned to throw in at the end. Take a moment to consider their plan. Then talk about the parts you like and how they fit with your proposal.

- Use gentle leading questions. Instead of making accusations ("That's an insult!") ask questions to solicit feedback ("What would you think if…").

- Don't just list objections. Propose solutions.

- When your opponent raises objections, say that you've already considered them. Use them to introduce the positive aspects of your proposal.

- Don't voluntarily list a range of options you'd be willing to accept. Your opponents will choose the one best for them, not you.

- Don't negotiate by phone unless you place the call. People receiving calls are at a disadvantage because they may not have their notes handy, be mentally prepared, or be in a quiet setting. If you receive a call when you're off-guard, suggest another call or meeting at a later, specified time.

- Be honest about your proposal's flaws; your opponent will assume you're honest in general.

■ Look for clues in what the other side says. They may say "It's not our policy," which is not the same as "It's impossible." Your reply, "If it were possible how would you do it?"

■ Try stating your ideal arrangement, and then immediately modify it. ("I'd normally need three weeks for a project like this but I could complete yours in two.")

■ Don't throw in anything for free. Make everything conditional. ("If I do...then would you...") Don't agree to the other side's request, and then ask for something. Why should they give it?

■ When making concessions let your opponent know that they are genuine but there may not be any more, especially if your opponent does not reciprocate.

Resources
→ *The Haggler's Handbook: One Hour to Negotiating Power*, Leonard Koren, W.W. Norton, 1991.
→ *Smart Negotiating: How to Make Good Deals in the Real World*, James Freund, Simon & Schuster, 1992.
→ *The Quick Interview & Salary Negotiation Book*, J. Michael Farr, JIST Works, Inc., 1995.

See Also
⇨ **Arranging Your Parental Leave**, *page 244.*
⇨ **Listen Up**, *page 70.*
⇨ **Arguing Productively**, *page 94.*
⇨ **Powerful Persuasion**, *page 96.*

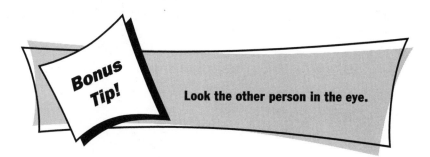

Bonus Tip!

Look the other person in the eye.

Section II: Communication Skills

Giving Clear Instructions

Whether you are a company president or a secretary you give directions, orders, suggestions, and requests daily. If those instructions are poor they can cause mistakes, safety hazards, and wasted time and money.

When that happens we often react by repeating—maybe at a louder volume—the same instructions that failed in the first place. But hearing usually isn't the problem. A better strategy is to change your message or the way you're sending it.

- Visualize the results you want before giving instructions. Break the task down into step-by-step procedures. Determine what people need to do the job.

- Tell people the purpose of the task, the desired end result, how to do it (not how NOT to do it), time needed, a deadline, what they'll encounter along the way, potential hazards and ways to deal with them, how they'll know if they've goofed, and reassurance that they can do it.

- Use illustrations and demonstrations when possible.

- Don't rush your directions, regardless of ambition or deadlines. Good directions save time.

- For complex jobs, give instructions for one part of the task at a time.

- Be consistent. Don't say that you want the job done one way, and then complain later that it should have been done another way.

- If you're a person of few words, elaborate more than usual when giving instructions so you don't leave people guessing. However, don't obscure your directions with excessive information.

- Say exactly what you mean. Use specific, direct, and concrete language that your audience understands. Avoid euphemisms, abstract ideas, and ambiguous terms.

- Don't let your instructions sound like orders, which most people resent. Help people understand why you want the task done this way. Link your directions to the organization's goals. Leave room for people to be creative and take responsibility for the job.

- Prevent misunderstandings by asking listeners how they'll approach the problem and why. Ask them to repeat your directions when you're done.

- Follow up. Make sure that people are following your plans, using correct and safe work methods, assuming their assigned responsibilities, and identifying hidden hazards or problems.

- If you're taking instructions, be active. Ask questions. Analyze.

- Be patient and open-minded as you listen to others' instructions. Don't jump ahead, second-guess the instruction giver, or assume you're too smart for the directions. Listen to the details.

Resources

➡ *Follow the Yellow Brick Road: Learning to Give, Take, and Use Instructions*, Richard Wurman, Bantam, 1992.

See Also

⇨ **Getting More Out of Meetings**, *page 18.*
⇨ **Communicating for Success**, *page 66.*
⇨ **Powerful Persuasion**, *page 96.*
⇨ **Negotiating for What You Want**, *page 98.*

Section II: Communication Skills

Bonus Tip!

Try to be clear, not clever.

Making Gossip Work for You

Psssst! Have you heard? Gossip can be good for you.

Many of us tend to think of gossip as a nasty way to sling mud at people. But gossip doesn't have to be negative or hurtful. When it's spread via the office grapevine it can be a helpful information source. Office gossip can reveal who has the real power at work and who is considered successful and why. It can tell you how you're regarded and it can enhance or tarnish your reputation.

If you're a manager the grapevine can help you learn more about employee attitudes and concerns.

- Engineer good gossip about yourself. Maintain a positive attitude at work so that whatever is said about you on the grapevine tends to be upbeat. Share credit with coworkers. Sincerely praise colleagues. You even could leak positive—but truthful—information about yourself. (Mention that you received a glowing thank-you note from a big client.)

- Establish positive relationships with people who know what's going on and who get things done. Include people from other departments. The more people you know, the more information you could pick up.

- Maintain positive or neutral relationships with people who seem to be against you. You might be able to keep them from spreading negative comments about you on the grapevine.

- Consider the differences in the ways most men and women perceive gossip. Men often avoid it, seeing it as a way to spread negative comments about people in their absence. And men may be nervous about joining the grapevine because they wouldn't want anything said about them that would make them look less competent than others, as Deborah Tannen notes in *You Just Don't Understand* (see **Resources** below). But women see gossip as a way to show interest in others and establish bonds by sharing information.

- Before you gossip ask yourself, "What is my intention for saying this?" If it's negative, forget it.

- Tap into trade gossip. Join professional associations. Get to know people who work for the competition. Learn from what's happening elsewhere.

- Be careful about what you say at work; say only what you'd be willing to have attributed to you. Be cautious about discussing personal problems. People might make erroneous conclusions based on what they hear. And unscrupulous people may seize power over you once they know your "secrets."

- When you hear false or damaging gossip about a boss or colleague consider telling that person. Your boss or colleague might appreciate getting a chance to clear up the problem. Don't reveal who is saying what or you could be cut out of the grapevine and become the subject of negative gossip yourself; or challenge the people spreading the false information; they may drop it just to avoid the confrontation.

- Don't react with vengeance if you are the subject of negative gossip. Take positive action to counteract it, either by confronting the gossiper or making sure others know the truth. Avoid sounding defensive.

Resources

➡ *You Just Don't Understand: Women and Men in Conversation*, Deborah Tannen, Ballantine, 1991.

See Also

⇨ **Building a Productive Network**, *page 206.*
⇨ **Communicating with the Opposite Sex**, *page 32.*
⇨ **Listen Up**, *page 70.*
⇨ **Projecting a Successful Image**, *page 110.*

Bonus Tip!

Don't participate in harmful, mean-spirited gossip.

SECTION III

Self-Improvement

Section III: Self-Improvement

CHAPTER

9

Chapter 9

Sharp Thinking

9-1 Positive Thinking Power

9-2 Projecting a Successful Image

9-3 Boosting Your Self-Esteem

9-4 Using Humor at Work

9-5 Setting Goals

9-6 Nurturing Your Creativity

9-7 Tapping Your Intuition

9-8 Making Better Decisions

9-9 Taking Smart Risks

Section III: Self-Improvement

9-1 Positive Thinking Power

Success is all in your head.

It's determined largely by your powerful thoughts. If they are positive and aimed at the future they'll help you reach your highest goals. But if they are negative and mired in the past, they'll dilute your energy and stall your career progress. Lurking in your subconscious, they could be behind job problems like procrastination, inappropriate comments, power abuse, constant complaints, or unprofessional actions.

- Visualize. Spend 90 seconds imagining how you'd be if you achieved all your goals. What will you look like? Where will you be? What will you be doing? How will you solve problems? Let that picture guide your thoughts and actions. Act like the person in that vision.

- Be your own leader, even if you're on a team or work for a dominant manager. Know who you are, what you want, and where you're going. Trust your intuition and be confident about your informed decisions.

- Consider working with a buddy (spouse, coworker, friend) as you both strive toward success. Meet every week to discuss your experiences, give each other feedback, and hold each other accountable for progress. Ask your buddy to alert you when you start speaking or acting negatively.

- Focus only on what you can control—yourself. Take responsibility for your problems. Blaming others robs you of control over your own life; it says that others have the power to make you take actions against your will.

- Address one weak attitude or negative habit at a time. With daily work it takes two to four weeks to develop new thought habits.

- Don't just dream about where you want to be in three months or three years. Write down your professional and personal goals. Identify skills you need to develop. Create a plan, with a timetable, for reaching your goals.

- Turn negative situations into positive ones by listing all the bright aspects of what seems to be a disaster. (Your boss may have rejected your proposal but you learned how to prepare three different kinds of reports in the process.)

- Nurture positive thoughts by taking positive actions. Try a new task at work, learn a new skill, help a coworker, or compliment a colleague.

- Surround yourself by positive thinkers who support your career goals and have the characteristics you want to develop.

- Spend the first 20 minutes of the day feeding your mind with rich, inspirational, educational material. Set a positive tone. Some people clear their minds of negative or distracting thoughts every morning by writing about whatever is on their minds for five to 10 minutes, or long enough to fill three pages of a notepad.

- Spend 15 minutes each evening reviewing the day's events. What could you have done better? What did you do well? What can you change tomorrow?

- Stop apologizing for your ideas ("This might not be a great idea but..."). State your opinions and proposals boldly and assertively ("I can find a way to fix that.").

Resources

➡ *Winning the Inner Game of Selling*, Matt Oechsli, Rough Notes, 1991.
➡ *1,000 Things You Never Learned in Business School: How to Manage Your Fast Track Career*, William Yeomans, Signet, 1990.
➡ *Your Own Worst Enemy: How to Overcome Career Self-Sabotage*, Andrew DuBrin, AMACOM, 1992.
➡ *The Psychology of Achievement* (audiotape program), Brian Tracy, Nightingale Conant, 1987, 800-525-9000, $59.95 + shipping and handling. Web address: http://www.nightingale.com.

See Also:

⇨ **Projecting a Successful Image,** *page 110.*
⇨ **Boosting Your Self-Esteem,** *page 112.*
⇨ **Setting Goals,** *page 116.*

Section III: Self-Improvement

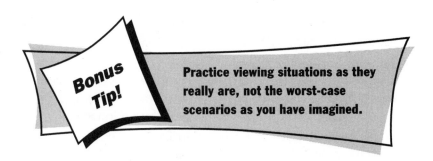

Bonus Tip!

Practice viewing situations as they really are, not the worst-case scenarios as you have imagined.

Projecting a Successful Image

Are you the victim of self-inflicted sabotage? That's when you sell yourself short to coworkers and supervisors with your language and behavior.

You are constantly instructing others how to view you. By sending negative or weak messages about yourself you're telling others to take you and your ideas less seriously.

This undermining is common, especially in women. The way to unlock yourself from this trap is to maintain high self-esteem and use some communication savvy.

- Pick up the physical traits of confident, assertive people. Stand straight, hold your head up high. Use a firm handshake, speak clearly, smile, and use strong and decisive body language. Look relaxed, but show that you have energy. Look at people with a strong gaze.

- Allow yourself to make mistakes. Everyone does. Learn from them. Don't dwell on past mistakes. That feeds a negative self-image.

- Don't put yourself down, especially at work. Making demeaning remarks about your appearance or skills, even in jest, projects a poor self-image.

- Display a proactive image. Speak up about how you or others could handle a problem early on. Don't portray yourself as a victim. Show that you are responsible for your own decisions and results.

- Gracefully accept compliments. Don't say that your project really wasn't much of an accomplishment, or that anyone could have done it, or that it contains mistakes.

- Don't undersell your own ideas ("I think this might be a good idea..." or "This might not make much sense but..."). Words like think, believe, and might are weak and signal that you have little faith in your thinking.

- When you've made a poor suggestion or handled a meeting improperly, face it. Go back to the key players and restate your position confidently. ("I didn't really express myself very well yesterday. What we really should do is..." Or, "I was having an off-day Tuesday. Let's talk about that problem again.")

- Be bold about asking for what you need from coworkers or supervisors. (Avoid "I know you're busy but..." and "I hate to bother you with this but...") Be direct. ("I need some of your time, please.")

- Don't allow others to interrupt you. Assuredly tell the other speaker that you're still talking, then and continue.

- Don't accept blame for others' moods or problems. ("I'm sorry I'm making you so angry.") Realize where your influence ends and where others' responsibilities begin.

- Make agreements with coworkers or colleagues to keep them from taking advantage of you. Commit major agreements to writing and stick to them. (Make a deal with a coworker over how to divvy up a project. Or specify acceptable times and lengths of meetings with a client.) When the other people don't hold up their end of the deal, refer to the agreement instead of making personal criticisms.

Resources
➡ *How to Win Friends and Influence People*, Dale Carnegie and Dorothy Carnegie, Simon & Schuster, 1981.

See Also
⇨ **Positive Thinking Power**, *page 108.*
⇨ **Boosting Your Self-Esteem**, *page 112.*
⇨ **Making Better Decisions**, *page 122.*
⇨ **Recovering from Mistakes**, *page 140.*

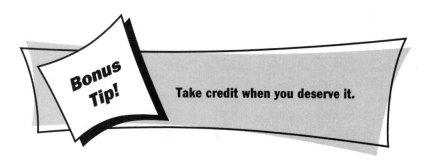

Bonus Tip!

Take credit when you deserve it.

Section III: Self-Improvement

Boosting Your Self-Esteem

It's trendy to talk about high self-esteem as an important part of mental health. But a healthy regard for yourself is important for career and business success, too.

"We have reached a moment in history when self-esteem, which has always been a supremely important psychological survival need, has now become a supremely important economic survival need as well," psychologist Nathaniel Branden writes in *The Power of Self-Esteem* (see **Resources** below).

You need confidence in your ability to think and cope with life's challenges to be productive, competitive, and creative in a demanding global marketplace.

- Trust your own informed decisions. Don't try to reach every conclusion by consensus or committee; you are qualified to make many decisions on your own.

- Notice how your work makes a difference in someone's life. What do your accomplishments mean for your colleagues, staff, customers, and family? Take satisfaction in those results.

- Don't base your self-esteem on factors that aren't in your control, such as the company's profit margin or the amount of your latest raise.

- Don't question your abilities when your supervisor demands more of you. Think about the skills you've learned so far. What do you know about learning unfamiliar subjects that could help you with these new challenges? Give yourself credit for what you've already accomplished.

- Take responsibility for your own success. Do what you can to master your job and understand how your work fits in the organization. Don't blame others for your career or job status.

- Don't define yourself solely in terms of your work or professional accomplishments. Your self-esteem will take a big hit if your job disappears or your accomplishments become sporadic. Develop other facets of your life, too—friends, family, community, or hobbies.

- Pick yourself up and keep going even when you fail to reach a goal. You may need to update, restate, or reschedule it. Also, examine the failure. Ask yourself, "What can I do about this? What did I overlook? What did I miscalculate?" Now, move on to the next challenge.

- Be true to yourself. Know what you want and need to reach your personal milestones of success. Make sure your work and goals are in line with your personal values. Tell people what you want at work, making it easier for them to give it to you.

- Share your accomplishments with coworkers and friends.

- Strengthen your work skills and confidence through education, training, and reading. Suggest that you help conduct a training session on a subject in which you have expertise.

- Try to help your boss solve problems. Show that you have some sharp ideas.

Resources

➡ *The Power of Self-Esteem*, Nathaniel Branden, Health Communications, 1992.

➡ *How to Raise Your Self-Esteem*, Branden, Bantam, 1988.

➡ *Overcoming 'Self-Esteem,'* (pamphlet), David Mills, Albert Ellis Institute, 45 East 65th St., New York, NY 10021-6593, 800-323-IRET, $1.50. Web address: http://www.rebt.org.

See Also

⇨ **Positive Thinking Power**, *page 108.*
⇨ **Setting Goals**, *page 116.*
⇨ **Making Better Decisions**, *page 122.*
⇨ **Recovering from Mistakes**, *page 140.*

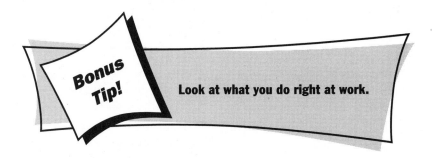

Bonus Tip!

Look at what you do right at work.

Section III: Self-Improvement

Using Humor at Work

Do you or the people you work with have Terminal Professionalism?

"People will tell you they've got it," humor specialist C.W. Metcalf says. "People will say, 'I'm dead serious.' And they will be." Dead, that is—and serious (see **Resources** below).

But it is possible to have fun at work and still be effective and successful. In fact, humor may be necessary for success. It sparks creativity, strengthens relationships, generates energy, and fosters positive attitudes.

- Don't assume that using humor at work means telling jokes. It's more an attitude than a stand-up comedy contest.

- Make having fun a career goal. Write it down and plan it.

- Be tolerant when you see people having fun at work. Unless it harms the quality of work over the long-term, it's doing more good than harm.

- Don't work harder when stress hits. Work looser. Look for the absurdity in your predicament. Think of what you could say if you were doing a comedy routine about it. Imagine what your favorite cartoon character would do in this situation.

- Encourage a lighter and more energetic atmosphere by bringing people together whenever possible (meetings, brainstorming sessions, annual picnics, sporting events, Friday morning donuts and coffee, Popsicle breaks on a hot day).

- If you work in a conservative atmosphere find clandestine ways to have fun. Wear Loony Tunes underwear. Listen to a comedy tape on your Walkman during breaks or lunchtime walks. Keep funny glasses in your glove compartment to wear while driving home.

- Design ways to quickly sprout a grin when you feel upset or out of control. Keep cartoons, jokes, buttons with funny sayings, or goofy-looking snapshots of yourself in a desk drawer or briefcase. Look at them before diving into a dreaded meeting or task.

- Listen to comedy tapes while commuting or during your lunch hour. Organize a comedy swap, Metcalf suggests. Have coworkers bring their favorite tapes to work and put them in a box. At the end of the day, everyone grabs a new tape for the ride home.

- Post jokes and cartoons in your office. Set up a "So you think it's tough around here..." bulletin board of cartoons and newspaper clippings. Be careful not to post material that could be offensive to others.

- Escape the weighty atmosphere of your workplace by having lunch or meetings at a stimulating, active, fun restaurant or gathering place. Lighten up a company lunchroom with a cartoon bulletin board, funny posters, or even a VCR-TV setup that plays funny TV shows or movies.

- Look for a sense of humor in job candidates. Do they laugh during the interview? Do they make you laugh? Did you have fun when you took them to lunch? Ask applicants to describe their most fun job or how they made a tough job enjoyable.

- Don't expect work to be fun all the time. It won't be. Strive for enjoying yourself at least some of the time.

- Avoid humor that's negative, sexist, racist, or abusive; joking when your motives are to insult or attain revenge; teasing others but not letting them tease you back; or joking about sensitive topics like baldness without asking the bald person if he minds.

Resources

➡ *Lighten Up: Survival Skills for People Under Pressure*, C.W. Metcalf and Roma Felible, Addison-Wesley, 1993.
➡ *The Light Touch: How to Use Humor for Business Success*, Malcolm Kushner, Simon & Schuster, 1992.
➡ The HUMOR Project, a humor and creativity think tank that sponsors workshops, *Laughing Matters* magazine, and a mail-order catalog, 110 Spring St., Saratoga Springs, NY 12866-3397, 518-587-8770. Web address: http://www.wizvax.net/humor/

See Also

➪ **Positive Thinking Power,** *page 108.*
➪ **Quick Stress Busters,** *page 128.*
➪ **Managing Stress for the Long-Term,** *page 130.*
➪ **I Hate My Job!** *page 136.*

Section III: Self-Improvement

Setting Goals

How often have you proudly made a list of goals for yourself, only to shove them in the back of a drawer and forget them? That doesn't mean that you can't accomplish big things. It does mean that you need a strategy to make your goals more achievable.

It is worth the trouble. Studies have shown that successful people set goals; others don't. Most of us won't grow or change without goals.

- Have a vision for yourself. What do you want to accomplish in your career? Your life? What's important to you? Dream. Soul search.

- Write down your goals. Specify what, where, when, who, how many, how often, and with what end result. Writing clarifies your thinking and creates a sense of action.

- Focus only on one or two big goals at once. Delegate or drop tasks that don't contribute to your goals. However, keep your goals balanced. Don't spend all of your time working on one area (career) at the expense of others (family, health).

- Write down all the steps you'll have to take to reach your goal before your deadline. Break that list of tasks down into smaller actions you can take this week, this month, and in coming months. Now you have an action plan.

- Write the steps on your calendar—starting with today—so they become part of your daily focus. Check them off your to-do list to build a sense of accomplishment and measure progress.

- Know what resources (time, money, equipment, education, expert guidance) you'll need to reach your goals. Make attaining them part of your action plan.

- Identify potential obstacles. Plan action steps to prevent them. Add the phrase "therefore, I will…" to the bothersome issues you've identified, suggests Jean Watson, speaker's coach and president of Watson & Associates, Tyler, Texas. ("Spending an hour on Goal A puts me behind in Project X, therefore, I will…")

- Overcome resistance by staying focused on the benefits of your goals. What will you get when you achieve them? A bonus? Control of your time? Less pressure from your boss? If your resistance is rooted in fear, realistically evaluate the risks you see. How bad are they, really? How likely is it that those problems will occur?

- Allow time for unexpected problems, delays, or revisions.

- Create a mental picture that shows you accomplishing your goal. Rehearse it internally until it becomes a reflex. Visualize the end result: what you'll be like, look like, act like, or have when you reach this goal. If possible, draw a picture of success as you define it and put it where you'll see it often.

- Reward yourself for small successes along the way.

- Adjust your goals as necessary to meet changing conditions or overcome unforeseen obstacles.

- Eliminate goals you don't believe in. You'll never get to them if you wrote them to please someone else or if they don't match your values. If you're stuck with a goal that someone else has imposed on you, negotiate a compromise or propose another goal that would serve both of you. If that fails, try to identify some kind of benefit you'll realize if you accomplish the goal, even if it's a reward from yourself.

Resources

➡ *Goal Setting*, Susan Wilson, AMACOM, 1994.

➡ *The Organized Executive*, Stephanie Winston, W.W. Norton, 1994.

➡ *The Successful Manager's Handbook: Development Suggestions for Today's Managers*, Brian Davis, Personnel Decisions, Inc., Minneapolis, MN, 1996, 800-633-4410, $54.95 + shipping and handling. Web address: http://www.pdi-corp.com.

➡ *Even Eagles Need a Push*, David McNally, TransForm Press, 1990.

See Also

▷ **Finding More Time in Your Day**, *page 8.*

▷ **Boosting Efficiency with Your Calendar**, *page 16.*

▷ **Positive Thinking Power**, *page 108.*

▷ **Balancing Work and Family**, *page 150.*

Section III: Self-Improvement

Nurturing Your Creativity

Doing the same old things the same old ways at work is not only boring, but it also drains success away from you and your organization.

Anyone can develop the creative spirit that is in high demand in today's competitive business climate. You don't have to be worldly, highly educated, or eccentric.

- Keep an idea list. Always have a small notebook handy for recording ideas that pop into your head. Review them periodically to see if any are ripe for use. Let your supervisor know that you keep such a list.
- Doodle. It activates creative juices.
- Build unstructured, free-thinking time into your schedule, even if it's just a few minutes a day.
- Broaden your ideas by becoming more of a generalist. Cultivate curiosity in many subjects. Adopt a hobby that seems unlike you. Spend time with people different from you. Propose to your boss that you spend two days this month outside your usual work area.
- Vary your daily routine to keep your mind flexible. Take a different route to work. Eat lunch at a different place with different people. Hold your next staff meeting at a new location.
- Invite different kinds of people with new perspectives to your meetings and brainstorming sessions (employees from another department, customers or potential clients). Don't rely on the same people and format all the time.
- Avoid conformist thinking. When everyone automatically agrees on a course of action at a meeting, table the issue for a few days or weeks until different approaches surface.
- Use lateral thinking. Look for ways to apply technology or concepts that work in one area to another issue.
- Allow your ideas to be illogical. Two concepts or objects that seem completely unrelated may have many links. An exercise you could try is to look for common qualities in two dissimilar objects, such as a lamp and a mushroom.
- Break rules.
- Spend time "what-iffing." Take a current project and come up with three what-if statements to help you think of new solutions. (What if we dropped that product line?)

- Feed your creativity with humor: read the funnies, listen to comedy tapes, or share funny stories before meetings.

- Help others churn out good ideas. Ask lots of questions, offer information, share your ideas, and praise unusual ideas.

- Counteract your fear of failure by focusing on what is going right or how you've learned from past failures. Reward yourself for creative successes.

- Create a support network for your creative ideas. Bounce them off of colleagues. Ask a senior manager to sponsor your concept.

- Don't push your wild ideas too far before you've done your homework. Analyze them enough to know if and how they would work. If you skip this step and your idea bombs people may be skeptical of other proposals from you.

Resources

➡ *99% Inspiration: Tips, Tales, and Techniques for Liberating Your Business Creativity*, Bryan Mattimore, AMACOM, 1993.

➡ *The Creative Corporation*, Karl Albrecht, Dow Jones-Irwin, 1987.

➡ *A Whack on the Side of the Head*, Roger Von Oech, Warner, 1993.

➡ Creative Whack Pack (64 cards featuring various creativity strategies) U.S. Games Systems, Inc.

➡ MindWare, catalog of toys, puzzles, games, books and other products designed to boost creativity and fun, 6142 Olson Memorial Highway, Golden Valley, MN 55422, 800-999-0398.

See Also

⇨ **Creative Problem Solving**, *page 48.*
⇨ **Using Humor at Work**, *page 114.*
⇨ **Tapping Your Intuition**, *page 120.*

Section III: Self-Improvement

Tapping Your Intuition

Have you ever been mystified at how a great idea just seemed to pop into your head? The force behind that phenomenon may not have been a great mystery. It may have been the power of your intuition, also known as a hunch, gut feeling, or instinct.

Intuition is built on knowledge and experience stored in your brain and mixed with new information. It can be a powerful tool for solving problems and making decisions. We all have intuition but we may be unsure how to harness it or be afraid of the results we may get.

- Make your mind a fertile ground for intuition. Constantly gather information from a variety of sources, even on seemingly unrelated topics. Read, observe, talk, and visit. The information will fuse together in your brain to bring you ideas later.

- Train yourself to spot gaps in your knowledge. Often recognizing what you don't know can spark intuition.

- Identify the specific result you want before trying to use your intuition. Knowing where you're going can help your brain pick out the best steps to take next. Visualization can help here.

- Revisit and redefine a problem frequently. Try to stir it up.

- Take a childlike view. Who says you can't do it that way?

- Try out your hunches. You'll never know how good they are until you review and test them.

- Do what feels right, even if it contradicts conventional wisdom.

- Don't question whether you're qualified to come up with an idea. Inexperience can make you bold.

- Take your brain somewhere else so you can be open to intuition: meditate, run, walk, or fish.

- Notice your body's reactions to intuition. How do you feel when you get a good idea? How does your stomach and chest feel when you get a bad idea?

- When you get what seems to be a bad idea, stick with it for a few minutes. Why does it feel bad? Is the reason you think it's a bad idea relevant? Have you overlooked an important factor? Distinguish between real obstacles and imagined ones.

- When you get a hunch, ask yourself if the facts seem to back it up. Would having more facts ease your uncertainty?

- Watch out for these enemies of intuition: written reports, constant analysis, strict structure, a requirement that everything must be precise and measurable, and detailed systems that control your every move at work.

- Try this method for tapping your intuition, called automatic association, from Albuquerque psychologist Audrey Gray. Write down two open-ended questions about a problem you want to solve. You should not be able to answer them with a yes or no. (How can I meet that deadline without ignoring the rest of my duties?) Now, close your eyes and imagine that you're walking to a schoolhouse in the forest. Inside is your teacher, who can be anyone you wish. Ask your teacher the first question and write down everything that comes to you. Write quickly and don't judge the ideas you get. Close your eyes again, return to the schoolhouse, and focus on the teacher. Imagine that you're really on the same wavelength. Ask the second question and write down the answers. Now walk out of the forest, open your eyes, and read the ideas you've gathered. You may find ideas that you never thought of before.

Resources
➡ *The Intuitive Manager*, Roy Rowan, Berkley, 1991.
➡ *Intuition*, P.O. Box 460773, San Francisco, CA 94146, 415-538-8171, $19.95/6 issues/year.
➡ *Dr. Marcia Emery's Intuition Workbook: An Expert's Guide to Unlocking the Wisdom of Your Subconscious Mind*, Marcia Emery, Prentice Hall, 1994.

See Also
⇨ **Creative Problem Solving**, *page 48.*
⇨ **Setting Goals**, *page 116.*
⇨ **Nurturing Your Creativity**, *page 118.*
⇨ **Making Better Decisions**, *page 122.*

Section III: Self-Improvement

9-8 Making Better Decisions

Making decisions can be intimidating. You face a problem or issue and wonder, "Where do I even start?" There may be dozens of choices, or you may not even know if a decision is necessary.

One facet of wise decision making is to focus as much or more on the process of making a decision as on the decision itself. Another key is to clearly identify and frame the issues so you can make a sound choice.

- Know the decision-making style of yourself and others who may be involved. Do you or they tend to be authoritarian, collaborative, compromising, hasty, deliberate, intuitive, or negotiation oriented? You'll make better decisions if you tune in to those tendencies and act to neutralize or exploit them.

- Define the problem clearly. What do you need or want to decide? Why? Keep asking why until you uncover your true purpose. (You may think you need a better copier technician but the real issue may be that you need a more reliable copier.)

- Look at why a decision is necessary. Why do anything? What happens if you do nothing? Must you make a decision now?

- Solve one problem at a time.

- Determine what kind of decision is necessary. Do you need to make a decision that meets minimum standards or is consistent with a policy? Analyze which option will work and which won't? Identify a single choice or several workable options?

- State your criteria. (This may be the most important step.) What do you want to achieve, preserve, and avoid? Now prioritize those objectives. Is it most important to achieve X or avoid Y?

- Gather information. Figure out what you need to know to make a good decision. But don't go crazy gathering too many details.

- Examine each objective or criteria and brainstorm ways to accomplish it. Look at how each option stacks up against your priorities. How many priorities does each solution satisfy?

- Hunt for ways to expand your choices. Consider doing the opposite of what you've come up with so far. Ask yourself what a child or your favorite role model would do. Try combining the best parts of several options to create one super alternative.

- Review your decision. What are the consequences of this choice? What could go wrong? How could you improve it? Be willing to drop a weak option.

- Go through this process on paper, except for minor decisions. Writing helps clarify issues and options.

- For uncomplicated decisions, draw a matrix to help you see how well your alternatives match your criteria. List your alternatives in columns horizontally across the top of a sheet of paper. List your criteria vertically down the left margin. Place a check mark wherever an alternative meets a criteria. The alternative with the most check marks could be your answer.

- For weighty or complex decisions, assign a point value to each criteria and see which alternative earns the most points.

- Consider whether someone else could or should make this decision.

- When you're stalled move away from the problem physically (take a walk or a fun break) or mentally (nap, daydream); or make a checklist of what you must have or do before you can proceed, then do it; or rate your feelings about the choices on a scale of one to 10. Involve an impartial person to provide different perspectives, better information, or political support.

Resources
→ *The Confident Decision Maker: How to Make the Right Business and Personal Decisions Every Time*, Roger Dawson, William Morrow, 1993.
→ *How to Make the Right Decision*, John Arnold, Ballantine, 1985.
→ *The Complete Problem Solver: A Total System of Competitive Decision Making*, John Arnold, John Wiley & Sons, 1992.
→ *Making Good Career & Life Decisions*, JIST Works, Inc., 1997.

See Also
⇨ **Getting More Out of Meetings**, *page 18.*
⇨ **Creative Problem Solving**, *page 48.*
⇨ **Tapping into Your Intuition**, *page 120.*

Section III: Self-Improvement

Taking Smart Risks

Skiers who choose only the easiest runs won't improve. Eventually, they must conquer their nervousness and try an intermediate or expert slope to develop skill and strength. Taking risks is at the heart of improvement.

It's the same in our working lives. We face all kinds of risks there: public speaking, new responsibilities, and unexpected career paths. To make the most of those risks or opportunities, we must overcome fear and anxiety and learn to choose smart risks.

- Know what you want so you can decide if this risk would meet your needs. What's important to you? What are your goals? Would taking this risk help you in those areas?

- Research the risk first. Don't go on hunches or the words of others. Find out what would improve your chances of success. Is this risk realistic? Is this the best time and place for it?

- Make sure there is a reasonable chance that you'll succeed if you take this risk. Or make your goal simply to learn. Then, even failing could be beneficial.

- Manage your fear. Don't try to eliminate it; that's unrealistic. Measure it instead. If you have a lot of fear (so much that you're paralyzed) this might not be the best time for that risk. If you have a little fear (you feel uncomfortable but still think you might be able to do it) push ahead.

- Tackle a particularly scary risk a little at a time. Give yourself some practice so you'll gain confidence and expertise for the next step. (If you're terrified of public speaking, try leading a small meeting or lunchtime discussion first. Then graduate to bigger groups.)

- Acknowledge your feelings about failure. It's normal and OK to feel angry, inadequate, and embarrassed. Discuss your feelings with a confidant who won't judge you. And remember that failing once doesn't mean you'll fail every time or most of the time.

- Look at the worst result that could occur if you take a risk and fail. It may not be that bad, or maybe it's something you could recover from readily.

- Don't wait for supervisors or others to dictate your next risk. Think about how you need to grow personally and professionally. Go for it on your own. Create your own opportunities.

- Don't confine all your risk-taking to work. Often that's what we do because it's easiest to see the payoffs there. Right now, choose a risk you can take in your personal life, something that will take time and effort. People who grow in their personal lives usually carry that excitement to their professional lives.

- Build a little risk in everything you do. If you feel perfectly confident about a meeting you're leading or a project you're organizing, you may not be stretching yourself enough.

Resources
➡ *Feel the Fear and Do It Anyway*, Susan Jeffers, Fawcett, 1988.
➡ *Risk-Taking for Women: How to Find the Courage to Get What You Really Want Out of Life*, Betsy Morscher, Everest House, 1982.
➡ *Taking Risks for Personal Growth* (audiotape), David Viscott, Psychology Today Tapes, 1985, 800-444-7792, $11.95 + shipping and handling.
➡ *Dare to Change Your Job and Your Life,* Carole Kanchier, Ph.D., JIST Works, Inc., 1995.

See Also
⇨ **Managing Your Career**, *page 194.*
⇨ **Setting Goals**, *page 116.*
⇨ **Recovering from Mistakes**, *page 140.*

Bonus Tip!

Take risks large enough to at least make you a little uneasy.

Section III: Self-Improvement

CHAPTER

10

Chapter 10

Coping with Work

Section III: Self-Improvement

Quick Stress Busters

Let's call it a bad day. Your boss moved up all your deadlines, the coworker who is supposed to assist you is out sick and, the copy machine is broken–again.

There are huge knots in your shoulders. You're clenching your teeth as you rush through five tasks at once. There's no time for a massage or stress management workshop. You need instant stress-reduction techniques that are easy to use at work.

- Talk about it. Ask a trusted coworker or friend for some new ideas for handling the problem. Find someone who will just listen while you blow off steam. But don't overdo it. Release that negative energy and move on.

- Use visualization. Imagine yourself somewhere that makes you happy and relaxed: a favorite vacation spot, at home in a warm bubble bath, or hiking in the woods. In a few minutes you can capture the pleasure of being there. Or think about something enjoyable you'll do when you leave work.

- If you're in the middle of a meeting cut the tension by creating a break. Call a time out to get something from your office or your briefcase or go to the rest room. This lets you stop the action, change positions, look around, get a different perspective, or just catch your breath.

- Have some fun. Take a minute to laugh with a coworker, call a friend, read the comics, or work on a task you really enjoy.

- Finish something. Give yourself a sense of accomplishment by tackling an easy, 10-minute task.

- Concentrate on breathing. If you're tense your breathing may be shallow, hurried, and erratic. Loosen up by taking a big cleansing breath. Then take easy, relaxed, deep breaths—in through your nose and out through your mouth. Breathe deeply from your stomach and lower abdomen instead of your chest.

- Give yourself a mini shoulder and neck massage. For headaches, cover your eyes with your hands for about 30 seconds. Then slide your palms to the sides of your head and gently make circles over both temples for about 30 seconds. Or use your finger tips to rotate your scalp in as many directions as you can.

- Try aromatherapy. Some salons, health food stores, and natural body care shops carry scented oils for relaxing. Place a drop on your fingertips and massage your temples or the indentation between the base of your skull and the top of your neck. Look for frankincense, ylang-ylang, sandalwood, rose, or bergamot. Scented candles may help too.

- Avoid caffeine and sugar. Try herbal teas, water, or wholesome foods instead.

- Use progressive relaxation. Start with your feet: tense them and then release. Now, your calves. Do this with your whole body, moving from one section to the next.

- Listen to calming instrumental music without dramatic or emotional passages. Try tapes with environmental sounds or soothing vocals. Check New Age or instrumental sections in music stores, health food or holistic book stores, nature gift stores, or your public library.

- Exercise. Stretch. Walk.

- Look for quick, minor adjustments you could make in your job. Could you ask your supervisor for more authority in a current project? Can you delegate a task? Ask for more feedback? Adjust your goals for the day? Improve the lighting or air flow in your work space?

Resources
➡ *The Working Woman's Guide to Managing Stress*, J. Robin Powell, Prentice Hall, 1994.
➡ *Learning to Relax* (audiotape), Arnold Lazarus, Albert Ellis Institute, 45 E. 65 St., New York, NY 10021-6593, 800-323-IRET, $9.95 + shipping and handling. Web address: http://www.rebt.org.
➡ *Psychology Today Tapes*, PO Box 400421, Des Moines, IA 50340, call 800-444-7792 for catalog.

See Also
⇨ **Using Humor at Work**, *page 114.*
⇨ **Managing Stress for the Long-Term**, *page 130.*
⇨ **Zapping Job Burnout**, *page 132.*

Section III: Self-Improvement

Managing Stress for the Long-Term

Excessive stress still burdens many working people, despite the fact that we've been hearing about how to handle it for years.

A 1991 study by Northwestern National Life showed that one-in-three Americans thought seriously about quitting work in 1990 because of job stress, one in three expected to burn out on the job soon, and 14 percent quit or changed jobs in the past two years because of job stress.

You can ease your heavy stress load by changing the way you approach difficult situations.

- Search for at least one positive aspect in your stressful work situation. What is working well and why? Can you apply one of those effective techniques to a problem?

- Don't try to always work at 100-percent capacity. One study of successful, highly productive people found that they tend to work at about 80 percent of their full capacity, where the difficulty was just manageable. When crises erupt, they push themselves to 100 or 110 percent. If you expect 100 percent of yourself all the time you'll become exhausted and less effective.

- Take responsibility for easing up on yourself. Don't wait for supervisors to tell you to slow down.

- Don't get caught up in a "who's-working-harder" contest with colleagues. If you feel that travel on weekends, frequent all-nighters, or working when you're ill is excessive, say so. You might find your colleagues feel the same way and will support your efforts to change the situation. As a group, bring possible solutions to your boss. You may achieve better results than if just one person complains.

- Give yourself time to feel sad, moody, or distracted if you've recently changed jobs, transferred, lost a promotion, or endured other major changes. Let yourself grieve those losses so you can move ahead.

- Slow down and savor special times (accolades from your peers or a long lunch at an elegant restaurant). Don't spoil them by thinking about the work you should be doing. Enjoy them as your payoff for hard work.

- Increase your rewards. What makes your stressful job worth it, anyway? Take more satisfaction from your accomplishments, schedule more vacations, and buy more little luxuries. If there aren't enough rewards and you can't create more, maybe you should change careers. However, don't expect to escape burnout by only changing jobs. You must change your approach to work.

- Park 15 minutes away from your workplace. You'll give yourself time to think and unwind while walking to and from work.

- Argue your convictions in a professional manner with your supervisors, even if it doesn't change anything. Honoring what's important to you helps prevent feelings of helplessness, a major cause of stress.

- Train yourself to stop and think when you encounter unexpected problems. Avoid knee-jerk reactions. The problem may look less severe after a quick analysis.

- Break up your heavy schedule by volunteering for a charitable or professional organization that your company supports.

- Make a long-term commitment to something or someone. "Long-term goals make short-term problems and sacrifices easier to bear," psychologist Ray Flannery writes.

Resources
➡ *The Relaxation Response*, Herbert Benson, Outlet Book Co., 1993.
➡ *The Joy of Stress*, Peter Hanson, Andrews & McMeel, 1987.
➡ *Career Success—Personal Stress: How to Stay Healthy in a High-Stress Environment*, Christine Leatz, McGraw Hill, 1993.
➡ *The Power of People Skills: A Manager's Guide to Assessing and Developing Your Organization's Greatest Resource*, Doug Stewart, University Press of America, 1993.
➡ *Beat Stress with Strength,* Stefanie Spera, Ph.D., and Sandra Lanto, Ph.D., Park Avenue Productions, 1997.

See Also
➪ **Working with Difficult People**, *page 30.*
➪ **Quick Stress Busters**, *page 128.*
➪ **Zapping Job Burnout**, *page 132.*
➪ **Balancing Work and Family**, *page 150.*

Section III: Self-Improvement

Zapping Job Burnout

Job burnout is a common malady, especially in workplaces where layoffs and organizational changes have stretched workloads and stress levels to new heights.

When you're burned out you are more than stressed out. You feel swamped, drained, and dissatisfied with your work. Motivating yourself to go to work is a chore. Effectiveness and productivity take a nose dive.

- Check whether your job expectations are realistic. Negative feelings hit when reality clashes with what you envisioned.

- Do whatever you can to get at least some control over your work. Talk to your supervisor about getting more responsibility instead of just more tasks to do. Discuss ways to break out of your dead-end job. Become more involved at work—volunteer to be on committees or offer new ideas regularly. Don't wait for assignments to be thrown at you.

- Look for diversions. You may need another stimulating outlet for your ideas and energy. Try community service work, part-time teaching, new hobbies, or socializing with people outside of your field.

- Spend less time with cynics or negative thinkers. They can sap your positive energy. Examine whether those negative attitudes are realistic and constructive or just excuses for not making improvements. What does it cost you in job satisfaction and performance to think negatively?

- Talk to others about your burned-out feelings. Trusted friends and colleagues can help you gain perspective. A career counselor can help if change seems overwhelming.

- Look for ways to get more positive recognition for your work. Sometimes burnout symptoms mean that you need more recognition. Ask your boss how you could get more feedback. Ask coworkers and colleagues for their feedback. Notice and take pride in the ways your work benefits customers or coworkers.

- Make your health a top priority. Exercise at least three times a week. Eat regular, nutritious meals that maximize your performance and energy. Get the right amount of rest for you at the times you need it most.

- Learn about stress reduction techniques such as deep breathing or meditation.

- Rejuvenate through time alone, intimacy with loved ones, and fun hobbies.

- Take a vacation, even if it's only a long weekend. This is especially important if you're one of those people who brags that you haven't taken a real vacation in years. Everyone needs a chance to recharge batteries. Spend your time off doing something entirely unrelated to your work.

- Cultivate enthusiasm for your work by getting in touch with the reasons you chose your field. Attend conferences and seminars, get more training, or take a sabbatical.

- Look at whether you are in the right job. Does it draw on your strengths instead of your weaknesses? Does it allow you to spend most of your time doing work you really enjoy? If not, think about a career change.

- Don't assume that a career change will fix everything. There may be underlying problems in the way you approach work that will cause burnout even in a new job. Also, career transitions themselves can cause stress.

Resources

➡ *What Color Is Your Parachute? 1997: A Practical Manual for Job Hunters and Career Changers*, Richard Bolles, Ten Speed Press, 1997.

➡ *You Don't Have to Go Home from Work Exhausted!* Ann McGee-Cooper, Bantam, 1992.

➡ *Career Satisfaction and Success,* Benard Haldane, Ph.D., JIST Works, Inc., 1996.

See Also

⇨ **Escaping a Career Pigeonhole**, *page 214.*

⇨ **Considering a Career Change**, *page 216.*

⇨ **Positive Thinking Power**, *page 108.*

⇨ **Addressing Workaholism**, *page 134.*

Bonus Tip!

Don't just react to burnout. Look at why it is happening.

Section III: Self-Improvement

Addressing Workaholism

"I don't have a life" is one way people describe the imbalance between work and the rest of their existence. It sounds like a joke, but it's really not funny. It does not reflect a healthy, happy, and effective way to live and work. It could reflect the underpinnings of workaholism, or work addiction.

Workaholism is more than burnout, long hours, or overachievement. It's a chronic and progressive pattern of using work to compensate for deficiencies in our lives, or making work the centerpiece of life at the expense of other important commitments.

Some characteristics of work addiction:

- Using your job to escape unpleasant areas of your life (marriage, children, relatives, household duties) or to feel better about yourself.

- Being a perfectionist.

- Hearing family and friends complain that you don't pay attention to them. Seeing them cover up for your work patterns. Having few friends away from work.

- Feeling guilty when you're not working. Thinking about work when you're supposed to be doing something else. Routinely taking work home and on vacation (if you take one). Hiding work or lying about how much you work.

- Being consumed by busyness and rushing. Failing to take time to think.

- Turning small problems into emergencies, giving yourself more reasons to work longer.

- Working for many hours or even days at a time with scarcely a break.

- Experiencing mounting physical problems such as inability to sleep, headaches, and digestive troubles.

Strategies for handling excessive devotion to work:

- Don't assume workaholism only happens to executives or people with exciting jobs. It strikes all kinds of people.

- Don't confuse working hard with work addiction. Hard workers who are balanced work overtime when necessary but don't feel compelled to do so routinely. They rest when tired and take time off. Work is only one part of their lives.

- Review your beliefs about work. Are they realistic? Are your work habits really virtuous? Do they match what you truly value in life?

- Identify what triggers your excessive behavior (taking a leadership role, setting goals, being asked to solve a stubborn problem).

- Question whether working longer or more compulsively truly makes you more productive. It probably has the opposite effect. Rushing, exhaustion, and obsessiveness lead to errors and poor quality work.

- Don't expect techniques like exercise or time management to fix a growing addiction. You'll need to address deeper issues.

- Get help through your company's employee assistance program or Workaholics Anonymous (see **Resources** below). Seek help immediately if you or others around you detect a steady decline in your life, or if you experience serious problems like blackouts, emotional deadness, and gnawing fear that you're in big trouble.

- Surround yourself with healthy, balanced people. Enlist their help and support.

- Tackle change one day at a time.

Resources
- *Working Ourselves to Death: The High Cost of Workaholism and the Rewards of Recovery*, Diane Fassel, HarperCollins, 1990.
- Workaholics Anonymous, in your local phone directory, or the WA World Service Organization, PO Box 289, Menlo Park, CA 94026-0289, 510-273-9253.
- Hazelden Foundation Information Center, programs and services for addictive disorders, PO Box 11, Center City, MN 55012-9900, 800-257-7800.
- *The Power of People Skills: A Manager's Guide to Assessing and Developing Your Organization's Greatest Resource*, Doug Stewart, University Press of America, 1993.

See Also
⇨ **Boosting Your Self-Esteem**, *page 112.*
⇨ **Managing Stress for the Long-Term**, *page 130.*
⇨ **Balancing Work and Family**, *page 150.*

Section III: Self-Improvement

I Hate My Job!

It's not uncommon to dislike your job at one time or another. But it's unhealthy and self-defeating to feel that way regularly. It's worse to feel that way and not do anything about it.

Taking positive action—even if it's just changing your attitude—can improve a dismal job situation.

- If your unhappiness stems from a big disappointment at work (not getting a promotion or choice assignment) talk it out with a friend or colleague. Avoid taking rash actions. Identify what you think you've lost (status, money) so you can plan how to compensate for the loss. Realize that life is a series of ups and downs. Just because your job is not going well now does not mean it will be that way forever.

- Analyze your negative position at work as if it were a business problem. List your strengths (why you should have received that promotion). Then honestly list your weaknesses (why you didn't get the promotion). Look for soft spots where you could improve.

- Ask trusted friends and coworkers to help identify your strengths and weaknesses. What common themes emerge?

- Pinpoint exactly why you're so unhappy. Does your work fail to interest or excite you? Are you neglecting the skills that bring you the most satisfaction? Are the working hours or environment unsuitable? How about the commute? Do you have too little autonomy? Do you cherish different values than your coworkers and supervisors? Do you have personal problems that may affect your work?

- Realize that it's your responsibility, not your employer's, to make yourself happier at work. The only way to do that is by changing what's under your control. Don't try to change what is outside that realm (your boss' personality or duties that are integral parts of your job).

- Think creatively about your job. Look for a project that will let you use some untapped skills. Develop new skills that will make you a master at your job. Look for an unsolved problem at work that needs fixing.

- Look for the positive angles in your job. It's probably better than being unemployed. In some way, it lets you help others or provide a useful service or product. It allows you to reach meaningful goals (being self-sufficient or putting your child through college).

- Improve your work relationships; they can help you overcome setbacks and unhappiness at work. Emphasize cooperation with coworkers instead of competition. Make it a project to make friends and be a friend at work.

- Speak up when you sincerely and seriously object to a plan, assignment, or action. Loyal opposition—dissent that is focused on the good of the group— is a vital part of healthy organizations. And it helps cut your stress by reducing your feelings of powerlessness.

- Get more of the emotional and spiritual support you need from family, friends, hobbies, church, community service, and the arts.

- Don't quit until you've explored every opportunity for improving your current job.

Resources
➡ *How to Be Happier in the Job You Sometimes Can't Stand*, Ross West, Broadman and Holman, 1991.
➡ *Career Satisfaction and Success,* Benard Haldane, Ph.D., JIST Works, Inc., 1996.

See Also
⇨ **Considering a Career Change**, *page 216.*
⇨ **Quitting**, *page 234.*
⇨ **Understanding Your Bothersome Boss**, *page 28.*
⇨ **Positive Thinking Power**, *page 108.*

Section III: Self-Improvement

Bonus Tip!

Don't expect work to provide all of life's joy.

Cooling Your Anger

You feel it rising in your chest—that red-hot anger. It might be your response to a reprimand from your boss, a complaint from a difficult customer, or an excuse from a coworker. Whatever its source, the emotion makes it difficult for you to continue work. Should you yell? Should you ignore it? Should you kick a wastebasket?

None of the above, anger experts say. They suggest a more thoughtful approach that involves taking responsibility for your own anger instead of claiming that you just can't control it.

- Strive to remain polite. Social rules like manners help us manage anger because they force us to maintain respect for others.

- Don't assume that it's always good to let out your anger. Often, expressing anger can worsen a touchy situation and spark more anger. Keep quiet unless expressing your feelings would change the other person's behavior, give you new insights into the situation, or somehow restore your sense of justice and control. It may be best just to let it out in private.

- Recognize that anger is the result of frustration—being backed into a corner or feeling that someone is not meeting your needs. Could you prevent an angry outburst by trying to meet your needs another way? Could you change your environment or relationships, or avoid certain people?

- Try the old count-to-10 technique. The idea is to create a buffer of time so your emotions can cool. Other approaches might be to take a walk, meditate, sleep on it, engage in some noncompetitive exercise, read, or watch a movie.

- Don't rely too much on talking out your anger with an uninvolved party. While this can be helpful, it could become harmful if all it does is allow you to relive and perpetuate the anger.

- Pinpoint what made you so angry. Did the person hit one of your "hot buttons?" What perceptions or interpretations did you have that triggered your anger? Are they valid? (Are you particularly touchy when you think someone is questioning your education, or judging you by your gender?)

- Empathize with the person who has aggravated you. Listen to that point of view. Have you ever felt that way?

- Keep focused on the current problem, not on old grudges or annoying personality traits.

- Use the energy generated by your anger for problem solving. Focus on the positive change you want to create.

- Learn to notice your own anger warning signs, such as a racing heart rate or stomach pains. Train yourself to take preventative action when you feel these changes.

- Keep an anger diary if you frequently feel angry. Note what triggers your anger: when, where, with whom, the intensity, its duration, and how you expressed it. What patterns do you see?

Resources

→ *Anger: The Misunderstood Emotion*, Carol Tavris, Simon & Schuster, 1989.
→ *Coping with Anger*, Paul Gelinas, Rosen Publishing Group, 1988.
→ RETHINK pamphlet series, Institute for Mental Health Initiatives, 4545 42nd St. NW, Suite 311, Washington, D.C. 20016, 202-364-7111, 50 cents per copy. E-mail:instmhi@aol.com. Web address: http://www.imhi.org/imhi.
→ *What to Do When You're Angry*, E. Dean Bevan, Rainbow Books, 1994.

See Also

⇨ **Understanding Your Bothersome Boss**, *page 28.*
⇨ **Working with Difficult People**, *page 30.*
⇨ **Handling Customer Problems**, *page 34.*
⇨ **Preparing for a Conflict**, *page 50.*

Bonus Tip!

Use humor to defuse your emotions, but avoid sarcasm and insults.

Section III: Self-Improvement

Recovering from Mistakes

We know that everyone makes mistakes, but that doesn't keep us from wishing we could undo ours. We'd take back an unwise comment or false statement we made at work, fix a problem that our oversight caused, or polish a bad impression.

Because we can't erase our goof-ups we sometimes choose to do nothing about them, thinking that it's better to not draw any more attention to them. But often, not fixing a mistake can be worse than the mistake itself.

- Be sure that you really have made a mistake and you aren't just being hard on yourself. Sometimes we tear ourselves down, overanalyze or obsess about what we do or say, imagining that we came off worse than we really did.

- Forgive yourself. Accept the fact that mistakes are unavoidable, especially if you're stretching in your job. Remind yourself how you've recovered from past mistakes. Look people in the eye to show them that you haven't lost your confidence.

- Analyze the mistake before trying to explain it to anyone. What were you trying to do? What did you forget about? Did you make one mistake or a series of errors?

- Tell your boss about the mistake before your boss finds out some other way. Everyone will be more likely to forgive you if you accept responsibility quickly. When you talk with your boss, focus more on repairing the damage than explaining it or assigning blame. Apologize and say that you understand what happened. You might add that your good intentions backfired. Promise that you'll be more careful in the future.

- Be prepared for anger from your boss. Don't argue back or make excuses, which may exacerbate your boss' irritation.

- If a high-level manager or customer will be questioning your boss about the mistake, be sure your boss has enough details to explain what happened and how it will be fixed.

- Offer to do whatever you can to help repair the damage (share the resulting workload, apologize to the customer). Be a problem solver.

- Don't overcompensate. Don't beg, grovel, or be overly sweet to whomever is offended.

- Search for a lesson. Do you need to relax more, prepare better, ask for help more, become more confident, or act more slowly? Watch for patterns, too.

If you repeat the same kinds of mistakes, you need to change something about yourself.

- Don't assume that you're ruined by one mistake. Most people are willing to overlook one error and judge you on the broader impression you make over time. Besides, many people feel compassionate and even charmed when others expose personal flaws and acknowledge mistakes.

Resources

➡ *Your Own Worst Enemy: How to Overcome Career Self-Sabotage*, Andrew DuBrin, AMACOM, 1992.

➡ *How to Be a Perfect Non-Perfectionist* (audiotape), Albert Ellis, Albert Ellis Institute, 45 E. 65th St., New York, NY 10021-6593, 800-323-IRET, $9.95 + shipping and handling. Web address: http://www.rebt.org.

See Also

⇨ **Dealing with Verbal Abuse,** *page 58.*
⇨ **Projecting a Successful Image,** *page 110.*
⇨ **Boosting Your Self-Esteem,** *page 112.*
⇨ **Taking Smart Risks,** *page 124.*

Bonus Tip!

Maintain your self-respect, despite your mistakes.

Section III: Self-Improvement

Flexing for Change

Being flexible is one of the key career and job survival skills for the 1990s and beyond. We need to adapt quickly to maximize the never-ending barrage of changes around us—layoffs, global competition, reengineering, and shifting consumer preferences.

To develop flexibility, think of change in exciting, positive terms. Respond to change for your own reasons instead of letting external factors push you around.

- Allow yourself to feel negative and confused when you first encounter a change. It's what you do next that matters. Acknowledge your concerns. Work through them with realism and maturity.

- Define yourself broadly so you have lots of room to absorb changes. If you draw too narrow a picture of yourself—who you are, what you like, and what you do—it's harder to welcome changes. They come too close to destroying your self-image.

- Do something unfamiliar every day. Change a routine for a week. Note how you overcame your internal resistance. Could you apply those techniques to other changes you face? How else have you successfully handled change?

- Hunt for signs of coming change. Keep a notebook of information tidbits or gut feelings. (The boss rejected my idea again; or, orders for that product are way up.) Review your notes daily to identify trends or spark insight. Listen to people. Watch the competition. Scan newspapers, books, magazines, junk mail, advertisements, songs, and TV shows. Watch organizations related to your work—unions, suppliers, and regulators. What trends are emerging?

- Take the good aspects of a situation and look for what's bad in them. Reexamine the bad aspects to spot the good.

- Position yourself at the edge of your department or industry, where your area meets another (where marketing meets production or where production meets customers), change expert William Bridges writes (see **Resources** below). There you'll find valuable information about consumer shifts, competition, government decisions, and internal moves.

- Use humor to reduce the threat of change, foster cooperation, and restore perspective.

- Educate yourself about upcoming changes. Read. Talk to experienced people. You'll be more prepared and less likely to resist.

- Be proactive. When an unwelcome change approaches you, set off your own series of small changes that could correct the situation or bring it to a head in a more managed way. Address small problems promptly so they don't turn into one big, prickly issue.

- Practice pushing your bottom line a little. Could you accept a bit more or less of something (one more day until the project is done, or $2 less than asking price)? Now, can you push it a little more?

Resources
➡ *The Flexibility Factor*, Jacquelyn Wonder and Priscilla Donovan, Ballantine, 1991.
➡ *Surviving Transition*, William Bridges, Doubleday, 1988.

See Also
⇨ **Managing Your Career**, *page 194.*
⇨ **Preparing for a Possible Layoff**, *page 236.*
⇨ **Using Humor at Work**, *page 114.*
⇨ **Nurturing Your Creativity**, *page 118.*

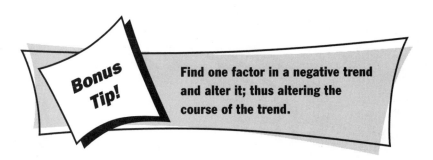

Bonus Tip!

Find one factor in a negative trend and alter it; thus altering the course of the trend.

Section III: Self-Improvement

CHAPTER

11

Chapter 11

Family Issues

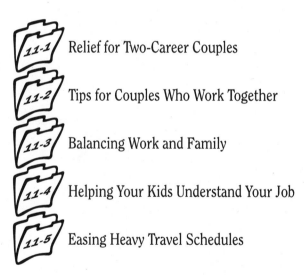

11-1 Relief for Two-Career Couples

11-2 Tips for Couples Who Work Together

11-3 Balancing Work and Family

11-4 Helping Your Kids Understand Your Job

11-5 Easing Heavy Travel Schedules

Section III: Self-Improvement

Relief for Two-Career Couples

If both you and your partner work, you might feel like pieces of taffy: pulled this way by your job, that way by your family, and another way by guilt or exhaustion.

When you're stretched out of shape it's tough to keep a relationship strong and intact—especially when time seems to evaporate before your eyes. But it's not impossible. Look at whether you're giving the best of yourself to your job and the leftovers to your partner.

- Use the people and communication skills you've learned at work on your partner (speak clearly without hidden meaning; give lots of positive, specific feedback; and involve your spouse when solving problems or making decisions).

- Concentrate on reserving some of your good qualities for your partner after work. Letting your negative traits hang out at home all the time won't buy you much understanding, respect, support, or encouragement.

- Use the time between the end of your work day and your arrival at home to recharge your energy. Listen to music or comedy tapes, take a brief walk, read, or give yourself a quick shoulder massage.

- Make returning home pleasant for both of you. Consider it part of your job to help rejuvenate your partner at the end of a work day. Allow yourselves a few quiet minutes to relax without being responsible for dinner, chores, or hearing complaints.

- Talk to your partner about what you do at work all day. Share some of the problems you deal with and decisions you've made. Your partner will be able to appreciate your work and empathize with you.

- Schedule appointments or activities with your partner on your calendar just as you would work commitments. Treat them as seriously as you would meetings with your boss.

- Don't stage a martyr contest to see who works hardest and suffers the most. What are you really trying to say when you list all the travails you've endured that day? Think about what you really want and ask for it directly. ("I need a hug." Or "I need some time alone." Or "I need some reassurance that I made the right decision.")

- Strive to appreciate each other's unique areas of success instead of trying to compete through your professional accomplishments. Value your differences.

- Set aside a block of time each week to be verbally intimate with your partner. No phones, no TV, and no interruptions. Concentrate on each other. Be open about what's on your mind and what might be twisting your relationship. The rules: listen, don't judge, don't try to fix the other's problems.

- Schedule solitude. Agree to grant each other a block of time every day or week just to be alone. Agree not to take it personally when your partner cashes in on that provision.

Resources
➡ *Power Partners: How Two-Career Couples Can Play to Win,* Jane Hershey Cuozzo, Mastermedia, 1990.
➡ *He Works She Works: Successful Strategies for Working Couples,* Jarne Carter and James D. Carter, AMACOM, 1995.

See Also
➪ **Listen Up,** *page 70.*
➪ **Tips for Couples Who Work Together,** *page 148.*
➪ **Balancing Work and Family,** *page 150.*

Bonus Tip!

Think about something good that happened today that you can share with your partner.

Section III: Self-Improvement

Tips for Couples Who Work Together

Some couples carry togetherness to an extreme—they work together. Working in the same department or building can provide a special dimension to your relationship, or it can produce a big strain. Couples need to treat this situation carefully so it won't complicate office politics or blur the lines between personal and professional lives.

- If you have a choice, look for workplaces with a collegial atmosphere, loose hierarchy, and little emphasis on office politics. Those are best for couples.

- Don't commit your partner to work on projects or work-related social functions without asking first. Better yet, tell coworkers to go to your partner directly with work-related issues.

- Tell your partner when you hear compliments about your partner's work. But be careful when you hear criticism. Pass it on only if it's constructive and you can shield the source's identity. This helps keep you out of office disagreements.

- Minimize calls and visits to your partner for personal business.

- Don't pretend to be an expert in your partner's field just because you hear your partner talk about it frequently. Don't let coworkers assume that you're an expert, either. Refer them to your partner.

- Minimize kissing, holding hands, and other displays of affection at work. In most workplaces those actions look unprofessional.

- Don't get involved in work conflicts involving your partner. Don't try to stick up for your partner or set the record straight. Let your partner handle it.

- Don't share with your partner too many details about how coworkers do their jobs or treat you. It could sabotage a good working relationship between your partner and those people.

- Don't talk or complain about your partner to coworkers. It will color their impressions of your partner.

- Don't ask your partner to reveal confidential information to you. It forces your partner to choose between loyalty to you and the organization. Plus, if there is an information leak you both would be suspect immediately.

- When you introduce your partner to a coworker for business purposes, just use your names and titles. You probably don't need to mention that you're a couple unless you are asked.

- Be careful about carpooling. It's great if your schedules usually are the same. But resentment builds when one person routinely has to delay going home because the other still is working.

- Limit shop talk when you're away from work. Some couples outlaw business discussions after a certain hour in the evening.

- Don't work together on key projects or form a coalition at work. Others may see you as a threat. Plus, it can be very difficult to be objective about business decisions when working so closely with your partner.

Resources

➡ *The Executive Dilemma: Handling People Problems at Work,* Eliza G.C. Collins, editor, John Wiley & Sons, 1985.

See Also

⇨ **Making Gossip Work for You,** *page 102.*
⇨ **Relief for Two-Career Couples,** *page 146.*
⇨ **Balancing Work and Family,** *page 150.*

Bonus Tip!

Maintain friendships and hobbies away from work and each other.

Section III: Self-Improvement

Balancing Work and Family

Balancing the pressing demands of work and family is a constant battle for many of us. In fact, surveys have shown that most Americans would take a slower career path if they could have more time with their families.

There are many ways to achieve that delicate balance, no matter what kind of job you do.

- Start with the notion that it takes thought and energy to make time for both work and family. It won't happen spontaneously.

- Know what you value in life. Set aside an hour or two to thoroughly evaluate what is really important to you. Be truthful. Don't adopt the values you think others want you to have. Now compare those values with the way you spend your time. Do you spend most of your time on the people and things you value most. Try drawing a pie chart in which the wedges are proportionate to the amount of time and energy you actually spend on different facets of your life. Now draw a second pie chart illustrating how you really want to spend your time. How well do they match?

- Have realistic expectations. Usually you can get some of what you want but not all, and not all in the form you prefer. You usually can't have and do everything all at once.

- Try writing a personal balance statement, as suggested by authors Ken Lizotte and Barbara Litwak (see **Resources** below). It is a brief one-sentence definition of what balance means to you. (I envision a life in which I achieve great things at work but also maintain a happy and loving family life; or, I want a life in which I have lots of friends, do lots of socializing, and am busy all the time.)

- View your life as a series of phases; you can concentrate on different priorities at different times. For example, you may wish to focus on your young family now but pour lots of energy into your career later.

- When deciding how to spend your time ask, "Is this the only chance I'll have to do this or can I postpone it?"

- Find ways to have at least some of what you love. Hiking with your kids once a month may be enough, instead of trying to do it weekly.

- Have a strong support network. Stay in touch with friends or family members you can talk to and rely on in a pinch. Call on them as soon as you need help.

- Don't try to do everything yourself. If possible hire someone to do chores like house cleaning, car washing, or lawn mowing—even occasionally. Spread family duties around so no one shoulders all the burden.

- Schedule family time on your calendar and honor it like a business appointment. Have regular family discussions to schedule activities you'll do together that week and keep everyone up to date about each other's schedules.

- Set specific limits for everything, from the energy you put into your job to the time you'll spend on family duties.

- Cultivate a positive attitude. Tell yourself that you're nowhere near the limit of your potential.

- Get creative about making the most of your limited family time. Keep the kids awake an hour later sometimes so you can be with them in the evenings; or get everyone up earlier for breakfast together; or meet your kids or spouse for lunch once in a while.

- Notice how developing your personal life can help you in your career. Many of the same traits that make you an appealing person, responsible spouse, and effective parent can make you successful at work, authors Stan Katz and Aimee Liu write in the book *Success Trap* (see **Resources** below).

- Reinforce your new habit of spending time on what's really important. Each evening make a mental list of the good things that happened to you that day. (You left work in time to attend your daughter's soccer game. You both felt good and you still finished your work the next morning.)

- Teach yourself to appreciate leisure and unscheduled time. Don't book your time off and weekends so heavily that you become a playaholic.

Resources
➡ *Success Trap,* Stan Katz and Aimee Liu, Dell Publishing, 1991.
➡ *He Works She Works: Successful Strategies for Working Couples,* Jaine Carter and James D. Carter, AMACOM, 1995.
➡ *Balancing Work and Family,* Ken Lizotte and Barbara Litwak, AMACOM, 1995.
➡ *Working Fathers: New Strategies for Balancing Work and Family,* James Levine, Addison-Wesley, 1997.
➡ *The Working Parents' Handbook,* Katherine Murray, Park Avenue Publications, 1996.

See Also
⇨ **Slowing Down Your Career,** *page 228.*
⇨ **Finding More Time in Your Day,** *page 8.*
⇨ **Relief for Two-Career Couples,** *page 146.*

Section III: Self-Improvement

Helping Your Kids Understand Your Job

What response would you get if you asked your kids to describe what you do at work all day? Blank stares? Wild misunderstandings?

Many children have false impressions or scant knowledge of their parents' work lives, even though work is a major part of adults' identities. You can help your kids understand more by talking with them about your job or taking them to work for a visit. This also helps them prepare to make their own career choices.

- Talk to your children about your job and its place in your organization. Ask what they'd like to do as grown-ups. Talk to your older kids about your training and education, goals you had as a youth, and goals you have now.

- Don't assume that your kids won't be interested in your workplace. Most kids are fascinated by anything their parents do.

- Bring home touchable pieces of your work—tools, scraps, samples, discarded supplies, blueprints, photos, boxes, and leftover promotional objects (with your boss' OK).

- Before taking your kids to your workplace ask what they would like to see there and who they would like to meet.

- Make visits fun and short (two hours maximum). Don't try to show everything in one visit. Think about what impresses them most. Plan the visit so two or three important aspects will stay with them.

- Keep visits simple for preschoolers. Show them where you go every day: your desk, coworkers' work stations, the cafeteria, a supply room, and even rest rooms.

- Keep older kids' interest by having coworkers explain their jobs, background, and goals. Introduce kids to positive role models.

- If kids aren't allowed in your work area meet them for lunch in the cafeteria or show them the lobby. If they're not allowed in the building at all show them the exterior, where you park and where you enter.

- Let your kids try out objects you use: a swivel chair, computer, adding machine, Dictaphone, order book, stapler, and copy machine. Older kids could help photocopy documents, staple reports, apply mailing labels, or cut material.

- After the visit talk about what they saw. What impressed them? How did it compare with what they expected? Did it encourage them to set new goals?

■ Have them draw pictures or write a paragraph about the visit. Collect writing, artwork, and photos in a scrapbook about Mom's or Dad's work.

Resources

→ *Finding Time for Fathering*, Mitch Golant and Susan Golant, Fawcett, 1992.
→ *The Father's Almanac*, S. Adams Sullivan, Doubleday, 1992.
→ The Take Our Daughters To Work Day project (a nationwide event, held each April, promotes exploration of career options for girls), Ms. Foundation for Women, 120 Wall St., 33rd Floor, New York, NY 10005, 212-742-2300. Web address: http://www.ms.foundation.org.

See also:

⇨ **Balancing Work and Family,** *page 150.*

Bonus Tip!

Bring home photos or videos of your workplace and coworkers.

Section III: Self-Improvement

Easing Heavy Travel Schedules

In many jobs frequent travel is part of the routine. But even if you enjoy travel, frequent long trips can cause problems in your work or personal life. You might feel out of touch with coworkers, family, and friends. You may not be able to do personal activities that you used to love. You may feel so frazzled and overwhelmed that when you return home you just want to be alone.

There are ways to cut your travel just a little while still being effective at your job.

- Use phone calls, faxes, teleconferences, or new video conferences more often instead of traveling (see **Resources** below). Many businesses have cut their travel budgets this way.

- Have a family meeting to discuss how much travel is OK. Discuss the results with your supervisor. If being home more often is crucial to your personal happiness, you'll have to tell your boss how much travel is too much. Explore with your boss ways to rearrange your schedule or duties so you can travel less.

- To avoid traveling on weekends, schedule meetings only on Tuesdays, Wednesdays, and Thursdays. If you must travel other days, schedule Monday meetings late in the day and Friday meetings early so you won't have to travel on weekends.

- Tell your boss in advance when you can't travel (anniversaries, birthdays, special school functions).

- While you're away call home daily so you can stay involved. Parents of young children could call at bedtime to read a story over the phone.

- Stay in touch with subordinates, coworkers, bosses, and clients with electronic mail, voice mail, and faxes. Ask for updates on projects, file daily activity reports, or pass along interesting tidbits of information.

- Bring family members along once in a while. Turning some trips in to mini-vacations is a way to build more family time into your schedule.

- If you're working late out of town on a Friday and have to be back there Monday, ask your company to fly your spouse out to spend the weekend with you. With lower weekend airline and hotel rates, it may be cheaper than flying you back home for the weekend, and you'll be in better shape mentally for the next week.

- Don't let the lure of frequent flier programs twist your travel plans into knots of inconvenient connections. Opt for the most convenient times and connections any airline can provide. You'll be less stressed out.

- When you're away, take an hour each day just for yourself. Relax or do something fun so you won't feel as if you are working around the clock when you travel.

- Keep your energy level up while you're away by eating light—lots of fruits, vegetables, and complex carbohydrates. Drink lots of water but go easy on the alcohol. Try to exercise at least a few times a week. Walk during lunch hours or between meetings. Make time to use your hotel's gym or pool.

- Don't bring home gifts for family members or friends expecting that they'll replace intimacy, involvement, or regular communication.

- When you get home make your top priority listening to family members about what happened while you were gone. When they're done, share your adventures and feelings.

Resources
➡ *Office on the Go*, Kim Baker and Sunny Baker, Prentice Hall, 1993.
➡ *The Business Travel Survival Guide*, Jack Cummings, John Wiley & Sons, 1991.
➡ *202 Tips Even the Best Business Travelers May Not Know*, Christopher McGinnis, Irwin Professional Publishing, 1994.
➡ *Consumer Reports Travel Letter*, Consumers Union, Box 53629 Boulder, CO 80322-3629, 800-234-1970, monthly, $39/yr.
➡ Kinko's copy centers offer video conference rooms and technical support, starting at about $150/hour, call 800-743-COPY for information and the site nearest you. Web address: http://www.kinkos.com.
➡ Management Recruiters International, Inc.'s Conferview system, the world's largest privately-owned network of video conference facilities, available on a rental basis, call 800-875-8200. Web address: http://www.mrinet.com/conferview.

See Also
⇨ **Avoiding Excessive Overtime Work**, *page 60.*
⇨ **Negotiating for What You Want**, *page 98.*
⇨ **Quick Stress Busters**, *page 128.*
⇨ **Balancing Work and Family**, *page 150.*

Section III: Self-Improvement

CHAPTER

12

Chapter 12

Details

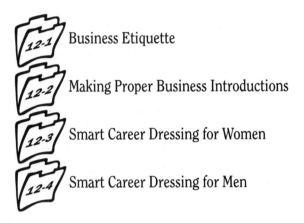

Section III: Self-Improvement

Business Etiquette

Today's more casual and high-tech workplaces make work easier but they also create new opportunities for rude and offensive behavior.

What are the rules now? How do you knock before entering someone's office when it's a cubicle without a door? How do you handle call waiting? How do you balance the frantic pace of your demanding job with the needs of coworkers and clients?

Learn the basics of good etiquette to help put people at ease and strengthen working relationships.

- Turn your pager down or off when you're in a meeting. Don't answer it immediately unless it's truly urgent. The people you are with deserve your attention first.

- Fax only material that is welcome and necessary; faxes are costly to receive and often hard to read. With important documents, mail originals to the recipients later for their permanent records. Don't use the fax for thank-you notes, invitations, or other personal correspondence.

- Don't make phone calls on your cellular phone when you suspect the reception may be poor or you won't be able to devote your full attention to the call (driving in heavy traffic or bad weather).

- If you have a call waiting, give the person you're already speaking with the choice of whether or not to hold. If you do answer the waiting call, take that caller's name and number and call back.

- Don't send back formal letters or memoranda with your reply scrawled in the margin (this might be OK for more informal correspondence). Show that you respect and value the writer's message by writing a separate reply. Do bother to respond when asked, even if it's to say that you haven't had time to review the material or don't wish to get involved.

- Try to reach a consensus among coworkers about playing music in your work area during work hours. What is appropriate and when? If you can't agree, listen to your music privately with earphones.

- Don't barge into someone's work area just because there is no door. Say "excuse me" from the perimeter and wait to see if you are welcome.

- Don't be rude to smokers, even if it seems politically correct. Don't make unsolicited comments about their appearance or health.

- Treat men and women with equal politeness and kindness. Don't extend extra courtesies to women solely because of their gender (holding doors open, standing when they leave the room).

- Don't continue typing or doing other work when you take a phone call. If you can't devote your full attention tell the caller you'll call back.

- Return all calls, even if they're answering machine messages, and even if only to say you're not interested in doing business with the caller.

- Avoid eating at your desk. It's unprofessional, messy, and rude to people who may come to your office to do business. Besides, you'll probably be more productive and refreshed if you grant yourself a 15- to 30-minute break away from the office. If you must eat at your desk close the door or turn away so others won't have to watch you.

Resources
➡ *The Little Black Book of Business Etiquette*, Michael Thomsett, AMACOM, 1991.
➡ *Don't Slurp Your Soup: A Basic Guide to Business Etiquette*, Betty Craig, Brighton Publications, Inc., 1991.

See Also
⇨ **Cubicle Survival Tips**, *page 20*.
⇨ **Using Your Fax Machine Wisely**, *page 38*.
⇨ **Voice Mail and Answering Machine Savvy**, *page 42*.
⇨ **Tuning Up Informal Speech**, *page 76*.

Section III: Self-Improvement

Bonus Tip!

Send handwritten thank-you notes for business gifts, favors, or entertainment.

Making Proper Business Introductions

Introducing people to one another can be intimidating. We become nervous about using the right names, the right phrases, and the right gestures.

Proper introductions are important because they help make people comfortable, broaden your circle of associates and clients, and reflect your manners and style.

- Mention first the name of the person to whom you're showing deference or honor. It could be your supervisor, a client, an out-of-town visitor, or an elected official.

- Everyone should stand during introductions—women included. Staying seated sends a message that the introduction really isn't important.

- Do shake hands, even if it's a man meeting a woman or two women meeting each other. Handshakes establish a personal link and are a welcoming gesture. Make yours firm.

- Hold drinks in your left hand so your right hand won't be cold and clammy when you shake hands (vice versa if you're right-handed).

- If your hand is sweaty or cold, try warming it or drying it off in your pocket or on your trousers or skirt. Don't apologize for your hand unless you're good at making jokes about it. You'll just draw more attention to it.

- It's perfectly OK to introduce yourself if you're networking, or if no one else can do it for you. Simply extend your hand and announce your name and your title or reason for being there.

- Call people by the name with which they were introduced. (Refer to Dr. Wilson as Dr. Wilson, until or unless she says "Oh, call me Elizabeth.")

- Don't use titles (Mr., Ms., Dr.) for every introduction unless the title is important in that setting or you know the person prefers the title. If you must use a title for a woman use Ms., unless she has told you she prefers Mrs. or Miss. If in doubt ask her preference ahead of time or check with someone in her office.

- Remember the name of the person you just met by concentrating on it as you are introduced. Use the name several times in your conversation. Also, try to form a mental link between the name and an outstanding characteristic of that person.

- If you don't understand the name of the person to whom you were introduced, ask to hear it again. You even could ask how it's spelled or inquire about its origin (this also helps you remember it).

- If you forget someone's name just admit it to the person. ("I'm sorry but I can't recall your name.") Many people will feel flattered that you care to learn it again. Other tactics might be to extend your hand and say your name; usually the other person will respond the same way; or start small talk with the person in hopes that something will trigger your memory or someone else will join in and use that person's name; or run through the alphabet—does the name begin with A? B? or C?

- Try these other memory tricks: silently make a rhyme with the name (Mark barks), think of words that sound similar (Adler and antler), create a picture in your mind of what the name means (Smith means blacksmith). Link details about the person (number of kids or home town) to the images or rhymes you just created (Sarah Adler parks her antlers in Minnesota).

- End the conversation with the person's name to pound it further in your memory. ("Nice to meet you, Bill.")

- Promptly record important or memory-jogging details about new acquaintances in your Rolodex or contact file, just as you would address and phone numbers.

- Don't panic if you forget these guidelines. Go ahead and do your best. Bend the rules to fit the situation if necessary.

Resources
➡ *The Memory Book*, Harry Lorayne and Jerry Lucas, Ballantine, 1986.
➡ *Don't Slurp Your Soup: A Basic Guide to Business Etiquette*, Betty Craig, Brighton Publications, Inc., 1991.

See Also
⇨ **Building a Productive Network**, *page 206.*
⇨ **Business Etiquette for the '90s**, *page 158.*

Section III: Self-Improvement

Smart Career Dressing for Women

You may not like to think that your style of dress and general appearance influence how you are regarded at work. But they do.

Dressing appropriately can be tricky for women. There is no universally accepted uniform akin to a man's suit, shirt, and tie. Women have to weed through many clothing choices that can send a variety of messages.

Acceptable styles vary by industry and location. But there are general guidelines that apply to most working women.

- Dress to create a first impression that says you're sharp, competent, respected, and serious about your work. Wear clothes that make you feel good and look good as you perform job tasks. Don't dress as if you're ready for a night out on the town or a day of lounging around the house.

- Know the accepted and preferred mode of dress for your workplace, industry, and geographical region. It's best to follow it somewhat if you want to be well-regarded. You may be able to stray from it a bit after you've proven yourself to be competent and valuable. Also consider what customers expect to see when they do business with you.

- Don't feel obligated to buy into every new trend, but do stay current with broad style changes.

- Stick to classic suits, coat dresses, and dresses with jackets when you're in a formal business setting or trying to win respect. Or upgrade two-piece dresses and mix-and-match separates by adding a jacket.

- Don't assume that you must look mannish to look professional. Look for business outfits with full cuts, bright colors, supple fabrics, soft collars, and interesting details.

- Don't wear skirts that are more than a couple of inches above your knees, especially if they ride up on your legs when you sit.

- Be cautious about slacks. They have become increasingly well accepted in many workplaces. Pants suits and slacks with a blazer look very professional. But in some industries and organizations people still may think they're not professional enough for a woman who wants to appear authoritative and competent. If you do wear slacks avoid tight-fitting styles.

- Avoid wearing blue jeans, T-shirts, sundresses, sweatshirts, sweatpants, and clothing that is sheer, very clingy, or otherwise too revealing.

- Wear shoes with heels of two inches or less. Avoid open-toe or sling-back shoes—they look too casual and flimsy. Don't wear athletic shoes unless they're required for your job. If you do wear them make sure they're clean and in good shape.

- Be judicious with jewelry. Choose items that look simple and well-made. Avoid jewelry that looks romantic. Items like unusual pins can serve as conversation starters.

- Keep fingernails at a reasonable length. Super-long nails are impractical for most workplaces and don't look professional. Save showy nail polish colors for off-duty times. When in doubt, go conservative.

- Don't use lack of money as an excuse for a worn, outdated, or inappropriate wardrobe. Invest in your work clothes just as you have your education. Put most of your money in good jackets, skirts, slacks, suits, and dresses; you can spend less on blouses and accessories. Update older outfits with new accessories. Shop in stores that sell quality, name-brand merchandise at discounts. Check out thrift or consignment stores; many have boutique areas reserved for high-quality clothing.

Resources
➡ *Work Clothes: Casual Dress for Serious Work.* J.S. Omelianuk, Alfred A. Knopf, 1996.
➡ *The New Professional Image: From Corporate Casual to the Ultimate Power Look,* Susan Bixler, Bob Adams Inc., 1997.

See Also
⇨ **Shining at a New Job**, *page 192.*
⇨ **Projecting a Successful Image**, *page 110.*
⇨ **Smart Career Dressing for Men**, *page 164.*

Section III: Self-Improvement

Bonus Tip!

Wear clothes with pockets to events where you'll be swapping business cards.

Smart Career Dressing for Men

Humorist Dave Barry has a simple way to gauge fashion correctness. "If, when you appear at the breakfast table, your wife laughs so hard that she spits out her toast, you should consider wearing a different tie," he wrote.

That's one way to determine if your business attire will have a positive effect on business leaders, coworkers, and customers. The other way is to seriously consider the image you project by your clothing.

Your appearance truly can influence your career. Fashion consultants tell stories about executives who refused to hire well-qualified people because the candidates looked unpolished. And no matter how casual our society has become, looking good attracts people to you and shows that you care about yourself and others.

- Know the dress codes of your organization and geographical region. Use them to determine how much personal style you can reveal through your wardrobe while still commanding respect.

- If you want the job, look the part. If you want the promotion, look promotable. If you want respect, dress as well or better than industry standards, image consultant Susan Bixler writes (see **Resources** below).

- Follow this rule of thumb from image expert Ken Karpinski (see **Resources** below): if you're comfortable working on your car in it, don't wear it to work. Even on casual dress days that would eliminate jeans, T-shirts, flannel shirts, and sweatsuits. It also eliminates anything that is worn, dirty, stained, ripped, a bad fit, or clearly designed for play or relaxation.

- For a business-like casual look try a jacket and good quality knit shirt without a tie; high-quality, muted-color sweater and shirt; or blazer and shirt with banded collar, no tie. Khaki and corduroy slacks are good, too.

- Buy quality fabrics, 100 percent wool, cotton, or silk that drape well. They cost more initially but look better and last longer.

- When you'll be meeting with others try to match their clothing style. When in doubt, go conservative. Conservative also is usually the best choice for job interviews, high-level meetings, or serious occasions.

- Broaden your tie collection. Bright, interesting ties are becoming more accepted even in conservative organizations. Ties also are a relatively inexpensive way to update and personalize a wardrobe, as are patterned socks, and striped shirts. And ties are a nice bridge to casual dress days when worn with a denim or khaki shirt. But don't wear conservative ties with casual shirts.

- If you're on a tight budget, choose one basic color on which to build your wardrobe, such as black, dark blue, or brown.

- Avoid short-sleeved dress shirts. They look unfinished and unprofessional. Also, don't wear a button-down shirt with a conservative suit—the shirt will look too casual.

- Buy the most expensive all-leather shoe you can afford. Keep shoes polished and scuff-free. Have at least two pairs of work shoes so each pair can air out while you wear the other. Avoid athletic shoes and sandals.

- Have your dress slacks pressed professionally and frequently. Wrinkles will ruin your look.

- Use accessories to make an impression, not to distract. Beware of items like bracelets, fraternity pins, or earrings that can alienate you from some clients or colleagues.

- Get wardrobe ideas and assistance from salespeople in a top-notch store or a personal wardrobe consultant. Flip through men's fashion magazines once in a while to see what's current.

Resources
→ *The First Four Seconds*, Martha Falke, Falcon House, 1990.
→ *The New Professional Image: From Corporate Casual to the Ultimate Power Look*, Susan Bixler, Bob Adams Inc., 1997.
→ *Red Socks Don't Work*, Kenneth Karpinski, Impact Publications, 1994.
→ *Mistakes Men Make That Women Hate*, Kenneth Karpinski, Cooper Square, 1994.

See Also
⇨ **Shining at a New Job**, *page 192.*
⇨ **Projecting a Successful Image**, *page 110.*
⇨ **Smart Career Dressing for Women**, *page 162.*

Section III: Self-Improvement

SECTION IV

Career Moves

Chapter 13

The Job Search

Chapter 14

Career Reinforcement

Chapter 15

Career Shifts

Chapter 16

Leaving Your Job

CHAPTER 13

Chapter 13

The Job Search

13-1 Using Information Interviews

13-2 Selling Yourself with Your Résumé

13-3 Composing an Electronic Résumé

13-4 Writing Super Cover Letters

13-5 Conducting an Electronic Job Search

13-6 Successful Job Interviews

13-7 Answering Interview Questions

13-8 Finding the Right Employer

13-9 Considering a Pay Cut

13-10 Handling Employment Recruiters

Section IV: Career Moves

Using Information Interviews

Two important parts of a successful job search are gathering information and finding jobs that are not advertised (most never are). A super technique for addressing both is the information interview. It's a brief, focused meeting with someone who knows about a field that interests you.

The goals of an information interview are to:
1. Get details about an occupation or industry.
2. Determine if you have the right skills for that field.
3. Learn about unadvertised jobs.
4. Do this while putting the other person at ease and not asking for a job.

- First, list everyone you know who could help you gather information or find knowledgeable contacts. Talk with your family, friends, neighbors, church members, colleagues, doctors, hair stylist, and insurance agent. Also look for names of potential contacts in newspapers, magazines, trade journals, and alumni publications. Find companies in the industries that interest you in the *Thomas Register of American Manufacturers*, in the public library's reference section, or on the Internet. Use your personal computer: tap into online information services like CompuServe, America Online, or Prodigy, which offer information on employers, employment opportunities, and related topics. Your eventual goal is to find contacts in your industry with hiring authority.

- List the contacts you've learned about, including phone numbers, occupations, and how you found out about them. Use a Rolodex, index card file, spiral notebook, three-ring binder with alphabetized sections, contact management software, or electronic pocket organizer.

- By phone or in a letter ask contacts for a 15- to 30-minute meeting within a specific week at their convenience. Mention how you got their names. Say that you're interested in their field or company and ask if they would help you by providing career information. Stress that you won't be asking for a job.

- Start with contacts who are least important in your job search. Practice with those interviews to build up your confidence.

- Before your meeting, use the library and your personal network to find out as much as you can about that industry or company.

- Ask how the person prepared for the job, the best and worst parts of the job, average starting salary, how to become qualified for this line of work, the average work week, types of problems and decisions faced at work, the usual career path in this field, and the names of others with whom you could talk. Also ask what need or challenge this organization faces; you might discover a new way to apply your skills.

- If you're interested in more than an entry-level position, ask how your skills would transfer to that field or company. Would additional education be helpful? How does this occupation differ from your preceding job?

- If people are too busy or unwilling to meet with you, look for ways to show them how they could benefit from seeing you, writes Hal Gieseking (see **Resources** below). Plan to write an article for a local or industry publication; then request an interview with the person you want to meet. Conduct your own mini–market survey to find out how customers regard the company's products. Now call the person you want to meet and say you'd like to share the results of your survey.

- If you do learn of a job opening during the interview, gather some details about it and find out whom to contact. Then go back to discussing the occupation or industry in general. Set up another time to talk about the job opening.

- Close by summarizing the specific details you have learned.

- After the meeting use your contact management system or notebook to record what you've learned and what you need to follow up on.

- Look for ways to pay back your contacts, such as participating in a fund-raiser their organization sponsors.

Resources
→ *The Career Coach*, self-guided audio- and videocassette program for job seekers, Kuselias Enterprises, Inc., North Haven, CT, 1997, 800-BESTJOB, $59.95 + shipping and handling.
→ *The Complete Job-Search Handbook*, Howard Figler, Henry Holt, 1988.
→ *30 Days to Finding a Good Job*, Hal Gieseking and Paul Plawin, Simon & Schuster, 1994.
→ *The Very Quick Job Search*, J. Michael Farr, JIST Works, Inc., 1996.

See Also
⇨ **Finding the Right Employer**, *page 184.*
⇨ **Building a Productive Network**, *page 206.*
⇨ **Escaping a Career Pigeonhole**, *page 214.*
⇨ **Considering a Career Change**, *page 216.*

Section IV: Career Moves

Selling Yourself with Your Résumé

A résumé is one of your most important pieces of employment equipment. It performs a big job—selling you and your unique combination of skills, experience, and qualities.

Even if you're not searching for a job now, periodically update your résumé (or at least create a rough draft) in case you need it quickly. Also, composing one is a good exercise for analyzing your strengths, weaknesses, and career plans.

- Do it yourself. Most people don't need to hire a résumé service. No one can sell you better than you because no one else knows you as well. However, do ask a knowledgeable colleague, friend, or advisor to review your résumé.

- Decide what you have to sell. Analyze your education and experience (what you can account for and verify) and how it relates to specific jobs and duties.

- Forget about the perfect format. There are many good ones. The best ones are brief. After listing your name and address, display your job objective, list your skills and experience related to that job, and then list specifics of past employment and education (start with the most recent). Good résumés are easy for an employer to scan and quickly discover why you would be a good match for the job. Get sample formats from résumé and job-hunting books in the library. Some job search experts recommend creating a brochure about yourself and your accomplishments, complete with photos, instead of or as a supplement to a standard résumé.

- Customize your résumé for different jobs and employers.

- Explicitly describe your job objective. Detail what you want to do, where, with whom, at what level of responsibility, and under what special conditions.

- Be specific about your skills. Show what you can do and how your skills match the requirements for this job. Ask the employer for the job description or requirements so you can highlight your most relevant strengths on your résumé. Or gather clues from the employment ad.

- Give details about past accomplishments (how many units, dollars, or people you handled; how often you performed certain duties; and under what conditions). Describe results and benefits to past employers.

- Don't focus on what you want out of the job, such as a new challenge or supportive atmosphere. Address what the employer wants and what you can offer the organization.

- Omit irrelevant personal information (age, marital status, height and weight, and hobbies). Include only information that demonstrates you have qualities the employer wants.

- Eliminate jargon (interface, modalities). Write in simple, clear, direct language.

- Use lots of action verbs (achieved, sold, created, organized).

- Check spelling and grammar repeatedly. Ask friends to help proofread.

- Use quality word processing and printing for a professional look. If you don't have your own computer equipment, use computers in public, school, or university libraries. Check with local copy centers too; some have computers for customer use at a small hourly fee. Some centers will design and produce your résumé with their desktop publishing equipment for about $25 and up. Or ask local United Way and unemployment offices if any organizations in your area offer clerical assistance to unemployed job seekers.

- Use white or cream-colored paper and matching envelopes, in most cases. Choose a clear, easy-to-read typeface.

- Carry your résumé with you everywhere. You never know when you'll run in to someone who knows of an opportunity for you.

Resources
→ *Beyond the Résumé: How to Land the Job You Want*, Herman Holtz, McGraw-Hill, 1984.
→ *The Damn Good Résumé Guide*, Yana Parker, Ten Speed Press, 1996.
→ *Résumés That Knock 'Em Dead*, Martin Yate, Bob Adams, Inc., 1995.
→ *Résumés That Get Jobs*, Jean Reed, Prentice Hall, 1990.
→ *Gallery of Best Resumes*, David F. Noble, JIST Works, Inc., 1994.
→ *America's Top Resumes for America's Top Jobs,*™ J. Michael Farr, JIST Works, Inc., 1998.
→ *Gallery of Best Resumes for Two-Year Degree Graduates*, David F. Noble, JIST Works, Inc., 1996.

See Also
⇨ **Writing Super Cover Letters**, *page 176.*
⇨ **Successful Job Interviews**, *page 180.*
⇨ **Returning to Work**, *page 230.*
⇨ **Conducting an Electronic Job Search**, *page 178.*
⇨ **Composing an Electronic Résumé**, *page 174.*

Section IV: Career Moves

Composing an Electronic Résumé

First there was the all-purpose résumé.

Then came the targeted résumé. Nurtured by the power of word processors, job seekers crafted several versions aimed at particular jobs, industries, or employers.

Now there's the electronic résumé. It's another important format job seekers need to know about—owing to employers' and search firms' growing use of computer systems to track the flood of résumés they receive.

It works like this. You send your résumé to an employer or search firm. Someone scans it electronically, placing it in the computer system. The computer then converts it to a standard text format. Now humans use computers to classify the résumé. They also search for résumés that contain keywords highlighting desired skills and experience.

Your goal is to write an electronic résumé that can be easily read by these computerized systems and easily retrieved by humans searching for the ideal candidate. You'll also need these techniques when using online employment services and online résumé banks or databases.

- Put your name on the very first line of your résumé, with nothing else on that line. The second line should be the first line of your address, and so on. Merging different pieces of information on one line, or using a column approach, makes it difficult for the computer to decipher it.

- In the text include lots of keywords and labels for yourself that could be searched by a computer. Forget about using action words and avoiding industry jargon. Keywords would be a foreign language or computer system you know, an area of study you've had, a job title you've held, a professional organization you've joined, an award you've won, a hot business trend you've tried, a prestigious university you've attended, or a Fortune 100 company you've serviced. Think like an employer: What keywords would you search for if you were trying to fill this position?

- Career expert Joyce Lain Kennedy recommends putting a keyword or qualifications summary at the top of your résumé, just under your name and address. It's a list of keywords, labels, and short phrases about you. List them from most important to least important. You might follow it with one or two sentences summing up your experience or career. You then would have a concise list of career highlights or more traditional, specific employment dates and titles (sprinkled liberally with keywords).

- Use only standard, clean-looking typefaces and high-quality printing with a laser printer. Anything else will scan poorly. Avoid italics, script, and underlines. Use boldface and capital letters sparingly. Don't use graphics, logos, or shading. Avoid horizontal or vertical lines. Check current résumé tip books for sample layouts.

- Send or deliver the original copy, not a photocopied version. Do not fold or staple it. Avoid faxing it, but if you must, set the fax machine to the "fine mode" to produce a cleaner copy.

- Send a cover letter with your résumé. Some employers will scan or save it. Use it to amplify your résumé and use more of those keywords.

- Call the company several days after sending your résumé to inquire whether you've been added to the applicant tracking system and if your résumé has been routed to any hiring managers. Find out if the computers had any trouble reading your résumé and offer to make changes. Make friends with the humans who keep the system moving.

- If you're e-mailing your résumé to a job bank or other online resource, protect your confidentiality by keeping your name or other identifying information out of the body of your résumé.

- For e-mailed résumés, write a good résumé title that sums up a lot of vital information about yourself in a very short space (Tech Writer/10 Yrs Exp/Cleve. or Controller/Health Co/CPA).

Resources

➡ *Electronic Résumé Revolution,* Joyce Lain Kennedy and Thomas J. Morrow, John Wiley & Sons, 1995.
➡ *National Business Employment Weekly Résumés,* Taunee Besson, John Wiley & Sons, 1996.
➡ *The Résumé Kit,* Richard H. Beatty, John Wiley & Sons, 1995.
➡ *Using the Internet and the World Wide Web in Your Job Search,* Fred E. Jandt and Mary B. Nemnich, JIST Works, Inc., 1997.

See Also
⇨ **Conducting an Electronic Job Search,** *page 178.*
⇨ **Selling Yourself with Your Résumé,** *page 172.*
⇨ **Writing Super Cover Letters,** *page 176.*

Section IV: Career Moves

Writing Super Cover Letters

Some people spend days, even weeks, perfecting their résumés but only minutes slapping together a routine cover letter. Not a good idea.

Your cover letter provides employers with their first impression of you. A good cover letter entices employers to learn more about you. A poor one encourages them to ignore you.

- Customize every letter. No generics.

- Start with an attention grabber; then get to the point quickly. Make sure the employer knows immediately what you want and why your letter is worth reading. Don't write your biography.

- Clearly explain how you could benefit the employer. Describe the value you could add or your biggest accomplishment at your preceding job. Describe how you have the qualifications, skills, or potential the employer seeks—and more. But don't repeat your résumé.

- Use the same keywords in your letter as in the employment ad. If your skills are different from what was requested, recast the job to fit you. ("I have the tenacity a successful sales director needs.")

- Conclude by asking for what you want: an interview and a chance to compete for the job. Say you'll be calling soon to schedule an appointment.

- Or close by indicating that you have choices, too. Say that you'd like more information about the job and would like to meet to discuss your mutual interests. Explain that you may want to schedule an interview after that meeting if you both think it's appropriate.

- Remember business writing basics: be brief (about three paragraphs, one-page limit), direct, polite, easy to read, and easy to understand. Use high-quality bond paper. Use good English and proofread repeatedly. Ask someone else to proofread, too.

- If you're sending an unsolicited résumé, don't tell the employer everything just yet. Give the employer a reason to get to know you better. The more points of contact you have, the better your chances of getting a job, says career management consultant and author Robert Riskin (see **Resources** below).

- Research the company before you write so you can reflect that knowledge in your letter. Use your public library, personal network, and professional associations.

- Try to address your letter to a real person instead of a title (Dear Personnel Director). Call the company and ask who has hiring responsibility for this job. Triple-check the spelling. If they tell you to send your résumé to the human resources department or follow the classified ad's directions, tell them that you're hoping to save the department some time. Or say that you're sending some important papers to the head of the department but you're not sure you have the correct name and title.

Resources
➡ *Kiplinger's Career Starter*, Jack O'Brien, Kiplinger Books, 1995.
➡ *Between Opportunities: A Survival Guide for Job Seekers and Career Changers*, Robert Riskin, Aar Dee Aar Publishing, 1992.
➡ *High Impact Résumés and Letters*, Ronald Krannich and William Banis, Impact Publications, 1994.
➡ *Gallery of Best Resumes*, David F. Noble, JIST Works, Inc., 1994.
➡ *The Quick Resumes & Cover Letter Book*, J. Michael Farr, JIST Works, Inc., 1994.

See Also
⇨ **Selling Yourself with Your Resume**, *page 172.*
⇨ **Composing Better Letters**, *page 84.*
⇨ **Choosing the Right Words**, *page 88.*
⇨ **Conducting an Electronic Job Search,** *page 178.*
⇨ **Composing an Electronic Résumé**, *page 174.*

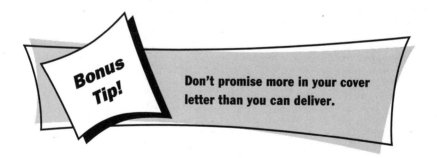

Bonus Tip!

Don't promise more in your cover letter than you can deliver.

Conducting an Electronic Job Search

Conducting an effective job search without a computer and modem is like crossing the country by bicycle instead of jet. You'll get there, but it will take you longer and be less convenient and far less direct.

"If you're not connected (to electronic information services), you are going to be passed over and will miss a good number of the opportunities that are out there," says James Gonyea, author of *The Online Job Search Companion.*

Through your computer and telephone lines you can become visible to employers around the clock (via résumé databases), find job leads that others never hear about (using electronic mail and public message forums), and research potential employers quickly (with business and media databases).

- Don't assume that only computer experts in high-tech fields can use electronic job search techniques. All kinds of job seekers and employers already use them.

- Start small. Ask if your public or university library has the Help Wanted USA microfiche compilation of classified employment ads from about 60 major metropolitan newspapers, updated weekly. Ask for electronic listings of magazine and journal articles you can study to research industries and employers.

- Don't despair if you don't have a computer. You probably know someone who does. Borrow it. Or rent computer time at libraries, college computer or career centers, or at commercial copy centers.

- Get software to help you define career paths, produce and mail résumés, and manage job search tasks. Select the best by scanning reviews in *Software Reviews on File* and *Computer Select* in your public library.

- Get a modem to link your computer to phone lines. Then you can use a commercial online service or an Internet provider for a monthly fee (see **Resources** below). Use these services to find job and résumé databases, career guidance, discussion groups in your field, corporate information, and e-mail services.

- Find out if there is an electronic version of your local newspaper and its classified ads. It's another research tool.

- Use your telephone to call job information hotlines, like the one the federal government has (see **Resources** below). Also, buy a telephone directory on

CD-ROM. For under $30 you'll have millions of business names in your computer. Sift through them to find potential employers with the characteristics you want.

- Use databases of corporate reports, newspaper and magazine articles, and other business information to build a target employer list and learn about specific companies. Dig up names of company leaders and their alma maters and past employers (maybe you have a connection with one of them). Find listings of helpful databases in the *Gale Directory of Databases,* Gonyea's and Kennedy's books, and online services (see **Resources** below). Ask career counselors or outplacement firms you know to use their databases. Check software stores and catalogs for databases you'd want to purchase.

- List an electronic version of your résumé with several electronic résumé databases for broad exposure to all kinds of employers, agencies, and recruiters. Look for them through your alumni association, professional or trade organizations, and major online services. Send your résumé for free to the Internet's Online Career Center (see **Resources** below).

- When paying a fee to put your résumé in a database, clarify how employers find it, how much exposure it gets, how many referrals you'd get per month, and if the database provider can help you rewrite your résumé so employers will select it more often.

Resources
➡ *The Online Job Search Companion,* James Gonyea, McGraw-Hill, 1994.
➡ *Electronic Job Search Revolution,* Joyce Lain Kennedy, John Wiley & Sons, 1995.
➡ *The Career America Connection,* the federal government's employment information service, 912-757-3000.
➡ Online Career Center on the Web at http://www.occ.com.
➡ Major online information services: CompuServe: 800-848-8199; America Online: 800-827-6364; Prodigy: 800-776-3449; and Delphi-Internet: 800-695-4005.
➡ *Using the Internet and the World Wide Web in Your Job Search,* Fred E. Jandt and Mary B. Nemnich, JIST Works, Inc., 1997.

See Also
➪ **Selling Yourself with Your Résumé,** *page 172.*
➪ **Composing an Electric Résumé,** *page 174.*
➪ **Writing Super Cover Letters,** *page 176.*

Section IV: Career Moves

Successful Job Interviews

The object of a job interview is to convince an employer that you are absolutely the best person for this job. Concentrate more on how you come across as a person than on your skills or potential.

- Spend a lot more time preparing for the interview than the interview actually will take.
- Ask for a job description or hiring criteria before the interview so you can describe your skills and accomplishments in terms of what the employer wants.
- Know what qualities the interviewer wants. Most are looking for knowledge, enthusiasm, confidence, energy, dependability, honesty, and pride in one's work.
- Know yourself. Do some soul searching on paper about your finest accomplishments and how they affect your career, your most significant failures and what you've learned from them, how well you work with authorities and others, and how others would describe you.
- Study the organization you're interviewing with. Get help from the public library reference desk, newspaper clippings, trade associations, Chamber of Commerce, Better Business Bureau, and professional associates. Look for information that will enable you to discuss how you could help the company reach its goals or fix a problem. Develop specific ideas for improving a particular department or product.
- Arrive at least 15 minutes early so you're not harried. Tardiness makes a bad impression.
- Dress appropriately for the job you seek. Avoid faddish clothing. Get ideas by visiting similar workplaces or asking colleagues, friends, or the employer's receptionist.
- Learn the correct pronunciation of the interviewer's name before you meet. Ask for help from the employer's receptionist or the person who scheduled your interview.
- Work hardest on the first five minutes of the interview.
- Anticipate questions you're likely to be asked.
- Always be honest. But do focus on the positive.
- Answer only what is asked. Too much information can make you appear overqualified or boring. Give some details; then ask if more are needed.

- Ask lots of questions. Inquire about the company's goals, whom you'd work for, working hours, what the interviewer likes and dislikes about working here, who had this job before, how successful that person was, what customers say about this company, and who makes the hiring decision. Ask about opportunities for advancement in this job and with this organization. Find out where people who have had this job in the past moved on to.

- Be dispassionate and factual about past employment troubles. It's OK to say you left a job because of a personality conflict. You might say that you probably could handle it better now or have learned a valuable skill because of the experience. Don't criticize your former or current employer.

- Show extreme interest and enthusiasm.

- Don't promise less than you're capable of delivering.

- If you're nervous, focus on the interviewer, not yourself. Pretend you're having coffee with a friend. Breathe deeply.

- Don't ask about money early in an interview. Ask about a salary range later if you feel there might be a good match.

- Ask for the job before you leave if you think it's the right one. Most candidates won't do this, so you'll be ahead of the competition.

- Write a thank-you note. Use it as one more opportunity to market yourself. Briefly mention another valuable quality you have or another detail that would help the employer see that you're the right choice.

Resources

➡ *Sweaty Palms: The Neglected Art of Being Interviewed*, H. Anthony Medley, Ten Speed Press, 1992.

➡ *The Career Coach*, self-guided audio- and videocassette program for job seekers, Kuselias Enterprises, Inc., North Haven, CT, 1997, 800-BESTJOB, $59.95 + shipping and handling.

➡ *The Quick Interview & Salary Negotiation Book,* J. Michael Farr, JIST Works, Inc., 1995.

See Also

⇨ **Answering Interview Questions**, *page 182.*
⇨ **Projecting a Successful Image**, *page 110.*
⇨ **Smart Career Dressing for Women**, *page 162.*
⇨ **Smart Career Dressing for Men**, *page 164.*

Section IV: Career Moves

Answering Interview Questions

"There are no stupid questions, only stupid answers," a favorite college professor of mine used to say.

That certainly is true when you're interviewing for a job. Some of the questions interviewers ask may seem weird, but most of them are not stupid. They're probably designed to uncover specific details. Plan for them.

- **"Tell me a little about yourself."** Before the interview prepare an honest, one- to two-minute speech including a brief introduction to yourself, your key accomplishments, your strengths as demonstrated by your accomplishments, the importance of those strengths and accomplishments to the employer, and how you could grow in this job, career expert Ron Fry writes (see **Resources** below). Avoid vague clichés such as "I like to work with people" or "I'm a hard worker."

- **"What are your weaknesses?"** Don't reveal serious flaws. Talk about a fairly old weakness that has been fixed. Or discuss a weakness positively. ("I suppose that my standards are so high that I get impatient with people who don't do their part.") Explain what you're doing to overcome the problem.

- **"What courses or extracurricular activities did you like best in college/high school?"** Talk about achievements, leadership, and how your activities relate to this job.

- **"What did you do in your last job? What kind of experience have you had?"** Discuss results and growth. Briefly describe how you spent your time during a typical day.

- **"Why did you leave your last job?"** If you don't have an acceptable answer, try framing your reply with any of these reasons: you want more challenge, the location wasn't right, there were virtually no opportunities for advancement, you want to work for a better company, or the company wasn't stable enough.

- **"You've been out of work for a while."** Or **"You've changed jobs quite often."** Describe your resilience and ability to handle adversity.

- **"Why do you want this job?"** One possible answer: "I've been evaluating my qualities lately and the tasks I enjoy. From what I've learned about this job, my skills are a good match."

- **"Tell me about the worst boss (or job) you ever had."** The interviewer might be trying to discover if you're a back stabber, complainer, or blamer.

Be objective. Acknowledge that there were conflicts over certain issues and then discuss what you learned from the experience.

- **"What is your impression of our company?"** Research the company ahead of time so you'll have thoughtful observations and questions.

- **"What books have you read lately?"** Or **"What movies have you seen?"** Tell what attracted you to the book or movie and what impressions you took away from it.

- **"Where do you see yourself in five years?"** Most employers want to know if you plan to stay awhile and if you have a career plan. If possible, mention that your career plan is flexible and you're eager to learn.

Resources

➡ *Between Opportunities: A Survival Guide for Job Seekers and Career Changers*, Robert Riskin, Aar Dee Aar Publishing, 1992.

➡ *101 Great Answers to the Toughest Interview Questions*, Ron Fry, Career Press, 1995.

➡ *Knock 'Em Dead 1997*, Martin Yate, Bob Adams, Inc., 1996.

➡ *Your First Interview: Everything You Need to Know to Ace the Interview Process and Get Your First Job*, Ron Fry, Career Press, 1995.

➡ *The Quick Interview & Salary Negotiation Book*, J. Michael Farr, JIST Works, Inc., 1995.

See Also

⇨ **Successful Job Interviews**, *page 180*.

⇨ **Tuning Up Informal Speech**, *page 76*.

Bonus Tip!

Use humor to help with a difficult or awkward question.

Section IV: Career Moves

Finding the Right Employer

Sometimes locating a new job can bring mixed feelings. You're happy that you've found it, but you have a nagging feeling that accepting the offer would be a mistake. You worry about whether the company is a good place to work.

There are many signs that will tell whether you've got a good match or if you'll wish you worked somewhere else in a few months.

Look for an employer who:

- Encourages informal and work-related communication between all levels of employees and management.
- Shows a lack of favoritism, bias, inequity, intimidation, or abuse. (The company may have an employee bill of rights or a well-developed diversity training program.)
- Tolerates individual styles.
- Allows and encourages positive humor at work.
- Designs jobs so employees can see the results of their work and feel they're making meaningful contributions.
- Shares success with employees financially and otherwise.
- Encourages employees to grow and learn.
- Doesn't expect employees to devote their entire lives to the company.
- Has established grievance procedures that employees follow and managers respect.

To uncover the true character of the company:

- Ask to meet the people you'd be working with. Ask them what the management is like. What are the ups and downs of working in their department? What benefits have they received by working there?
- Ask those questions of other employees too. Talk with them in informal meeting places like the company lunchroom. Be suspicious if the company is unwilling to allow this.
- Ask about the organization's values. What does it stand for? What is important here? What kind of employees do they value most?
- Ask employees and managers for examples of when they had fun working here.

- Gather information about the company's pay and benefits from managers, human resources officials, industry contacts, and trade associations. Ask employees how they feel about their pay and benefits. How would your pay and benefits compare with that of other employees? With similar companies? What does this tell you about the company's ability to pay and its commitment to job security and fairness?

- Use your network of contacts outside the company to find and talk to former employees, industry analysts, competitors, and customers.

- Interview the person who interviews you. Why did the people who previously held this position leave? How successful were they? What is the company's turnover rate? Its philosophy? Its biggest problems? Its growth plans?

- Be tenacious about getting the information you want. Write out your questions ahead of time so you won't forget any during the interview. Don't allow the interview to end until you get your answers.

Resources

➡ *A Great Place to Work: What Makes Some Employers So Good—and Some So Bad*, Robert Levering, Random House, 1988.

➡ *The 100 Best Companies to Work for in America*, Robert Levering and Milton Moskowitz, Currency/Doubleday, 1993.

➡ *Companies with a Conscience*, Mary Scott and Howard Rothman, Citadel Press, 1994.

➡ *The Right Job for You,* J. Michael Farr, JIST Works, Inc., 1997.

See Also

⇨ **Using Information Interviews,** *page 170.*
⇨ **Successful Job Interviews,** *page 180.*
⇨ **Making Better Decisions,** *page 122.*
⇨ **Conducting an Electronic Job Search,** *page 178.*

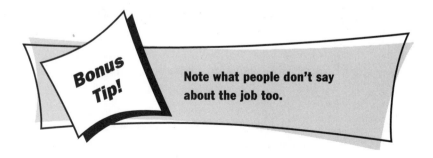

Bonus Tip!

Note what people don't say about the job too.

Section IV: Career Moves

Considering a Pay Cut

When you finally get a good job offer after months of job hunting, you may be tempted to settle for less compensation than you had before just so you can be employed again. But should you?

Maybe not, some career experts advise. Taking a pay cut while your job skills remain valuable and current can hurt more than your bank balance.

- Don't assume that you'll have to take a cut. That assumption would show that you have a poor self-image and are too willing to sacrifice before employers ask, says Marilyn Moats Kennedy, managing partner of Career Strategies, Wilmette, Ill. Employers won't pay full price for your work if you indicate that money isn't important or is highly negotiable.

- Know what you're worth, considering your level of skills, education, experience, and responsibilities. Get salary averages from industry contacts, professional associations, or your state or federal Bureau of Labor Statistics (see **Resources** below). Most employers will pay for quality employees.

- Know the market. Salaries are affected by the size of the job and company and whether your skills are in high demand or scarce. Larger companies generally pay better and compete more for workers from other large, well-paying companies. Small companies may pay less with fewer benefits but may be better places to work. Some employers might expect you to take a cut if you're switching industries or specialties. However, Kennedy says that many people get at least a 10 percent increase for a lateral move and 20 percent for a higher-level job. Refer again to what you are worth in the job market.

- Don't give a number when an employer asks what salary you want. Say that you expect the organization to be competitive and fair if you are the best person for the job. Ask what the salary range is for this job. If you have developed skills and can be productive immediately, you should be in at least the middle of the range.

- Ask if the salary offer is firm or negotiable. If it's low but firm and you really want the job, ask for a six-month salary and performance review. Or ask for a signing bonus, which allows the company to pay more without upsetting its own salary limits.

- Say, "Would you consider $50,000?" instead of "I want (or I need) $50,000." Note that asking for much more than the offer may require approval from high-level managers, which could mean delays and heavier scrutiny of whether you're the best candidate.

- Take the long view. It may be better financially to take a salary cut for a job with great future potential than to stay unemployed until you get another good offer.

- Think about what accepting a pay cut says about you. Your supervisors and coworkers might conclude that you're not worth a higher salary and lose respect for you. *You* may believe it, too, and lose self-esteem.

- Don't expect to be paid well for lengthy service at another company. New employers care about your current skills.

Resources

➡ *Between Opportunities: A Survival Guide for Job Seekers and Career Changers*, Robert Riskin, Aar Dee Aar Publishing, 1992.

➡ *Kennedy's Career Strategist* (newsletter), Career Strategies, 1150 Wilmette Ave., Wilmette, IL 60091, $59/10 issues. 800-728-1709. E-mail: mmkcareer @aol.com.

➡ U.S. Department of Labor, Bureau of Labor Statistics, Inquiries and Correspondence, Washington, D.C., 202-606-7828. Web address: http://www.stats.bls.gov.

See also

⇨ **Finding the Right Employer**, *page 184.*
⇨ **Asking for a Raise,** *page 202.*
⇨ **Making Better Decisions**, *page 122.*

Section IV: Career Moves

Handling Employment Recruiters

Receiving a call from an employment recruiter, or headhunter, can be tricky. Will you let yourself be flattered and forget to ask tough questions? Will you pass up an opportunity because you're happy where you are?

Companies hire recruiters to find qualified employees, usually for middle- and upper-level jobs. Many recruiters specialize in certain fields. They usually target successful, satisfied, and stable employees and executives with solid references.

Knowing how recruiters work will prepare you to deal with them successfully.

- Listen to the recruiter, even if you think you're not interested. You may find that the job offers greater challenge, relocation, or a salary hike. Plus, you don't want to be rude to a recruiter who may have better opportunities for you later.

- Check out the recruiter as you listen. Does it appear that the recruiter only is fishing for names? Does the recruiter's pitch match what you know about jobs, opportunities, and salaries in your industry? If not, be wary.

- Watch out for recruiters who are too complimentary, guarantee success, and seem determined to place you no matter what. Keep your own interests and priorities in mind. You'll want to work with someone who is genuinely likable, honest, and cooperative.

- Ask for and check the recruiter's references (both people placed in jobs and clients who hired people the recruiter located).

- Check the recruiter's credentials. Is the recruiter a Certified Personnel Consultant? Affiliated with national personnel, recruiters, or search consultants associations? A member of a trade or professional association related to the recruiter's specialty? You might even call the associations (get numbers from the public library) to see if the recruiter is a member in good standing and if there have been any ethical complaints filed against that person. Also ask if the recruiter carries errors and omissions insurance to cover mistakes that may cause you problems in your job or career.

- Expect that you may not immediately know which company the recruiter represents. Often companies want their names revealed only to serious contenders. Plus, recruiters don't want you to contact the company and get the job yourself, causing them to lose their fees.

- However, do expect to find out which company you're dealing with after you send a résumé and express serious interest in a job.

- Make sure your résumé is top-notch. It should be clear and concise. It should spotlight your most valuable talents and experiences and position you for the kind of job you want next. The recruiter may keep it around for future opportunities.

- Don't give references when you first send your résumé. Wait until you're sure you're interested and you know the company involved. It's a good idea to sign a release form saying that current references, such as your present boss, will not be called until you say it's OK.

- Research the company the recruiter represents. Get information from professional colleagues, industry journals, professional and trade associations, *Standard and Poors Register of Corporations*, newspaper and magazine articles in your local library, the local Chamber of Commerce and Better Business Bureau, city offices of consumer affairs, and the state attorney general's office.

- Never pay a recruiter a fee. Fees always should be paid by the company trying to fill a position.

Resources

➡ *How to Get a Headhunter to Call*, Howard S. Freedman, John Wiley & Sons, 1989.

➡ *Kennedy's Pocket Guide to Working with Executive Recruiters*, James H. Kennedy, ed., Kennedy Publications, 1996.

➡ *Directory of Executive Recruiters 1997,* Kennedy Publications, 1996.

See Also

⇨ **Selling Yourself with Your Résumé**, *page 172.*
⇨ **Finding the Right Employer**, *page 184.*

CHAPTER

14

Chapter 14

Career Reinforcement

Section IV: Career Moves

Shining at a New Job

A few weeks into my first real job I batted a softball smack into the Big Boss' head at the company picnic. It was a dramatic way to make an impression, although I wouldn't recommend it.

There are more effective ways to make a new job a memorable success and establish yourself as a valuable employee.

- Dare to be just a little different, consultant and author Debra Benton advises (see **Resources** below). Don't try to be weird or brash, but do look for small changes you could make in your attire, behavior in meetings, memoranda, or attitude that will make you stand out.

- Don't complain. Your supervisors will resent you and may be tempted to look for a replacement. If you do disagree with your organization or boss, discuss your objections politely, professionally, and constructively. Suggest alternatives. But accept the final decision and look for ways to make it work. Show that you support your organization's mission.

- If this is your first "real" job, stop thinking of yourself as a student. Show confidence, knowledge, and a take-charge attitude. Be self-motivated. Start on an assignment right away, without waiting for the boss to push you along. Think about what you're doing; explore whether there might be a better way.

- Do the job right and work faster and smarter than required.

- Expect and accept grunt work and unpopular shifts. Everyone must pay the dues. Your challenge: see them as opportunities. Tackle them with efficiency, diligence, resourcefulness, and a positive attitude.

- Don't expect to learn everything from first-line supervisors—they often are inexperienced, inept, or dead-ended. Watch rising stars and high-level managers instead.

- Be on time or early. Don't steal time from your employer by regularly coming in late, leaving early, or using lots of company time for personal business.

- Ask lots of questions. You'll learn a lot and show that you're a good listener.

- Look for signs that tell you when the real work is done in your organization (maybe after 5 p.m. or on Saturday mornings). Show up then so you can learn and make useful contacts.

- Learn about other parts of your company and the people who work there. Get away from your desk or workstation for lunch. Volunteer for assignments that take you away from your cubicle or department.

- Get the Big Boss to notice you. It's less scary than you think. When you pass the chief in the hall, say hello and introduce yourself. Next time, make a comment or ask a question. Third time, mention that you'd like to meet to talk about a particular topic, project, or issue.

- Use humor. It can help you release tension, put others at ease, and make you more appealing.

- Treat small tasks as if they were important large jobs.

- Expect to make mistakes. Own up to them and try to correct them. Don't try to blame others. Assure your boss that you've learned from them. Don't let fear of failure keep you from taking risks. You'll learn from risks, and errors are easier to recover from early in your career.

- Be politely assertive. Don't wait for others to invite you to speak at a meeting; they probably have their own agendas.

Resources
➡ *Lions Don't Need to Roar: Using the Leadership Power of Professional Presence to Stand Out, Fit In, and Move Ahead*, Debra Benton, Warner, 1994.
➡ *Making It on Your First Job When You're Young, Ambitious and Inexperienced*, Peggy Schmidt, Peterson's Guides, 1991.
➡ *Job Savvy: How to Be a Success at Work*, LaVerne L. Ludden, JIST Works, Inc., 1998.

See Also
⇨ **Growing with a Mentor**, *page 200.*
⇨ **Communicating for Success**, *page 66.*
⇨ **Projecting a Successful Image**, *page 110.*
⇨ **Recovering from Mistakes**, *page 140.*

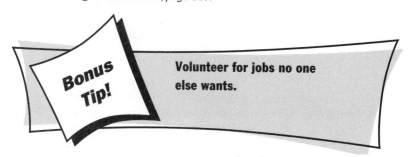

Bonus Tip!

Volunteer for jobs no one else wants.

Section IV: Career Moves

Managing Your Career

Smart business owners develop strategies to make sure their companies stay afloat in tough times. You can do the same for your career. Use shrewd career management to boost your value as an employee, keep a good job, and end up where you want to go.

The key is to practice these career management techniques now, while you're still employed.

- Look for new skills, experiences, and responsibilities. Try to pick up three major accomplishments or new skills every six months. Get on interdepartmental project teams. Trade jobs temporarily with someone in another department. Get as much training as possible. Be able to do more than one job at your company.

- Show an entrepreneurial spirit. Take risks, use current trends to create more business for your company, and design better ways to do your job. Move away from what's familiar and comfortable.

- Become known as a helpful, resourceful coworker, career consultant Marilyn Moats Kennedy says (see **Resources** below). Don't be overly concerned about what is your job and what's not. Pitch in when it will benefit the group.

- Analyze your performance by pretending to apply for your own job. What qualities would your boss seek? How could you become a better candidate? How would you convince your boss that you'd bring more value than expense?

- Avoid what career consultant and author Robert Barner calls "image lag"— an outdated notion about who you are, what you do, and what you're good at (see **Resources** below). (You say you're inept with computers, but actually you've developed useful word processing skills. Or you think you're hot because of an award you won three years ago.) Ask for formal or informal critiques on your current abilities from people outside your work group, peers, subordinates, professional associates, and clients.

- Identify the "hot buttons" of the key players in your organization (cost containment, quality improvement). Find ways to tie your work to those areas.

- Be tuned in to job market changes. Read a variety of publications to keep abreast of consumer trends, new products, and innovative companies. Attend professional association meetings. Call human resources managers at organizations that fit your target interests and ask what long-term needs and job opportunities they see in their organizations.

- Develop a career marketing plan. Include your present career situation, opportunities, and problems. Outline specific goals, action steps, and deadlines. Post them where you can see them every day.

- Keep a success journal with details of major projects and accomplishments, Barner recommends. Mention highlights to your boss occasionally.

- Listen to what adversaries say about you. You could learn a lot about how others perceive you.

- Get exposure and develop credibility by writing articles for your company newsletter, local newspaper, or trade journals.

Resources
➡ *Lifeboat Strategies: How to Keep Your Career Above Water During Tough Times or Any Time*, Robert Barner, AMACOM, 1994.
➡ *Guerrilla Tactics in the New Job Market*, Tom Jackson, Bantam, 1993.
➡ *The 110 Percent Solution: Using Good Old American Know-How to Manage Your Time*, (audiocassette) Mark McCormack, Random House, 1991.
➡ *Career Shock*, James Cotham, Berkley, 1992.
➡ *Hardball for Women: Winning at the Game of Business*, Pat Heim and Susan Golant, Lowell House, 1992.
➡ *Kennedy's Career Strategist* (newsletter), Career Strategies, 1150 Wilmette Ave., Wilmette, IL 60091, 800-728-1709, $59/10 issues. E-mail: mmkcareer @aol.com.
➡ *Career Satisfaction and Success,* Benard Haldane, Ph.D., JIST Works, Inc., 1996.

See Also
⇨ **Growing with a Mentor**, *page 200.*
⇨ **Staying Current in Your Job**, *page 208.*
⇨ **Considering a Career Change**, *page 216.*
⇨ **Setting Goals**, *page 116.*

Section IV: Career Moves

Shattering the Glass Ceiling

Despite much attention paid to the situation, relatively few women have reached advanced levels in their organizations. A study of women executives done by Catalyst showed that in 1995 women made up 46 percent of the U.S. labor force but they were 10 percent of all corporate officers, held 2.4 percent of companies' highest titles, and were 1.9 percent of companies' top earners.

A 1993 study by the National Association for Female Executives found that there are few women in senior or powerful positions even in female dominated fields and companies known for having good working conditions for women.

It's true that changing this scene requires action on the part of business leaders. But there are many effective steps women and minorities can take to reach their goals.

- Find a good role model who successfully balances the personal and professional aspects of life and who shares your values.

- Reassess your career timetable. Envision your career spread out over your entire life, moving from one stage to another. Many women move from seeking success to being disillusioned by it to seeking balance between personal and professional life.

- Measure yourself by your own ruler of success, not someone else's. You may not need to be an executive to feel successful.

- Find out how key decision makers in your company react to people who take advantage of the company's family-friendly policies. Will you be sabotaging your career if you use options like flextime? If so, you'll need to take other steps to maintain visibility and demonstrate commitment.

- Choose your jobs strategically. Focus on making or saving money for your company. Go for jobs that have authority, budget responsibility, and easily quantified results (sales, investment banking, money management, consulting, or small, entrepreneurial companies and departments). Learn which fields or departments the companies in your industry watch for new leaders.

- Ask to be included in important meetings and projects related to your work; don't wait for leaders to invite you.

- Always know what you're talking about. Prepare thoroughly for meetings and presentations. Continually learn and sharpen your skills. Become an expert; it gives you confidence and deflates others' objections to working with you.

- Use well-timed humor to break through a sober atmosphere. You'll knock down others' defenses.
- Keep a positive attitude. Don't bash your adversaries. Grousing sabotages your effectiveness and makes it hard for others to accept and work with you.
- Learn the origins of your coworkers' cultural biases. It will be easier to not take them personally.
- Listen and think before speaking. You'll earn others' respect.
- Build power 1990s-style; it comes from knowledge, vision, commitment, and shared responsibility instead of muscle or craftiness.
- If you don't get what you want, look elsewhere for greater opportunities and a better match for your skills and style. Find good companies for women through your personal network, professional associations, and annual surveys published by magazines like *Working Woman* and *Working Mother*.

Resources

→ *Breaking the Glass Ceiling: Can Women Reach the Top of America's Largest Corporations?* Ann Morrison, Randall White, Ellen Van Velsor and the Center for Creative Leadership, Addison-Wesley, 1992.
→ *Success and Betrayal,* Sarah H. Bray and Nehama Jacobs, Franklin Watts, 1986.
→ *Games Mother Never Taught You: Corporate Gamesmanship for Women,* Betty Lehan Harragan, Warner, 1992.
→ The National Association for Female Executives, P.O. Box 469031, Escondido, CA 92046. Web address: http://www.nafe.com. 800-634-6233. Membership: $29/year.

See Also

⇨ **Growing with a Mentor,** *page 200.*
⇨ **Escaping a Career Pigeonhole,** *page 214.*
⇨ **Communicating with the Opposite Sex,** *page 32.*

Advancing Without a Promotion

It's time to face up to a workplace fact of the 1990s: many of you will become stuck in your jobs. You'll hit a career plateau, a place where you seem tethered to your current job level, despite good qualifications for other positions. Job openings above you will be limited. You'll feel restless and bored.

Plateaus have become more common as companies continue to eliminate middle management jobs. Making matters worse, there are millions of qualified baby boomers out there, all trying to grab and keep the same scarce advanced positions.

- Don't assume that you're not a valued employee just because there are no promotions available for you. Objectively look at your skills and accomplishments. You may see that you still can be an effective member of your organization even in your current job.

- Take the initiative. Don't wait for your boss to tell you you're on a plateau. And don't assume that something will open up soon. If you've had the same job and responsibilities for the last several years, it's time to sit down and discuss your future with your supervisor.

- Revise your expectations. Maybe some of your career goals don't make sense anymore in the current job market. Continue to adjust your goals as the job market changes.

- Don't assume that if you only work longer and harder, you'll get to move up. You may wind up focusing on action instead of results, and it's results that will help you advance.

- Note that in today's flattened organizations status and titles may be less important than in the past. Are you measuring your worth against outdated standards? Do you have what leaders in your organization value in employees and prospective leaders?

- Don't make rash decisions to leave your job. Analyze the job market. It may not be much better elsewhere. Also, know what's going on in your own company. Opportunities may open up if there are plans for expansion, reorganization, or renewing a commitment to a particular business goal or division. If your organization seems poised to scale back, you'd be wise to start looking around early.

- Expand your position by looking for new responsibilities. Grab middle management tasks no one else wants. Design new ways to improve the company, even if you weren't asked to do so.

- Gain visibility from your new duties and projects by making sure higher-ups know you were responsible for those good results.

- Keep track of your accomplishments by listing them weekly in a notebook or calendar. It will help you identify your strengths and weaknesses so you can improve the skills you use in your current job. The list also can help you fine-tune career goals and keep your résumé current.

- Look for ways outside your job to make professional contacts, gain experience, and achieve a sense of accomplishment. Join community boards, local trade groups, professional associations, volunteer organizations, or your college alumni association.

- Avoid tying too much of your happiness in life to your job. Make sure you have enough outside interests and relationships to provide you with fun, challenges, and creative outlets.

Resources
➡ *The Plateauing Trap: How to Avoid It in Your Career…and Your Life,* Judith Bardwick, AMACOM, 1986.

See Also
⇨ **Managing Your Career**, *page 194.*
⇨ **Staying Current in Your Job**, *page 208.*
⇨ **Considering a Career Change**, *page 216.*
⇨ **Boosting Your Self-Esteem**, *page 112.*

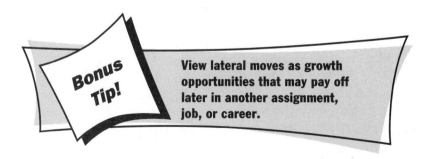

Bonus Tip!

View lateral moves as growth opportunities that may pay off later in another assignment, job, or career.

Section IV: Career Moves

Growing with a Mentor

No one said you have to engineer your career development all alone. Get guidance, support, perspective, and information from a mentor—someone with solid experience and skills in your field.

Building a relationship with the right mentor is a great way to develop in your job and prepare for future career moves. It's also a smart way to fortify your career in the face of growing competition for high-level jobs. And some experts say having a good mentor is imperative if you want to advance to higher levels in your organization or field.

- Determine what kinds of help you need: managerial, technical, general feedback, street smarts, or support and encouragement. Seek a mentor with strengths in those areas.

- Look for established mentoring programs through your employer, trade or professional association, or local Chambers of Commerce. Or seek a mentor independently by posting notices in company newsletters, checking with members of your professional network, or contacting former teachers or professors.

- Search for a mentor whose background, values, and style are similar to yours. There should be mutual respect. You should believe that you can learn from your mentor and feel safe asking this person almost anything. Your mentor should be knowledgeable and respected in your field and have good connections in your organization.

- When you find a potential mentor, volunteer to help with special projects and put in extra hours with that person. See how you work together. You don't have to ask the person point blank to be your mentor—although you could.

- Take the time necessary to establish a good working relationship. Learn about each other. Build a personal bond, not just a business relationship. Meet on a regular basis to talk and review projects. Look for challenging ways you and your mentor can collaborate on assignments.

- Set goals together and commit them to paper. Also, think about what your mentor will get out of this. Ask about your mentor's expectations.

- Reciprocate when your mentor needs help or a different perspective. The best mentor-protégé relationships are mutually beneficial.

- Be willing to face unpleasant truths about yourself that your mentor might point out.

- Listen to your mentor's advice. If you don't accept it, explain why. Don't ask for other opinions behind your mentor's back. Tell your mentor why you need more information before making a decision, and ask for suggestions about who else you could talk with.

- Be prepared to deal with jealous coworkers who feel you're getting special treatment through your mentor relationship. Don't let it stop you.

- Stay in touch with your mentor with a phone call or note every week or two.

- Don't expect your mentor to do your work or solve your problems for you. That still is your responsibility.

- Expect your relationship with your mentor to change as you grow. Eventually, you won't need your mentor's constant guidance. You may shift your relationship to a different plane (maybe one in which you are more like equals). Whatever the case, split on positive terms so your ex-mentor does not become an enemy.

Resources
➡ *Women, Mentors, and Success,* Joan Jeruchim and Pat Shapiro, Fawcett Columbine, 1992.

See Also
➪ **Managing Your Career,** *page 194.*
➪ **Building a Productive Network,** *page 206.*

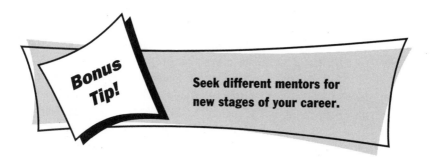

Bonus Tip!

Seek different mentors for new stages of your career.

Asking for a Raise

OK, so your company isn't throwing money around these days. But you've been in your job for a while now. Your supervisors rave about your work. You want a raise. How do you get one?

Usually, it doesn't hurt to ask. It shows that you're taking control of your career. Not asking could indicate that you lack self-confidence and a true understanding of your worth to the company.

To be successful, you'll have to be bold but realistic.

- Make sure that you've been visible (offer comments and ideas often), indispensable (do essential projects, develop key skills), and pleasant to your boss (give positive feedback, be friendly).

- Make sure your boss knows what size raise you'd consider an insult. Does your boss have the impression that you'd be grateful for anything or that money isn't important to you? Or does your boss know that you'd protest a tiny raise?

- Time it right. Don't ask when your boss just grappled with a difficult problem or received a bad quarterly report. Don't wait for your annual review. Exploit good opportunities. Strike when your organization is in good financial shape. Do it when you've handled a project successfully, assumed extra work, made your department look good, or been praised by other organizations.

- Use evidence and make rational arguments. Show letters of praise from clients, supervisors, and others who count. Cite your successful projects. Talk about how you've saved money or made money for the organization, even indirectly. Mention the skills and natural abilities you've used. Show how your job responsibilities have increased.

- Know what you're worth. What are others with similar jobs paid? Get answers from friends with access to payroll or budgets, industry or professional associations, magazine articles containing salary surveys, state or federal bureaus of labor statistics (see **Resources** below), help wanted ads, your public library, and online services like CompuServe or America Online. Or ask colleagues to anonymously write their salaries on index cards and place them in a box so one of you can compile a list and share it with everyone.

- Use specific numbers in your request.

- Aim high, within reason. It provides room to negotiate.

- Learn how your organization sets salaries. Are they based on years of experience, performance, or preset minimums and maximums? Who has the authority to adjust salaries?

- Don't argue that you need the money, haven't had a raise in a while, or should get the same raise as a coworker. Employers give raises when employees do their work with superior skill.

- Watch your company's quarterly and annual reports for percentage increase in earnings. That's the amount that net profit increased from last year to this year. If the number went up last year, ask for the same percentage increase. If you work for a highly successful division, ask for more.

- Don't threaten or act hostile; it's unnecessary and counterproductive.

- Consider whether your boss is trying to send you a message by not giving you raises. Calmly ask your boss if there is a problem with your work. Listen carefully.

- If you don't get a raise, ask why. Also ask what you could do in the next few months to get one.

Resources
➡ *Games Mother Never Taught You: Corporate Gamesmanship for Women*, Betty Lehan Harragan, Warner, 1989.
➡ *The American Almanac of Jobs and Salaries*, John Wright, Avon, 1994.
➡ *Dynamite Salary Negotiations: Know What You're Worth and Get It*, Ronald L. Krannich and Caryl Rae Krannich, Impact Publications, 1997.
➡ U.S. Department of Labor, Bureau of Labor Statistics, Inquiries and Correspondence, Washington, D.C., 202-606-7828. Web address: http://www.stats.bls.gov.
➡ *Annual salary guide for accounting, finance, banking and information systems positions*, free from local Robert Half International and Accountemps offices, or Robert Half corporate offices, 2884 Sand Hill Rd., Suite 200, Menlo Park, CA 94025, 415-926-1300 or 800-804-8367.

See also
⇨ **Considering a Pay Cut**, *page 186.*
⇨ **Negotiating for What You Want**, *page 98.*

Declining a Promotion

In a society that values moving up, what do you do when you want to stay put? How do you refuse a promotion—especially when they're so scarce these days—and not doom your career?

Surveys show that more and more workers are putting personal and family considerations ahead of career choices. And some of today's workers just don't want to move up in a bruising business climate of growing competition and constant change.

- Assess the flexibility of your organization. Is it acceptable to refuse a promotion for personal reasons? In some redesigned, flatter organizations it may be OK and even welcomed. In other companies, refusal could relegate you to dead-end jobs. If that's the case, it may be best to look for work at an organization that values the skills you've perfected at your current level.

- If you're offered a promotion you don't want, talk with your boss about unfinished business in your current job. Discuss the skills you still want to develop and how you'd strengthen them (special projects, more education).

- Convince your boss that you'd be more valuable to the organization in your current position than the next level up. (You'll be an expert and bring in credibility, you'll be happier and more productive, or you'll help the organization become more technically advanced.)

- If you're asked to leave a technical position you love for management, propose that you become a master technician instead (senior engineer, nursing specialist). Your organization could create a career ladder for people who don't want to be managers. The key would be showing your boss how highly developed technical skills would benefit the organization.

- If you'd be interested in a promotion later, tell your boss. Don't let your boss assume that you never want to move up and that don't want to be considered for future promotions. Work out a plan with your boss detailing how you could prepare for a move later.

- Be careful when supervisors try to convince you that you'll grow into a job for which you're not ready. What may happen is that gradually they'll whittle the job down to what you can handle. You won't be using your skills wisely, and your bosses won't value you as highly.

- Stop yourself if you're tempted to take a promotion solely because you want a change. Examine your experience and competence. How else could you use your skills and be challenged without moving up to a job that you don't really want? Look at different jobs, other companies, starting your own business, or trying new activities outside of work.

■ Use creative incompetence, as Laurence Peter wryly suggested in his books. Make your superiors believe that you're a good employee who shouldn't be promoted. How? Be just a little eccentric without decreasing your job performance. (Keep an impossibly messy desk, leave your desk drawers open when you leave for the day, look slightly rumpled or dress in outdated styles, or park in the company president's parking spot periodically.)

Resources
➡ *The Peter Prescription*, Laurence Peter, William Morrow, 1974.
➡ *The Peter Principle*, Laurence Peter and Raymond Hull, Buccaneer, 1996.

See Also
⇨ **Managing Your Career**, *page 194.*
⇨ **Advancing Without a Promotion**, *page 198.*
⇨ **Slowing Down Your Career**, *page 228.*
⇨ **Balancing Work and Family**, *page 150.*

Bonus Tip!

Some promotions may be better for your employer than for you.

Building a Productive Network

One of the best forms of career insurance you can have is a well-developed, current network of people.

Those people—ranging from colleagues to customers to folks you meet around town—are resources who could help you do your job better, accelerate your career, reveal new opportunities, and develop new ideas. They have information that could help you, and they know others who have valuable information, too.

- Network with a goal in mind (finding job opportunities, getting publicity). Seek people who have the information you need for that goal.

- Don't establish network relationships only to promote yourself or sell your product or services; you'll turn people off.

- Grow your network by joining professional or alumni associations and other groups that interest you. Get their membership directories. Ask people you deal with professionally and personally if they know someone who could help you. Use your personal computer to find people through online information services like CompuServe or America Online.

- Look for networking opportunities in unusual settings, such as your spouse's club picnic, a church service, the library, or an airport. Strive to have a diverse assortment of contacts.

- When you find someone who could help you, invite that person to lunch or a brief meeting for a one-on-one discussion. When you meet, clearly state what you're looking for. If you meet for lunch, pick up the bill.

- Always carry business cards in your pockets, briefcase, wallet, glove compartment, and gym bag. Order simple cards at a quick print shop or discount office supply store (under $20 for as many as 1,000).

- Use an easily accessible system to record contacts' names and the information they have. Categorize them in some way (college pals, prospective clients) in a large Rolodex, an index card system, a loose-leaf notebook, a three-ring binder with plastic pages designed to hold business cards, or a contact management computer program with cross referencing.

- Keep track of when and why you contacted a person, the results, and when you should contact that person again. Also record details of when people ask you for help.

- Don't expect big favors out of people you've just met or with whom you have lost touch.

- Give as much as you take. Build a reputation as a valuable network member who is helpful, resourceful, respectful, sincere, and considerate. Pass on information that may help other networkers, even if they haven't asked for it.

- If you can't fulfill a network member's request right now, offer your future help. But don't make promises you can't keep.

- Exercise your network daily with brief visits, phone calls, or notes. Use a phone call or postcard to follow up with new acquaintances promptly.

- Be specific when you ask for help. Know exactly what you want, from whom, by when, and in what form. Get to the point quickly about what you want, but not so quickly that you sound curt or rude.

- Give polite, prompt, and sincere thanks for any help you receive. A personal, handwritten note works well.

- Clean out your network periodically. Eliminate people and organizations who don't serve your goals, don't help when asked, or don't have the kinds of information you need.

- Expand your network by providing services: speak to local organizations, write articles for trade publications, or be an officer in a professional or service organization.

Resources
→ *Is Your 'Net' Working? A Complete Guide to Building Contacts and Career Visibility*, Anne Boe, John Wiley & Sons, 1989.
→ *The Secrets of Savvy Networking: How to Make the Best Connections for Business and Personal Success*, Susan RoAne, Warner, 1993.
→ *Dig Your Well Before You're Thirsty,* Harvey Mackey, Doubleday, 1997.
→ *Networking for Everyone,* L. Michelle Tullier, Ph.D., JIST Works, Inc., 1998.

See Also
⇨ **Using Information Interviews,** *page 170.*
⇨ **Managing Your Career,** *page 194.*
⇨ **Growing with a Mentor,** *page 200.*
⇨ **Shattering the Glass Ceiling,** *page 196.*

Staying Current in Your Job

As companies continue to lay off and reassign employees, some workers—especially middle-aged and older ones—may feel a little paranoid. They may fear that bosses and coworkers see them as out of touch or too expensive to keep around.

Those fears can become the foundation for self-fulfilling prophecies; but they don't have to. Employees of any age can take steps to stay in touch with the latest trends that affect their work.

- Don't socialize and discuss work with only your peers. Seek perspectives and opinions from people in different age groups who have different values and experiences.

- Don't be the last to know. Develop networks so you learn about your organization's values, plans, and trends as they emerge instead of after they're in place. Keep up with changes in your field through professional organizations. Keep up with changes in your community through civic, social, or church organizations.

- Continually set and work on professional goals, even if you already have sizable accomplishments. Adjust the goals regularly to stay in line with changes in your organization and industry.

- Get feedback on your work from a variety of sources, not just current supervisors. Ask other supervisors, peers, new employees, or professional associates and subordinates.

- Don't let yourself become a stereotype. Keep your dress, habits, lifestyles, interests, and hobbies current.

- Use your experience, contacts, and perspectives to help your organization. Look for ways to share your expertise with others. But also practice listening as much as or more than you talk. This helps you tune in to changes at work and shows that you're willing to soak up new information.

- Show interest in expanding your skills at all stages of your career. Ask your supervisors to include you in training programs even if you're considered an old pro. Look for training and development opportunities that give you hands-on, skill-building practice and immediate feedback.

- Demonstrate your interest in change. Volunteer to take on new responsibilities, work on a cutting-edge project, or lead a strategic planning session.

- Unchain yourself from the traditional American life sequence of education first, work second, and leisurely retirement last. Why jam all your training and work into the early part of your life? Consider going back to school and starting another career or related job in your middle or later years. Don't assume that your current job will be your last, even if you are older.

Resources
➡ *Unretirement: A Career Guide for the Retired, the Soon-to-be Retired, the Never-Want-to-be Retired*, Catherine D. Fyock, AMACOM, 1994. Available through Innovative Management Concepts, P.O. Box 905, Prospect, KY 40059, 800-277-0384.

➡ *America's Workforce Is Coming of Age: What Every Business Needs to Know to Recruit, Train, Manage and Retain an Aging Workforce*, Catherine D. Fyock, Lexington Books, 1990. Catherine D. Fyock, AMACOM, 1994. Available through Innovative Management Concepts, P.O. Box 905, Prospect, KY 40059, 800-277-0384.

➡ *How to Stay Employable: A Guide for the Midlife and Older Worker*, American Association of Retired Persons, 1994, Stock no. D14945, available free from AARP, 601 E Street, NW, Washington, D.C. 20049, 800-424-3410. Web address: http://www.aarp.org.

➡ SeniorNet, a nonprofit organization that teaches computer skills to older adults, using 110 learning centers in 32 states. Membership: $35/year. To find the center nearest you contact SeniorNet at One Kearny St., Third Floor, San Francisco, CA 94108, 415-352-1210. Web address: http://www.seniornet.org.

See Also
➪ **Managing Your Career**, *page 194.*
➪ **Escaping a Career Pigeonhole**, *page 214.*
➪ **Going Back to School**, *page 220.*
➪ **Setting Goals**, *page 116.*

Bonus Tip!

Schedule time each week to learn or experience something new.

Section IV: Career Moves

Choosing the Right Seminar

Today's competitive business and employment climate requires employees to regularly update their job and communication skills. You need to do this to keep your career moving in the right direction. Employers want you to do it so you can improve productivity and profit.

There are thousands of training companies and colleges out there, offering courses on everything from projecting a professional image to reading financial reports. Choosing the right one can be confusing. You'll want to be sure the seminar will address the areas you're interested in and give you high-quality information.

- First, know what you want to learn. Clues are everywhere. How is your job or industry changing? Has your supervisor asked for improvements? Do you feel unqualified for your job? Do you want another job? Have subordinates or colleagues been dropping hints about your weaknesses?

- Find seminars or courses through your employer's training department, colleagues, professional associations, local colleges and universities, local school district adult education programs, or training and consultant directories in public libraries. Or ask your employer if the company uses a seminar search and management service that would be accessible to you (see **Resources** below).

- Pay attention to the price differences in seminars. One-day training sessions offered by national companies can vary from $59 to $149 or more. Two-day sessions can cost $200 or more. Generally, the lower the price, the more participants will be accepted and the more the instructors will lecture. A higher-priced seminar may offer more one-on-one attention and some frills (a better meeting room, snacks or meals, more take-home materials). Ask the course registrar for details.

- Talk to the training company about the workshop ahead of time. If it's a big company, ask for the seminar development department. Clearly outline your skills and desired improvements. Then ask if this course will help. An ethical company will tell you if its seminar isn't right for you.

- Have realistic expectations. One-day workshops provide a broad overview and lots of practical tips and techniques. They're good refreshers. They don't offer theories, in-depth discussions, or heavy interaction with the instructor. If you want those features, look for courses that last a few days or longer.

■ Check out local training companies through the local chapter of the American Society of Training and Development (see **Resources** below). Also ask for references and check the Better Business Bureau. Some companies may permit you to observe part of a seminar for free, especially if you might sign up other coworkers or colleagues.

■ During the seminar listen carefully, take notes, join discussions, and ask questions. Filter everything through this question: How could I use this at work? Jot down your ideas. If you're not willing to work, don't waste your time and money on the session.

■ Don't put your course materials on a shelf when the session is over. Review them periodically. Look for new ways to apply the information so you won't forget it.

Resources

➡ The American Society of Training and Development (ASTD) can help you find local chapters, 1640 King St., PO Box 1443, Alexandria, VA 22313, 800-628-2783. Web address: http://www.astd.org.

➡ Trainet, ASTD's online search service, helps locate trainers, seminars, conferences, materials, and prepackaged courses on specific topics, for a fee. Call ASTD (see above).

➡ *The Linton Trainers Resource Directory*, Linton Publishing, 1996.

➡ *Consultants and Consulting Organizations Directory,* Gale Research, 1996.

➡ Seminar search and management services are hired by employers to locate professional and technical training programs for employees and assist with registration. Two are Seminar Clearinghouse, International, Inc., PO Box 1757, St. Paul, MN 55101-0757, 800-927-0502. Web address: http://www.seminarnet.com.; and First Seminar, 175 Cabbot St., Lowell, MA 01854-3635, 800-321-1990. Web address: http://www.firstseminar.com.

See Also

⇨ **Managing Your Career**, *page 194.*
⇨ **Advancing Without a Promotion**, *page 198.*
⇨ **Staying Current in Your Job**, *page 208.*
⇨ **Going Back to School**, *page 220.*

CHAPTER

15

Chapter 15

Career Shifts

Escaping a Career Pigeonhole

Sometimes you can be so skilled at what you do and so perfect for your job that no one can imagine you doing anything else.

That's not a problem if you like your job. But what if you really want something else—a different job, a position in a different department or a completely different career? It takes thought and planning to convince your supervisor and others that you can perform other jobs well, too.

- Make sure you're willing to invest lots of your own time and energy to make this change. Don't expect your employer to provide all the training and necessary experience.

- Map out a plan for reaching the new career goal. What education and training will you get? Who will guide and support you? What projects will you work on? What is your deadline?

- Talk to your supervisors about your goals. Ask what they think you need to get that other job. An annual performance review is a good time to do this. Talk to other influential people, too—other managers, human resources officials, and leaders in the department you're interested in.

- When talking with supervisors, frame your desire to move in terms of "Here is what I can do for this organization…" Don't stress that your main goal is to get out of your current job.

- Demonstrate that you want to get experience and knowledge that would be useful in another job. Volunteer to work on different kinds of projects, work teams, or committees. Subscribe to professional journals or read them in public or university libraries.

- Get educated. Take advantage of your company's training programs. Find out if your organization offers financial or other support for college courses or professional seminars. Educational background is no guarantee, but you probably won't get the job without it.

- Look for learning opportunities outside of work. Get management experience by overseeing projects for a volunteer agency or your church. Or learn a new technical skill by helping with a community project.

- Help find and train a successor. Your supervisors won't want you to switch positions if you truly are the only one who can do your job.

- Take advantage of your company's job postings. Consistently bid for jobs in the department in which you're interested. If you build your skills simultaneously, you probably will get at least an interview.

- Join professional organizations in your area of interest. Find them in the *Encyclopedia of Associations*, published by Gale Research Co., in your library's reference section. Attend local chapter meetings to meet people who can provide guidance and opportunities. Check newspaper business and entertainment sections and local business magazines for meeting listings.

- Be willing to make a downward move. You might have to start at the bottom in your new department.

- Be persistent and patient. It may take months or years to reach your goal.

Resources
➡ *1,000 Things You Never Learned in Business School: How to Manage Your Fast-Track Career,* William Yeomans, NAL-Dutton, 1990.
➡ *Career Satisfaction and Success,* Benard Haldane, Ph.D., JIST Works, Inc., 1996.

See Also
⇨ **Advancing Without a Promotion,** *page 198.*
⇨ **Choosing the Right Seminar,** *page 210.*
⇨ **Considering a Career Change,** *page 216.*
⇨ **Setting Goals,** *page 116.*

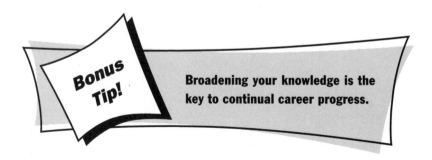

Bonus Tip!

Broadening your knowledge is the key to continual career progress.

Considering a Career Change

The idea of finding a new career sounds appealing when you're unhappy with your job, facing a significant lifestyle change, or worried about your company's new direction. However, it can produce a storm of conflicting emotions; your choices may seem endless and severely limited at the same time.

The key to uncovering the right career is to mix what you enjoy and do well in new ways that pertain to other jobs.

- Find support. Look for objective people or a career counselor who will encourage you to try new avenues to find what you want. Don't listen to negative thinkers or people who tell you to be thankful for what you have.

- List and rank your values, wants, needs, interests, and goals. Think about what you enjoy most and want out of life. Review everything from intellectual needs to your ideal workplace to your favorite leisure activities. Use your imagination to learn more about what you really enjoy and want to do. What would you do with a year's sabbatical? What would you say about yourself on a large billboard?

- List broad career categories that combine your top-ranking values, wants, needs, interests, and goals.

- Look at using old skills in new ways. List the skills you now have and enjoy. Think of them as building blocks that you can rearrange. Your goal will be finding work where you can use those skills. (You could break down plumbing into analyzing a problem, selecting the right tools and materials to fix it, and having manual dexterity.)

- Identify your skills by writing descriptions of the jobs you've held. Look for patterns and similarities in the verbs you've used.

- After you've selected a few career possibilities, list all the pros, cons, and possible consequences of each choice. What do you possess that would help you in that field, and what would hurt your progress?

- Consider crazy ideas and old dreams. Don't automatically settle for what is convenient or easy.

- But don't forget reality. Do you have the necessary skills? Could you meet your financial obligations with that career? Will you be happy with the working conditions? Can you get the resources necessary to make this change?

- Make career choices for your own reasons, not someone else's.

- Consider options other than changing careers, such as reshaping your current job or doing more of what you love outside of work.

- Learn all you can about your career choices. Read. Interview people in those fields. Attend trade shows or professional association meetings for that industry. Conduct research in your public library.

- Don't rely on help-wanted ads to find new careers. Instead, look for potential employers or clients with needs you can meet or problems you can solve. Often these needs aren't even articulated in the form of a job listing. (A company might need photographs but may not have planned to hire a staff photographer. You could demonstrate how you would solve that problem for the company.) There are unlimited problems in the world, so there are unlimited job opportunities.

Resources
→ *What Color Is Your Parachute? 1997: A Practical Guide for Job Hunters and Career Changers*, Richard Bolles, Ten Speed Press, 1997.
→ *Where Do I Go From Here With My Life*, John Crystal and Richard Bolles, Ten Speed Press, 1982.
→ *Guerrilla Tactics in the New Job Market*, Tom Jackson, Bantam, 1993.
→ *Wishcraft: How to Get What You Really Want*, Barbara Sher and Anne Gottlieb, Ballantine, 1986.
→ *Pathfinders*, Gail Sheehy, Bantam, 1997.
→ *The Inventurers: Excursions in Life and Career Renewal*, Janet Hagberg and Richard Leider, Addison-Wesley, 1988.
→ *Dare to Change Your Job and Your Life,* Carole Kanchier, Ph.D., JIST Works, Inc., 1995.

See Also
⇨ **Using Information Interviews**, *page 170.*
⇨ **Escaping a Career Pigeonhole**, *page 214.*
⇨ **Finding a Good Career Counselor**, *page 218.*
⇨ **Going Back to School**, *page 220.*

Section IV: Career Moves

Finding a Good Career Counselor

If you're seeking a new career after investing several years in your old one, you probably need objective advice and support that goes beyond how to write a résumé. Self-study may be helpful, but it may not be enough. You may need a good career counselor to help you through your search.

■ Locate a good counselor by asking friends, associates, and members of your network for referrals. Check with local colleges, a community career center, or your local phone book.

■ Check credentials of prospective counselors, such as accreditation by the National Board for Certified Counselors, membership in the American Counseling Association, a master's degree in social work or counseling, or education, psychology, or human behavior. Contact the National Board for Certified Counselors (see **Resources** below) for a list of certified counselors in your area and guidelines on selecting a counselor.

■ Ask prospective counselors how they approach situations such as yours. What services are they likely to provide?

■ Check references.

■ For major career changes, steer clear of people who mostly rely on personality or aptitude tests or who focus mostly on résumés, cover letters, and interviewing techniques. You probably need to examine deeper issues.

■ Choose a counselor who shows interest and enthusiasm. A good one will want to know what you love, what you care about, and what you dream about. Look for a good problem solver, goal-setter, and mentor. Look for someone with whom you could develop a lasting professional or friendly relationship.

■ Choose a counselor with broad resources: local and national contacts in many fields, access to job information and market analyses, and knowledge about educational opportunities.

■ Check your local newspaper's business calendar or local business magazines for job search resource and support groups. Also check with your local YMCA, YWCA, United Way, major churches in the area, and career-planning and placement services at local colleges and universities.

■ If your career problems involve substance abuse, family difficulties, or emotional problems, seek a specialist or a career counselor with a background in those areas.

- Expect to pay an average of $70-$80/hour, or a few hundred dollars for several sessions and tests.

- Don't automatically seek a career counselor if you enjoy your work but dislike your company or supervisor. You may just need to change jobs.

- Switch to another counselor if, after several sessions, you don't feel energized and able to make necessary changes. You don't want to just talk about your career development; you need to gain knowledge and confidence, which translates into action.

Resources
➡ The National Board for Certified Counselors, 3 Terrace Way, Suite D, Greensboro, NC 27403, 910-547-0607. Web address: http://www.nbcc.org.
➡ The American Counseling Association, 5999 Stevenson Ave., Alexandria, VA 22304-3300, 703-823-9800. Web address: http://www.counseling.org.
➡ *Career Counselling*, Robert Nathan and Linda Hill, Sage Publications, 1992.

See Also
⇨ **Considering a Career Change**, *page 216.*
⇨ **Quitting**, *page 234.*
⇨ **Understanding Your Bothersome Boss**, *page 28.*
⇨ **I Hate My Job!** *page 136.*

Bonus Tip!

Choose a counselor who believes in you.

Going Back to School

Changing careers and boosting your income are two reasons to continue your education. Others include strengthening yourself in your current job and making yourself more marketable.

There are many decisions you'll need to make before continuing your education. Do you need a degree or just a few courses? Should you try a traditional four-year university, a private college that caters to working people with busy schedules, or a computer-enhanced, online program?

- Don't wait until you think you'll have more time. You may never have it. If the idea of returning to school seems overwhelming, take it one step at a time: first focus on applying, then getting transcripts, then registering, and then taking the first course.

- Don't decide alone. Talk to professionals in your chosen industry, career counselors, academic advisors, and college career center counselors to find out what education you need.

- Choose a program you can stick with. It should fit your lifestyle and career plans and be conveniently located. Also consider the types and times of courses, amount of out-of-class work, instructors' backgrounds, whether you can get academic credit for life and work experience, and success rates for placing graduates in their fields.

- Find out whether the institution is accredited. Most public four-year institutions and many private ones are accredited regionally by organizations such as the North Central Association of Colleges and Schools. They generally accept credits and degrees from other regionally accredited institutions, which is important if you want to transfer credits or continue your education at another institution later. Some business and technical colleges may be accredited through other associations, but their credits may be not widely transferable.

- Check with your employer to see if the company will cover all or part of the cost of your continued education. Show how your education could benefit the company.

- Don't assume you can't get financial aid because you are employed. Check with the financial aid officers of the institutions you're considering. Many can qualify for a low-interest government subsidized loan (see **Resources** below).

- Rally family members' support. Discuss how your course work will change household schedules and workloads.

- Talk to your supervisor about new scheduling or vacation requirements you may have. Give as much notice as possible when you need flexible scheduling or extra time off to meet college schedules.

- Take a hard look at how you spend your time; you'll need several hours a week for part-time course work. Read while waiting for appointments or traveling; temporarily eliminate TV and magazines; periodically leave work 30 minutes early to study at a library for an hour; devote some lunch hours to studying; get up an hour earlier twice a week to study or read.

Resources

➡ *The Adult Student's Guide to Survival and Success,* Al Siebert and Bernadine Gilpin, Practical Psychology Press, 1997.

➡ *The College Board Guide to Going to College While Working,* Gene Hawes, College Entrance Examination Board, 1985.

➡ Financial Aid Resources for Women, free fact sheet from Women Work! The National Network for Women's Employment, 1625 K Street NW, Suite 300, Washington, D.C. 20006, 202-467-6346, E-mail: womenwork@ worldnet.att.net.

➡ *College After 30: It's Never Too Late to Get the Degree You Need,* Kim Baker and Sunny Baker, Bob Adams, Inc., 1992.

➡ *Back to School: A College Guide for Adults,* LaVerne L. Ludden, Park Avenue Productions, 1996.

➡ *Luddens' Adult Guide to Colleges and Universities,* LaVerne L. Ludden and Marsha Ludden, Park Avenue Productions, 1997.

See Also

➪ **Choosing the Right Seminar**, *page 210.*
➪ **Experience Through Internships**, *page 222.*
➪ **Shifting to Part-Time Work**, *page 224.*
➪ **Finding More Time in Your Day**, *page 8.*

Experience Through Internships

Internships aren't just for students anymore.

Adults who want to change careers, re-enter the workforce, or explore different aspects of their field can use internships to get valuable hands-on experience and make professional contacts. Often they can lead to permanent employment.

Internships are monitored work and learning experiences. They can be full- or part-time, paid or unpaid, or short (one month) or long (one year). They may be in private industry, public institutions, or volunteer organizations in your city or another state.

- Use internship directories to find opportunities in many fields, companies. and locations (see **Resources** below). Most guides list a contact person, details of the internship, and application details. Find directories in public or university libraries, university placement offices, career development centers, or bookstores. Also check in your library's catalog files for books about internships in specific industries.

- Look for internship notices in trade journals, on campus bulletin boards, and through alumni associations, public officials, government agencies, public interest groups, and volunteer coordination centers.

- Don't overlook internships or job-swapping options within your current organization. You may be able to convince your employer to create an internship just for you, with the help of your supervisor, mentor, or human resources liaison.

- Call your top choices to get more details. Apply as you would for a permanent job. Research the organizations, send inquiries directly to those who would be responsible for hiring an intern, send résumés, and set up interviews. Then, follow up. Be persistent.

- Don't despair if the organization you choose doesn't have an established internship program. Locate a person within the organization who has influence and authority to hire an intern. How? Talk with people in your network, the organization's human resources office, or the department in which you're interested. Discuss how interns cost less than regular employees, have knowledge and skills that allow them to accomplish real work, offer fresh perspectives, and create a pool of potential future employees.

- Before you start your internship discuss your short-term goals with your supervisor. Try to balance your learning goals with the needs of your employer.

- Treat an internship seriously. Maintain good work habits, as you would for a permanent job. Be a responsible employee with a positive attitude.

- Expect that you might be assigned some "go-fer" or menial work. Be a flexible team player. But if you feel you should do more advanced work, talk to your supervisor about how you're ready for more challenges.

- Know your rights as an intern. You may be covered under the federal Fair Labor Standards Act. Don't stay where you're being exploited or treated unfairly. Get information from your local office of the Wage and Hour Division, U.S. Department of Labor (see government listings in your phone book) or state labor departments.

- Squeeze all you can out of your internship. Volunteer for different tasks to broaden your experience. Visit other departments. Observe the experts and ask them questions. Attend a variety of meetings and presentations.

- Keep a journal of your experiences and the feedback you receive.

- Get a letter of reference from your internship supervisors before you leave.

Resources
➡ *The National Directory of Internships*, Amy Butterworth and Sally Migliore, eds., National Society for Internships and Experiential Education, 1991.
➡ *Internships 1994: On-the-Job Opportunities for Students and Adults*, Michele Fetterolf, ed., Peterson's Guides, 1993.
➡ *America's Top 100 Internships 1995*, Mark Oldman and Samer Hamadeh, Villard, 1994.
➡ *The Experienced Hand*, Timothy Stanton and Kamil Ali, Carroll Press, 1987.

See Also
⇨ **Using Information Interviews**, *page 170*.
⇨ **Successful Job Interviews**, *page 180*.
⇨ **Shining at a New Job**, *page 192*.
⇨ **Building a Productive Network**, *page 206*.

Section IV: Career Moves

Shifting to Part-Time Work

People with demanding personal lives often feel they must choose between two extremes. One is to give up their careers entirely and tend to family or other needs. The other is to overload themselves with full-time careers and equally demanding personal lives.

There is a middle ground for some people. It is temporarily turning your full-time career into a part-time one. Working part-time (35 hours a week or less) allows you to shift your priorities for a while, but not give up the ground you've covered so far professionally.

Besides having a young family, other reasons for working part-time include going to college, having more time for leisure or volunteer work, or starting a business.

- Plan ahead for a smooth part-time switch. Establish yourself as a valuable, experienced, loyal, and accomplished team member. Earn the support of peers and subordinates now, while you are a full-timer. Make colleagues and bosses aware of your devotion to your career. Establish a good rapport with the person who will decide if you can work part-time.

- Talk to other part-time workers in your company or industry to learn from their experience.

- Build a proposal to present to your boss. Cover every detail. What duties would you handle and how? How would you cover emergencies? What's the minimum and maximum number of hours you'll work each week? How much do you want to be paid? Would you continue to be a manager? Will you work at home? Will you still receive vacation and sick-time pay? What about other benefits? Does your organization have policies about part-time workers? Would you return to full-time status sometime later?

- Call your state labor department to see if you are covered by laws that prohibit discrimination against part-time employees.

- Look at the impact working part-time will have on your salary and benefits. Which benefits are most important to you? Do you want to be paid hourly, receive a portion of your full-time salary (half your full-time salary for 20 hours/week), or be paid based on results? Ask for a higher salary if you give up certain benefits, or vice versa.

- Examine several scheduling options such as working a half-day every day, two-and-a-half full days/week, two full days one week and three full days the next, two days/week in the office and one day/week at home, or one full week on and one full week off.

- Emphasize to your boss how part-time work would be good for your company. An organization that supports part-time schedules retains high-performing, experienced workers. It spends less time and money searching for replacements. Its employees take shorter parental leaves. Plus, part-timers tend to be loyal and grateful. And they usually become experts at delegating, planning, setting priorities, and time management.

- If your supervisor argues that it will be tough for people to reach you if you work part-time, note that most full-timers only are available part-time because of meetings, training, and trips. Talk about your plan for staying in touch through phone calls, voice mail, fax, electronic mail, regularly scheduled activity reports, and attendance at staff meetings.

- Before you start, sign an agreement with your supervisor detailing hours, responsibilities, pay, benefits, and other expectations. Plan to re-evaluate in three months.

- Be prepared for negative reactions from some coworkers. Remind them that you don't receive the same salary and benefits as they do.

Resources
➡ *The Part-Time Solution*, Charlene Canape, Harper & Row, 1990.
➡ Association of Part-Time Professionals, Inc., 7700 Leesburg Pike, Suite 216, Falls Church, VA 22043, 703-734-7975. Membership: $20–$45. Web address: http://www.mbinet.mindbank.com/aptp.
➡ 9 to 5, National Association of Working Women, 231 W. Wisconsin Ave., Suite 900, Milwaukee, WI 53203, 414-274-0925. Job Survival Hotline (open to all): 800-522-0925, 10 a.m.-3:50 p.m. EST, Monday-Friday. Membership: $25/year.
➡ *Breaking Out of 9 to 5,* Maria Laqueur, Peterson's Guides, 1994.

See Also
⇨ **Job Sharing**, *page 226.*
⇨ **Slowing Down Your Career**, *page 228.*
⇨ **Balancing Work and Family**, *page 150.*

Job Sharing

Job sharing offers many benefits for employers and employees. It's a flexible work arrangement for qualified employees who can't or don't want to be confined to a traditional 40-hour work week. Usually their jobs can't be done effectively part-time.

In job sharing, two people work together in a job usually done by one person. It's been used effectively by banking employees, attorneys, editors, and teachers. It's ideal for parents of young children, people who care for elderly relatives, and workers who want to gradually phase into retirement.

- Use job sharing for work that can be divided easily or that involves two different sets of skills.

- If you're job hunting and want to try job sharing with a new employer, look for one with a history of flexible work arrangements, concern for employees, and openness to new ideas.

- Learn about job sharing and be able to educate employers about it. Depending on the arrangement, it can be costly to an employer in administrative expenses, benefits, extra equipment, and training. But it can save money by cutting turnover and absenteeism and by improving continuity, scheduling, and productivity.

- When searching for a job-sharing partner look for compatibility (professionally and personally), cooperation, and excellent communication skills.

- Make a list of specific skills each partner can bring to the job. Think about interpersonal skills, creativity, managerial savvy, writing, negotiating, manual or technical skills, financial know-how, and research talents. Divide the work according to aptitudes, interests, and fairness.

- Go after a job as a team. Submit a joint résumé to emphasize your team's strengths; or submit a joint cover letter with separate résumés. Ask that you be interviewed together.

- Set up a schedule where partners work alternate days or weeks; or one could work mornings and the other afternoons. For good communication, partners should overlap schedules every day or once or twice a week.

- Split most jobs and salaries in half for job sharing. But 75-25 splits and other arrangements also have been successful, depending on the job and the needs and skills of the partners.

- Encourage employers to try job sharing on a pilot basis first. Set a time limit of a few months and review the arrangement before making more long-term commitments.

- Set clear ground rules for partners and employers. Describe the job carefully and outline each person's responsibilities.

- Communicate with your partner through regular meetings, memoranda, a daily log book, tape recordings, phone, voice mail, e-mail, or on a write-on/wipe-off whiteboard.

- Be open about your arrangement when talking with coworkers so you can soften negative reactions. Deal with jealousy by noting that you have a flexible arrangement but only receive part-time pay. Ask your supervisor to demonstrate support for your job-sharing team. Talk with coworkers about how the arrangement benefits the company.

Resources
➡ *The Job Sharing Handbook*, Barney Olmsted and Suzanne Smith, Ten Speed Press, 1985.
➡ New Ways to Work, 785 Market St., Suite 950, San Francisco, CA 94103, 415-995-9860, Web address: http//www.nww.org. Membership: $75 for companies and organizations, $35 for individuals.

See Also
⇨ **Finding the Right Employer**, *page 184.*
⇨ **Shifting to Part-Time Work**, *page 224.*
⇨ **Slowing Down Your Career**, *page 228.*
⇨ **Arranging Your Parental Leave**, *page 244.*

Bonus Tip!

Keep coworkers informed about your team's schedules and responsibilities.

Section IV: Career Moves

Slowing Down Your Career

Several recent studies have shown that many working Americans would take a slower career path if they could spend more time with their families. If you are one of those working people, there are several career slowdown plans you could try.

You might drop out of your job for a few years, refuse promotions or demanding assignments, stick to an eight-hour work day, work a flexible schedule, cut travel or work part-time. Do consider the many issues involved first.

- Plan for a possible career slowdown before you really need it. Show your employer now that you are a valuable employee; you'll be more likely to get support for your career shifts later.

- Think long-range. What happens to your financial goals (retirement, college for the kids) if you slow down? What if your spouse's earning power drops while you're on the slow track? Will your future earnings potential rebound if you return to the fast track?

- If you're a man, consider how you may counteract the stigma our society attaches to men who slow their careers for family reasons. Depending on the values in your organization, your supervisors and colleagues may view you as uncommitted to your career.

- Try to find more family time by cutting other activities (recreation, community work) before you jump into a big career change.

- Evaluate what work means to you. If it is central to your self-image will diminishing that role harm your self-concept or cause resentment? Can you adjust your self-image and redefine the role of work in your life?

- Analyze how much time per week you truly must devote to your career to keep it accelerating. Maybe only a few extra hours a week would be enough, and could keep you from taking drastic steps.

- Accept trade-offs. You may have to settle for less personal time if you want a challenging, well-paid job; or you may have to take less challenging work and a smaller salary to get a looser schedule.

- Don't try to be the perfect employee and parent simultaneously. Accept different priorities and successes at different times.

- Maintain a reasonable work pace—at least temporarily—by starting at low status when you take on new career challenges; or work like an apprentice, developing expertise slowly.

- Ease your work pace in your current job by cooperating more and competing less. Share information, trust others, and share credit.

- Look for new role models. Can you learn from colleagues you previously thought were unambitious?

- Consider a variety of flexible work options: part-time work, job sharing, phased retirement, telecommuting, flexible and split scheduling (working at variable or unusual times), and compressed work weeks (working 40 hours in fewer than five days).

- When job hunting, seek employers who support a healthy balance between work and family. Look for understanding bosses, a history of accepting flexible work arrangements, leave policies that recognize the needs of sick children or elderly relatives, and on-site or nearby child care.

Resources

➡ *Downshifting: Reinventing Success on a Slower Track*, Amy Saltzman, Harper Collins, 1992.

➡ *Success Trap*, Stan Katz and Aimee Liu, Dell, 1991.

➡ *The Father's Almanac*, Revised, S. Adams Sullivan, Doubleday 1992.

➡ *Finding Time for Fathering*, Mitch Golant and Susan Golant, Fawcett, 1992.

➡ *When Mothers and Fathers Work: Creative Strategies for Balancing Career and Family*, Renee Y. Magid, AMACOM, 1987.

➡ *Out of the Rat Race* (newsletter), Gregory Communications Group, PO Box 95341, Seattle, WA 98145-2341, $12/year, $2/sample issue.

➡ *Time Off from Work: Using Sabbaticals to Enhance Your Life While Keeping Your Career on Track,* Lisa Angowski Rogak Shaw, John Wiley & Sons, 1995.

See Also

⇨ **Declining a Promotion**, *page 204.*

⇨ **Shifting to Part-Time Work**, *page 224.*

⇨ **Avoiding Excessive Overtime Work**, *page 60.*

⇨ **Balancing Work and Family**, *page 150.*

Section IV: Career Moves

Returning to Work

Many people put their careers on hold while they raise children, take a sabbatical, return to school, enjoy extended travel, care for a seriously ill relative, or pursue a demanding personal goal.

But returning to work can be scary. How will you fall back into the groove? Will people think you're out of touch?

The best way to jump back into your career after a break like that is to never leave your career completely.

- Evaluate your professional goals frequently while away from your job. Adjust them every year or so to keep them current and relevant.

- Keep your skills and networks current through reading, professional organizations, and workshops and courses. Stay in touch with your former employer and coworkers. Join supportive groups related to your profession or interests (see **Resources** below).

- Every year you're away from your job ask yourself: What am I doing this year to ease my way back into the workforce?

- Use your time off to investigate new career paths and ideal jobs and schedules. Know what salary you'll want when you return. Remember to figure in child care or elder care costs, taxes, work clothes, and lunches.

- Expect that you may have to re-enter the work world at a lower salary and status level than before. But plan to negotiate for other desirable job features such as flexible hours, less travel, or different benefits.

- Work part-time or do occasional freelance or consulting work during your leave. Attend professional association meetings. Write articles for association newsletters or trade publications.

- Choose volunteer work that will help you. Check into organizations related to business or your industry (Chamber of Commerce, trade groups, United Way fundraising).

- Frame your unpaid experiences as homemaker, parent, volunteer, or student in terms of business or employment skills (managing, communicating, problem solving, making or saving money).

- Be up-front with employers about the gap in your résumé. Say that you made a deliberate decision to stay home and spend time with your young family (or whatever). Show how you've had a career plan in mind the whole time. Follow with a description of what you did during that time, how you kept current in your field, and how you developed other skills.

- Be prepared for changes that have occurred in the workplace during your absence (streamlined organizations, fewer middle management jobs, heavy emphasis on quality and customer service, workforce diversity). Re-evaluate your strengths and adjust your career plans accordingly.

- Update your job-seeking skills. Today's job market requires highly focused, assertive techniques that rely heavily on personal networks. Read the latest job-seeking advice books for ideas.

Resources

➡ *Maternity Leave: The Working Woman's Practical Guide to Combining Pregnancy, Motherhood and Career*, Eileen Casey, Green Mountain Publishing, 1992.

➡ *The Résumé Guide for Women of the '90s*, Kim Marino, Ten Speed Press, 1992.

➡ The Federation of Organizations for Professional Women (referral service affiliated with 20 women's groups), 1825 I St. NW, Suite 400, Washington, D.C. 20006, 202-328-1415. E-mail: fopw@dgs.dgsys.com.

➡ American Business Women's Association, 9100 Ward Parkway, PO Box 8728, Kansas City, MO 64114, 816-361-6621. Web address: http://www.abwahq.org.

➡ The American Association of University Women, 1111 16th St. NW, Washington, D.C. 20036, 800-326-2289. Web address: http://www.aauw.org.

➡ Women Work! The National Network for Women's Employment, 1625 K Street NW, Suite 300, Washington, D.C. 20006, 202-467-6346. Web address: http://womenwork@worldnet.att.net.

See Also

⇨ **Selling Yourself with Your Résumé,** *page 172.*
⇨ **Building a Productive Network,** *page 206.*
⇨ **Staying Current in Your Job,** *page 208.*
⇨ **Setting Goals,** *page 116.*

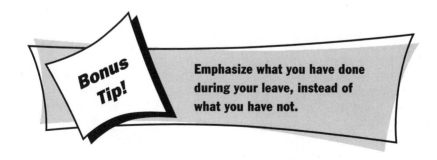

Bonus Tip!

Emphasize what you have done during your leave, instead of what you have not.

Section IV: Career Moves

CHAPTER

16

Chapter 16

Leaving Your Job

16-1 Quitting

16-2 Preparing for a Possible Layoff

16-3 Coping with Job Loss

16-4 Reacting to an Unfair Dismissal

16-5 Planning Now for Early Retirement

16-6 Arranging Your Parental Leave

Quitting

Anyone who's been miserable at a job can tell you it's a lousy way to spend 40 or more hours a week. If you're in that situation, you may be right to plan to quit. But don't act rashly; there are right and wrong ways to leave a job.

Ask yourself these questions before you quit:

- Is this a good company to work for? Are the benefits, perks, bonuses, and career advancement possibilities too good to give up?

- Is this a good time economically to leave your job? What is your personal financial situation? How is the economic health of your industry and the area in which you live?

- Do you have another job lined up? Don't quit unless you do.

- Have you let a single incident force your decision?

- What truly is making you unhappy at work? List what you like and dislike about your job and weigh the lists against each other. Can you repair or compensate for the negatives without quitting? Could you communicate better with coworkers or bosses? Request a transfer? Discuss the problem with a supervisor, the human resources department, or your company's employee assistance program?

- Do you always think work would be better somewhere else? Be realistic, no job is perfect.

- Look at your role in the situation. Do personal difficulties affect your work? Do you work hard and smart enough? Are your work problems rooted in your own behavior and attitudes?

If you decide to quit, engineer a positive departure.

- Tell your supervisor first, not coworkers or colleagues. When you meet with your supervisor sandwich the negative between the positive. For example, first thank the supervisor for the opportunities you've had; then say that you've determined the position just isn't right for you; and finish by thanking the supervisor for the training or support (or whatever) you've received.

- Ask for letters of recommendation before you leave.

- Don't bad-mouth your employer to others. Your paths may cross again.

- Give adequate notice. Some guidelines: at least a week for new employees, two weeks for employees of a year or more, and three to four weeks for a senior employee who may be difficult to replace. Be prepared to leave immediately if asked.

- Send personal notes of thanks to supervisors and associates who have been supportive. Don't let those valuable relationships die.

- Know what will happen to your benefits (health insurance, retirement, company-sponsored savings plan) before you officially cut ties.

- Look at this as a learning experience. What have you learned about working with various types of people or your aptitude for your line of work? What qualities should you seek or avoid when looking for your next position?

Resources
➡ *Martin's Magic Motivation Book: How to Become an Anointed One in Your Organization*, Phyllis Martin, St. Martin's Press, 1984.

See Also
⇨ **Advancing Without a Promotion,** *page 198.*
⇨ **Considering a Career Change,** *page 216.*
⇨ **Understanding Your Bothersome Boss,** *page 28.*
⇨ **I Hate My Job!** *page 136.*

Bonus Tip!

Offer to help train your successor.

Preparing for a Possible Layoff

If you want to rebound quickly after a layoff heed these words: rely on yourself, starting now.

"The key to success in tomorrow's workplace is self-evaluation, self-confidence, and self-reliance!" James Cotham writes in his book *Career Shock* (see **Resources** below). He goes on to say, "But there's more: Self-preservation! Self-planning! Self-preparation! Self-initiative! Self-discipline! All are required. In a word, self-management."

The key is to practice self-management now, while you're still employed.

- Don't assume that you'll never be laid off or your job eliminated. In fact, the issue may be when you'll be laid off, not if.

- Get flexible financially, especially if you're over 35. Have money reserved to cover unexpected job changes in the short-term and for retirement in the long-term.

- Keep in touch with people who have interviewed you for other jobs and with employment recruiters you've met. They may know about a good opportunity next time around.

- Make sure your network includes people outside of your division or company. Use them to learn about the job market and to help you get the word out discreetly that you may want to change jobs

- Gather information to update your résumé. List major accomplishments in your current job. Get details from your old management-by-objective files, monthly activity reports, and performance reviews. Start a success folder or journal for information about accomplishments and new skills.

- Be alert. Watch for signs that your company or industry plans to pare jobs. Evaluate media reports about trouble at your company or division. Monitor business, political, and lifestyle trends that may affect your industry. Take heed if you start getting poor performance reviews, less desirable assignments, or less attention from the key players in your organization. Have people who joined your organization at the same time as you moved up to better positions than you? Do you seem to be clashing more with your supervisors lately? Has your company recently bought another company or been bought?

- Notice new job skills that are increasingly in demand. Do you have them? Get them by working on different kinds of projects, taking continuing education courses, and reading or helping colleagues who do have them. Brush up on the basics, too: writing, speaking, listening, organizing, problem solving, computer literacy, Total Quality Management, basic accounting, cost analysis, and project management.

■ Prepare for interviews now. Read books and articles about how to present yourself and answer tricky questions.

■ Know your career needs and desires so you're ready to evaluate new opportunities quickly. What satisfies you at work? What do you dislike? What would your ideal job be? Who is your role model? What are your salary and benefit requirements? What trade-offs would you accept (a smaller salary for a job with more visibility)?

Resources
➡ *Career Shock,* James Cotham, Berkley, 1992.
➡ *Lifeboat Strategies: How to Keep Your Career above Water during Tough Times or Any Time,* Robert Barner, AMACOM, 1994.
➡ *The Very Quick Job Search,* J. Michael Farr, JIST Works, Inc., 1996.

See Also
⇨ **Managing Your Career,** *page 194.*
⇨ **Building a Productive Network,** *page 206.*
⇨ **Staying Current in Your Job,** *page 208.*
⇨ **Coping with Job Loss,** *page 238.*

Bonus Tip!

Start updating your career goals and plans today.

Coping with Job Loss

It's been said that no one ever died from being fired or laid off. That may seem hard to believe if you've just been shoved out of your job, but it's probably true. Being fired can be a beginning instead of an end.

When you've just lost your job:

- Save your emotions for later. You've got lots of serious issues to think about. Don't cloud your head or the atmosphere by reacting emotionally or making a scene at work.

- If you don't feel in control, ask your supervisor if you can meet again in a day or two to discuss important issues.

- Make a list of questions: How much severance pay will I receive? How long does my insurance coverage last? Am I due money from profit-sharing, savings, or pension plans? Will you pay me for unused vacation time? What kind of reference will you give me? What does my contract say about being released?

- Don't further weaken the relationship between you and your employer. You'll both lose if you become angry or uncooperative. Be polite, humble, courteous, and calm. You never know when you might need each other again.

- Immerse yourself in another activity immediately after the termination. Participate in a favorite sport or hobby, attend a movie or show, or go out with friends.

- Give yourself at least a few days to work through the shock by using the support of friends and family. Then give yourself lots of time to feel grief, sadness, and anger.

- Find out about out-placement and job-search services available through your company and local agencies. Check with the human resources office, state labor or employment departments, large churches or local council of churches, support group notices in newspapers, and local bulletin boards.

- Take positive action to help you move ahead and regain control of your career (dig up data for your résumé, get a job-search book, call network members, investigate retraining or relocating). These steps are better for the long run than relying mostly on coping mechanisms like seeking financial assistance or personal counseling.

- Keep a sense of order in your life. Awaken at a reasonable hour, dress neatly, and plan an agenda for the day.

If you were fired for performance or behavior problems:

- Expect it to take effect immediately. It probably will be easier on everyone if you leave right away instead of trying to finish the work day.

- Find out why you were fired. What could you have done differently? Contemplate your part in the problems that led to dismissal. Re-evaluate strengths you want to maintain and weaknesses you need to improve. Have you had similar job problems in the past? What patterns do you see? Some caring, honest friends and colleagues, or a good career counselor can help here.

- Don't fight your boss' decision in most cases (except in instances of outright discrimination). Would you want to return where you're not wanted, anyway? Focus on moving forward.

- Don't hang around your old workplace. Your boss probably will not reverse the decision. Plus, communications will become awkward.

- In future job interviews be honest—but not nasty—about why you were fired. Briefly explain why the relationship didn't work. Ask prospective employers questions that will help you determine if you've got a good match in personalities, styles, values, and skills.

Resources
➡ *The Survivor's Guide to Unemployment*, Tom Morton, Pinon Press, 1992.
➡ *How to Bounce Back Quickly After Losing Your Job*, Holly Smith, VGM Career Horizons, 1993.
➡ *When Smart People Fail: Rebuilding Yourself for Success*, Carole Hyatt, Viking/Penguin, 1993.

See Also
➪ **Preparing for a Possible Layoff**, *page 236.*
➪ **Reacting to an Unfair Dismissal**, *page 240.*
➪ **Boosting your Self-Esteem**, *page 112.*

Reacting to an Unfair Dismissal

Being fired usually is traumatic. It's even more gut-wrenching when you feel you've been dismissed unfairly.

Your options may seem somewhat limited, but there are several steps you can take to attempt to receive fair treatment.

- Realize that the law generally is on the side of the employer. No law gives employees an automatic right to keep their jobs, even if the reason for the dismissal is morally wrong.

- Safeguard yourself before you lose your job. Check what's in your personnel file every six months. Make brief notes of every significant meeting with your boss. Demand a formal performance review at least once a year. If your employer won't put it in writing, type up your own summary and ask the employer to sign it. If you've responded to criticism, write a note detailing what you've done. Ask that a copy be placed in your personnel file. Also document pay raises or decreases, scheduled pay increases you never received, changes in work assignments, commendations, and reprimands.

- Know your rights. Read your employee handbook. Contact the local Equal Employment Opportunity Commission about wrongful termination. Get advice from your union, if you have one, or national employees associations (see **Resources** below).

- Ask the person dismissing you for a written explanation of why you were fired. Try to get it before you leave the premises. Or write the employer a letter saying that you want to clarify the reasons for your dismissal on such-and-such date. State that you understand you were fired for the following reasons. Ask that the employer advise you in writing by a specific date if your understanding is incorrect. Send the letter via certified mail.

- Check for evidence that your employer had a breach of good faith and fair dealing (firing you so you can't collect sales commission or misleading you about negative aspects of the job).

- Know the risks of taking your employer to court. Employees often lose those fights, which can cost thousands of dollars. Employers could dig up personal information about you to use in court. And other employers might not want to hire you once you've sued.

- Consider using mediation or arbitration to solve your dispute quickly and inexpensively. Contact your local bar association or arbitration services listed in the Yellow Pages (see **Resources** below). Or consider the inexpensive, easy-to-use small-claims or conciliation courts in your county.

- Find a good employment lawyer by asking people you know for referrals. Also check with the local bar association, legal aid clinics, the nearest law school, minority rights groups, or national workers rights groups.

Resources

➡ *Your Rights in the Workplace*, Dan Lacey, Nolo Press, 1992.

➡ The 9 to 5 Job Survival Hotline, 800-522-0925, 10 a.m.-3:50 p.m. EST, Monday-Friday (run by 9to5, National Association of Working Women, Milwaukee, WI).

➡ The American Arbitration Association, a private, non-profit dispute resolution service, listed in local phone books, or contact them at 140 W. 51st St., New York, NY 10020, 800-778-7879, Web address: http://www.adr.org/, to find the office nearest you. Ask for the free pamphlets, *National Rules for the Resolution of Employment Disputes* (for nonunion employees and employers), *Labor Arbitration Rules* (for unionized workplaces), or *Resolving Employment Disputes* (for employers).

➡ U.S. Arbitration and Mediation, a private for-profit service, helps resolve disputes for a fee. Offices are listed in local phone books or contact 800-373-0915 to find the office nearest you.

See Also

⇨ **Coping with Job Loss**, *page 238.*
⇨ **Unethical or Unlawful Employers**, *page 52.*
⇨ **Handling Sexual Harassment**, *page 56.*

Bonus Tip!

Get your job description in writing while you're employed.

Planning Now for Early Retirement

In the last couple of decades many people have decided they want to retire in their 50s or early 60s. They hope to pursue personal or professional interests while they still have lots of energy, drive, and good health. Others may be unexpectedly tempted by early retirement offers from their cost-cutting companies.

Retiring will affect your family, health, self-image, and social life. It requires careful analysis and advance planning years before you make the change.

- Clearly define what retirement means to you. Would you quit work completely? Cut back to part-time? Work as a consultant or private contractor? Try another career? Find a similar full- or part-time job at another company?

- Research your dreams before retiring. What's involved in starting your own business? Returning to school? Part-time teaching?

- Start making financial plans for retirement as early as possible, even while you're in your 20s and 30s. Start planning other aspects of your retirement in detail five years or more ahead of when you plan to retire. Revisit and update the plans often.

- Spend lots of time on financial planning. Consider your resources, income, health, insurance, financial obligations and lifestyle. Make a future budget, factoring in inflation, to see if your dreams match your means. Get help from a professional financial planner (see **Resources** below), take advantage of company-sponsored retirement counseling programs or take a financial planning course from your local community college. Another option is to get inexpensive financial planning software for your personal computer.

- Realistically think about what you want your days to be like after retirement. Consider your personality, style, aptitudes, and values. Plan to stay busy — research has shown that people who remain active live longer and stay happier.

- Plot your anticipated post-retirement schedule on a calendar. Do you have a lot of leftover time? Find outlets for those hours now, before you retire and become bored.

- Be prepared to face a lot of pressure if your company offers an early retirement plan. Some supervisors may urge you to go, but others may not want to lose you. Put your own needs and wants first.

- Don't assume that your family will know exactly what you're planning just because you've mentioned it a few times. Discuss it in detail. Plan it together. Expect some resistance, especially if your spouse is not employed. Spouses often worry that you'll be infringing on their territory.

- Don't underestimate retirement's impact on your social life. You won't see your work friends as often and won't have as much in common with them. Plan to make new friends who share your postretirement interests.

Resources

➡ *The Complete Retirement Handbook: For Anyone Who Will Ever Retire*, Forest J. Bowman, University Press of Kentucky, 1989.

➡ *Feathering Your Nest: The Retirement Planner*, Lisa Berger, Workman, 1993.

➡ International Association for Financial Planning, 5775 Glenridge Dr. NE, Suite B300, Atlanta, GA 30328-5364. Web address: http://www.iafp.org. 800-945-4237; and the Institute of Certified Financial Planners, 7600 E. Eastman Ave., Denver, CO 80231, 800-282-7526, Web address: http://www.icfp.org. Each provides free referrals to financial planners in your area.

➡ *Look Before You Leap: A Guide to Early Retirement Incentive Programs*, American Association of Retired Persons, stock no. D13390, free by contacting AARP, 601 E. Street, NW, Washington, D.C. 20049, 800-424-3410. Also, a 20-page booklet, *Planning Your Retirement*, stock no. D12322, is available free from AARP.

➡ *Healthy, Wealthy, & Wise: A Guide to Retirement Planning*, Park Avenue Productions, 1998.

See Also

⇨ **Staying Current in Your Job**, *page 208.*
⇨ **Going Back to School**, *page 220.*
⇨ **Shifting to Part-Time Work**, *page 224.*
⇨ **Job Sharing**, *page 226.*

Arranging Your Parental Leave

Setting up a fair parental leave that suits both you and your employer requires research, knowledge of your needs, and savvy negotiating skills.

This is true whether or not you're covered by the 1993 Family and Medical Leave Act. The law guarantees qualified employees at companies with more than 50 employees up to 12 weeks of leave for the birth or adoption of a child, or the serious health condition of a close family member or yourself. But even if you work for a smaller employer you still may get the leave you want; smaller organizations often can be more flexible and creative.

- Know which federal and state leave laws apply to you and your employer (FMLA, Pregnancy Discrimination Act). Get information at public and university law libraries, the state labor department, your human resources department, or women's professional associations.

- Learn about your company's parental leave policies, practices, and philosophies. Find out how the company has treated pregnant workers or new parents in the past. Learn what other companies have done (see **Resources** below).

- Don't start negotiating for your leave when you announce your pregnancy or your spouse's pregnancy. Let the news sink in. But do say something positive about your work and that you intend to return to your job.

- Establish how much leave would be good for you, your baby, and your employer. Many doctors and companies propose that new mothers take off six weeks after birth. Others recommend at least four months. If you're the mother-to-be, consider whether you'll be breast-feeding, the expected health of you and the baby, and the amount of sleep and support you'll get at home. Overestimate the time you think you'll need.

- Think about whether you'll ask for pay and benefits during your entire leave or only a portion of it.

- Plan how you'd like to return to work—full-time, part-time, part-time leading into full-time, sharing a job, or telecommuting? Do you want your old job back or would you accept a comparable job in another department?

- Remind your employer of your value. Mention training, knowledge, experience, contacts, money you bring in, results you produce, and awards and honors.

- Plan for how your work will be covered during your absence. Consider mothballing some of it and using coworkers, temporary workers, or college interns for other parts. Don't promise to work while on leave. You'll need to rest and concentrate on parenthood.

- Present your proposal in writing at a well-timed, private meeting with your boss. Put the final agreement in writing.

- If you can't get all the leave you'd like negotiate other benefits (retaining health insurance while on leave, returning part-time).

- Bring disputes to the Wage and Hour Division of the U.S. Department of Labor (check government listings in your phone book) if you're covered by federal laws. If you're not covered by federal or state laws suggest that you resolve disputes with mediation or arbitration. (Check with local bar associations or arbitration services listed in phone books.) Or investigate whether your state labor agency or women's commission would sponsor your case in court.

Resources
➡ *Everything a Working Mother Needs to Know*, Anne Weisberg and Carol Buckler, Doubleday, 1994.
➡ *Maternity Leave: The Working Woman's Practical Guide to Combining Pregnancy, Motherhood, and Career*, Eileen Casey, Green Mountain Publishing, 1992.
➡ *Your Rights in the Workplace*, Dan Lacey, Nolo Press, 1992.
➡ Women's Bureau Clearinghouse has information about women's workplace issues, 200 Constitution Ave. NW, Washington, D.C. 20210, 800-827-5335 or 800-347-3741, 11 a.m.-4 p.m. EST, Monday-Friday. Web address: http://www.dol.gov/dol/wb.
➡ Women's Legal Defense Fund, 1875 Connecticut Ave, NW, Suite 710, Washington, D.C. 20009, 202-986-2600. Family and Medical Leave Act fact sheet, free with stamped, self-addressed envelope. Also offers *Guide to the Family and Medical Leave Act*, $3.95. E-mail: info@wldf.org.

See Also
➪ **Shifting to Part-Time Work**, *page 224.*
➪ **Job Sharing**, *page 226.*
➪ **Returning to Work**, *page 230.*
➪ **Negotiating for What You Want**, *page 98.*

Section IV: Career Moves

Notes

These experts, articles, and other resources provided information for the tips in this book. The author wishes to express her appreciation for their ideas. Other books and resources are listed in the **Resources** section after each topic. The **Bibliography** section also lists books used by the author.

Section I: Working Smart
Chapter 1: Productivity

1-1. **Finding More Time in Your Day:** David Luna, Luna & Associates, Albuquerque, NM; "How Not to Waste Time on the Telephone," Deirdre Boden, *Bottom Line Personal* (newsletter).

1-2. **Improving Your Filing System:** "Get Control of Clutter," Eleanor Berman, *Working Mother*, Aug. 1990.

1-3. **Controlling Paperwork:** BIS Strategic, Norwell, MA; Quill Corp., Lincolnshire, IL.

1-4. **Managing Your Reading Material:** Mildred Bunch Langston, time management consultant, Albuquerque, NM; Kelly Summers, ground water scientist and technical writing consultant, Albuquerque, NM; Peter Balleau, groundwater consultant, Albuquerque, NM; "Reading Lesson: How to Absorb More...Faster," Eric Bienstock, *Boardroom Reports* (newsletter), June 1, 1990; Paul Scheele, adult learning expert and developer of the PhotoReading course, Learning Strategies Corp., Wayzata, MN.

1-5. **Boosting Efficiency with Your Calendar:** Bill Gupton and Suzan Gupton, Creative Management Services, Albuquerque, NM; Margaret Bunch Langston, time management consultant, Albuquerque; Ann McGee-Cooper, leadership development coach, Ann McGee-Cooper & Associates, Dallas, TX.

1-6. **Getting More Out of Meetings:** "Make Every Meeting a Career Opportunity," Milo Frank, *Management Digest*, May 15, 1989; "Making the Most of Meeting Time," Peter Tobia and Martin Becker, *Training & Development*, August, 1990; "Meetings Can Be Much More Meaningful," *Boardroom Reports* (newsletter), June 15, 1990; "Seven Surefire Steps to Running an Effective Meeting," Jim Jubak, *Self*, May, 1990.

1-7. **Cubicle Survival Tips:** Stacey Wolf, president, Cubicle Cues, Inc., Cordova, TN; Barbara Brazil, public affairs manager, Intel, Rio Rancho, NM; "Your Walls Speak Volumes," *Communication Briefings* (newsletter), Volume IX, Number XI.

1-8. **Working at Home Successfully:** Jim Theiss, telecommuting systems analyst, US West Communications, Lakewood, CO; Kathleen Christensen, professor, environmental psychology, City University of New York Graduate School, New York, NY; "Mission Control—Home Offices Are Becoming a Must for Everyone," Dan Gutman, *Success*, Nov. 1989.

Chapter 2: Relationships

2-1.   **Making Your Boss Your Partner:** "Managing the Baffling Boss," J. Kenneth Matejka and Richard Dunsing, *Personnel*, Feb. 1989; "Ideas to Help Reporters Get the Help They Need," Roy Peter Clark, *American Society of Newspaper Managing Editors Bulletin*, Dec. 1987.

2-2.   **Understanding Your Bothersome Boss:** "Managing the Baffling Boss," J. Kenneth Matejka and Richard Dunsing, *Personnel*, Feb. 1989; "Ideas to Help Reporters Get the Help They Need," Roy Peter Clark, *American Society of Newspaper Managing Editors Bulletin*, Dec. 1987.

2-4.   **Communicating with the Opposite Sex:** Susan Greer, human relations consultant, Solutions, Albuquerque, NM; Robin Parker, communications consultant, Albuquerque, NM.

2-5.   **Handling Customer Problems:** "Customer Service Perceptions and Reality," Wendy Becker and Richard Wellins, *Training & Development*, March 1990; "Customer Service Behavior Spelled Out," Keith Wilcock, *Training & Development*, Nov. 1989; "Managers Tipsheet," *Working Woman*, Oct. 1989.

Chapter 3: Technology

3-1.   **Using Your Fax Machine Wisely:** Larry Baker, president, Time Management Center, Inc., St. Louis, MO; Dan Stamp, chair, Priority Management Systems, Inc., Bellevue, WA.

3-2.   **Comfortable Computer Tips:** Ruth Krug and Fran Wilkinson, University of New Mexico, Albuquerque; NM; *About Working with VDTs*, (booklet) Channing L. Bete Co., Inc., South Deerfield, MA, 1988; Julia Lacey, computer consultant, CRT Services, Inc., Kerrville, TX; Naomi Swanson, ergonomics and occupational stress researcher, National Institute of Occupational Safety and Health, Cincinnati, OH.

3-3.   **Voice Mail and Answering Machine Savvy:** Donald Weiss, Self-Management Communications, Inc., St. Louis, MO.

3-4.   **Maximizing Your Electronic Mail:** Lynn Closway, manager of media relations, American Express Financial Advisors, Minneapolis, MN; Ellen Dowling, Professional Training Company, Albuquerque, NM.

Chapter 4: Conflicts at Work

4-1.   **Creative Problem Solving:** Mike Bell, management consultant, Englewood, CO; "The Secrets of Much, Much Better Problem Solving," William Miller, *Bottom Line Personal* (newsletter), June 15, 1991; "Everyone Is Creative," Michael Ray, *Bottom Line Personal*, Aug. 15, 1990; "Secrets of Much Better Problem Solving," Gerald Nadler, *Bottom Line Personal*, Sept. 15, 1990.

4-2.   **Preparing for a Conflict:** Corinne Taylor, vice president, Conflict Management Inc., Albuquerque, NM; "Managing Difficult People," Ellen Dowling, *Employee Services Management*, Feb. 1989; "Attacks Handled by Advance Practice," *The Pryor Report* (newsletter), Vol. 6, No. 1A.

4-4. **Working with a Drug or Alcohol Abuser:** Steve Anderson, president, Comprehensive Counseling Associates, Albuquerque, NM; Joe Cotruzzola, owner, Management Institute, Albuquerque, NM.

4-5. **Handling Sexual Harassment:** "Have a Sexual Harassment Policy—and Make It Known," *Laborwatch* (newsletter), Berens-Tate Consulting Group, Omaha, NE, Nov. 1991; "Sexual Harassment, Fact or Fiction," *Excelling!* (newsletter), Herman Associates, Inc., Fairlawn, OH, Winter 1992; Anita Alvarado, administrator, University of New Mexico sexual harassment policy, Albuquerque, NM; Ray Armenta, investigator, U.S. Equal Employment Opportunity Commission, Albuquerque, NM; Frank Miranda, contract compliance officer, Albuquerque Human Rights Office; New Mexico Commission on the Status of Women, Albuquerque, NM; Daniel Fee, EEO Consulting Group, Cahokia, IL.

4-6. **Dealing with Verbal Abuse:** Alan Lovejoy, principle, Lovejoy & Lovejoy, human and organization consultants, Denver, CO.

4-7. **Avoiding Excessive Overtime Work:** Jessica Glicken, president, Women's Economic Self-Sufficiency Team, Albuquerque, NM; Sandy Pope, executive director, Coalition of Labor Union Women, New York, NY; "The Overtime Bind," Diane Cole, *Working Mother*, April 1990.

Section II: Communication Skills
Chapter 5: Clear Messages
5-1. **Communicating for Success:** Carol Cox Smith, author, Albuquerque, NM; "Twenty Three Ways to Improve Communication," Lester Tobias, *Training & Development*, Dec. 1989.

5-3. **Listen Up:** Denny Garber, co-owner, Perceptions Seminars and Consulting, Albuquerque, NM; "The Art of Active Listening," David Lewis, *Training & Development*, July 1989; "What's That You Say?" Richard Neal, *The Executive Educator*, Nov. 1991.

Chapter 6: Speaking
6-2. **Tuning Up Informal Speech:** ManagersEdge (audiotape series, tape #3), "Impromptu Response," Sharon Crain, 1987; Jean Watson, speaker's coach, Watson & Associates, Tyler, TX.

6-4. **Using Visual Aids:** "The Layman's Guide to Presentation Design" and "Presentation-Graphics Software," Robin Raskin, *Home-Office Computing*, July 1989.

Chapter 7: Writing
7-1. **Composing Better Letters:** Marjorie Shapiro Stein, writer and communications teacher, University of Phoenix, Albuquerque, NM; "Writing Better and Faster," Frank Grazian, *Communication Briefings* (newsletter), Vol. IX, No. V; "In Practice," *Training & Development*, Dec. 1989.

7-2. **Writing Effective Memos:** Ellen Dowling, co-owner, Professional Training Co., Albuquerque, NM; Debra Benton, Benton Management Resources, Fort Collins, CO.

7-4. **Smashing Writer's Block:** Marcia Yudkin, creativity consultant, Boston, MA.

Chapter 8: Communicating with a Purpose

8-2. **Powerful Persuasion:** Gina Agostinelli, assistant professor, psychology, University of New Mexico, Albuquerque, NM; "How to Win an Argument," William Rusher, *Bottom Line Personal* (newsletter), Aug. 15, 1990.

8-4. **Giving Clear Instructions:** "Do It Right the First Time: Job Briefing Can Prevent Problems," C. Roger Smith, *Laborwatch* (newsletter), Berens-Tate Consulting Group, Omaha, NE, Oct. 1992.

8-5. **Making Gossip Work for You:** "The Scoop on Office Gossip," Lynne Cusack, *Working Mother*, March 1992.

Section III: Self-Improvement
Chapter 9: Sharp Thinking

9-1. **Positive Thinking Power:** Norma Milanovich, president, The Alpha Connection, Inc., Albuquerque, NM; "Self-Esteem Bolsters Success," Eugene Raudsepp, *National Business Employment Weekly*, July 6, 1986.

9-2. **Projecting a Successful Image:** Denny Garber, president, Perceptions Seminars, Albuquerque, NM; *Powerful Communication Skills for Women* (audiotape), Brenda Robinson, Sourcecom, 1987.

9-3. **Boosting Your Self-esteem:** Vivian Harris, speaker and trainer, Albuquerque, NM.

9-4. **Using Humor at Work:** C.W. Metcalf, change and stress management consultant, Fort Collins, CO; "Building Fun in Your Organization," David Abramis, *Personnel Administrator*, Oct. 1989.

9-5. **Setting Goals:** Jean Watson, speaker's coach, Watson & Associates, Tyler, TX; Al Walker, trainer and professional speaker, Columbia, SC; "The Power of Goals," Don Wallace, *Success*, Sept. 1991.

9-6. **Nurturing Your Creativity:** "Breaking the Cycle That Stifles Innovation," Alex Kozlov, *Psychology Today*, October 1989; "Endangered Species: New Ideas," Gareth Morgan, *Business Month*, April 1989; "The Great Freedom of Corporate Life: to Question," Leonard Silk, *Business Month*, April 1989.

9-7. **Tapping Your Intuition:** Audrey Gray, psychologist, executive trainer, and consultant, Albuquerque, NM.

9-8. **Making Better Decisions:** Keith Parsons, associate, John Arnold ExecuTrak Systems, Waltham, MA; Lex Stapp, training specialist, Honeywell, Albuquerque, NM.

9-9. **Taking Smart Risks:** Vivian Harris, speaker and trainer, Albuquerque, NM; "Four by Four," Marc Bassin, *Training & Development*, July 1989.

Chapter 10: Coping with Work

10-1. **Quick Stress Busters:** Catherine Hebenstreit, therapist, *Empowering Through Choices,* Albuquerque, NM; Louis Nuanez, account executive, F.J.'s Nature's Products, Albuquerque, NM, "Your New Role: Stress Buster," Nick Nykodym, Ian Miners, and Susan Gedeon, *Management World*, May/June 1989; Cy Stockhoff, emergency medicine and stress management trainer, University of New Mexico, Albuquerque, NM; "Instant Stress Relievers," *Practical Supervision* (pamphlet), Professional Training Associates, Inc.

10-2. **Managing Stress for the Long-Term:** Thomas Sims, psychologist, Behavior Therapy Associates, Albuquerque, NM; "Surviving Burnout: The Malady of Our Age," Stanley Modic, *Industry Week*, Feb. 20, 1989; *Employee Burnout: America's Newest Epidemic*, Northwestern National Life, 1991; "Is Your Company Asking Too Much?" Brian O'Reilly, *Fortune*, March 12, 1990; "Stress," Ray Flannery, *Bottom Line Personal* (newsletter), July 15, 1991.

10-3. **Zapping Job Burnout:** "Beating Those Burnout Blues," Marie Moneysmith, *Savvy*, November 1986; "How to Battle the Causes of Burnout," William Brown, *National Business Employment Weekly*, July 6, 1986.

10-5. **I Hate My Job!** "Fall in Love with Your Job Again," Louise Tutelian, *Working Mother*, Dec. 1991; "Disappointment on the Job," Diane Cole, *Working Mother*, Aug. 1990.

10-7. **Recovering from Mistakes:** "How to Turn Around Bad First Impressions," Barry Lubetkin, *Bottom Line Personal* (newsletter), March 15, 1991; "So You Made a Mistake!" Diane Cole, *Working Mother*, Aug. 1991.

Chapter 11: Family Issues

11-1. **Relief for Two-Career Couples:** Marsha Hardeman, management trainer, Images, Ltd., Albuquerque, NM; Maryhelen Snyder, psychologist, Albuquerque, NM.

11-2. **Tips for Couples Who Work Together:** Julia Bristow-Romo, assistant cashier, and Patrick Romo, assistant vice president, Sunwest Bank, Albuquerque, NM; Peggy Schoof and Clay Wright, owners, Desert Gem Productions, Inc., Albuquerque, NM; Max DeLara, human resources manager, Citicorp Credit Services Inc., Albuquerque, NM.

11-3. **Balancing Work and Family:** Beverly Nomberg, counselor, Human Affairs International, Albuquerque, NM; Corinne Taylor, vice president, Conflict Management, Inc., Albuquerque, NM.

11-4. **Helping Your Kids Understand Your Job:** Diane Cushman, health and family programs specialist, The St. Paul Companies, St. Paul, MN; *Employers/Employees Guide—Take Our Daughters to Work*, Ms. Foundation for Women, New York, NY.

11-5. **Easing Heavy Travel Schedules:** Dan Martinez, owner, Uniglobe Torres Travel, Albuquerque, NM; Roberta McLaughlin, organizational development consultant, Charter Oak Consulting Group, Albuquerque, NM; "Till Travel Do Us Part," Richard Leider, *Training & Development*, May 1991.

Chapter 12: Details

12-1. **Business Etiquette for the '90s:** Maria Everding, *Manners for Success,* St. Louis, MO.

12-2. **Making Proper Business Introductions:** Maria Everding, *Manners for Success,* St. Louis, MO; "Gaining the Winning Edge with Business Etiquette," Ann Marie Sabath, *Communication Briefings* (newsletter) Oct. 1989; "Remember Names Better Than a Computer," Andrew Robin, *Prevention*, December, 1989; *Sales Upbeat*, Vol. C, No. 10, The Economics Press, Inc., 1986.

12-3. **Smart Career Dressing for Women:** Louise Spicer, national president, American Business Women's Association; Pearline Motley, ABWA'S 1993 American Business Woman, Kansas City, MO; Nancy Gove, ladies department manager, Liemandt's, Minnetonka, MN; *Career Dressing That Works,* (pamphlet) Naturalizer Shoes.

12-4. **Smart Career Dressing for Men:** Anita Kasle, international fashion consultant, Fashion Your Image, Carmel, IN.

Section IV: Career Moves

Chapter 13: The Job Search

13-1. **Using Information Interviews:** Chris Kuselias, president, Kuselias Enterprises, Inc., North Haven, CT; Prudence Davis, career counselor and out-placement consultant, The Career Center, Albuquerque, NM; Elizabeth Craig, Craig Group International, Minneapolis, MN.

13-5. **Conducting an Electronic Job Search.** Michael Willis, career management consultant, Syracuse, NY; James Gonyea, director, America Online Career Center.

13-7. **Answering Interview Questions:** Prudence Davis, career counselor and out-placement consultant, The Career Center, Albuquerque, NM.

13-8. **Finding the Right Employer:** Cheryl Eckstam and David Cady, career and human resources specialists, Minneapolis, MN.

13-9. **Considering a Pay Cut:** Robert Riskin, career management consultant and author, St. Paul, MN; *Kennedy's Career Strategist* (newsletter), May 1993, Career Strategies, Wilmette, IL.

13-10. **Handling Employment Recruiters:** Terry Keyes, senior vice president, Professional Personnel Placements, Albuquerque, NM.

Chapter 14: Career Reinforcement

14-1. **Shining at a New Job:** Debra Benton, Benton Management Resources, Fort Collins, CO; Jack Miller, president, Quill Corp., Lincolnshire, IL, "Attitudes That Employers Don't Like," Robert Half, *Bottom Line Personal* (newsletter), Feb. 28, 1993.

14-2. **Managing Your Career:** "Choreographing Careers," Barry Grossman and Roy Blitzer, *Training & Development*, Jan. 1992; "How to Make Your Career Dreams Come True," Nella Barkley, *Bottom Line Personal* (newsletter), July 15, 1990; Robert Barner, vice president, Parry Consulting Services, Inc., Jupiter, FL; "New Career Traps: 1991...And How to Avoid Them," Nella Barkley, *Bottom Line Personal* (newsletter), Dec. 31, 1990; Debra Benton, Benton Management Resources, Fort Collins, CO; Jack Miller, president, Quill Corp., Lincolnshire, IL, "Attitudes That Employers Don't Like," Robert Half, *Bottom Line Personal* (newsletter), Feb. 28, 1993.

14-3. **Shattering the Glass Ceiling:** Jo Kirchner, vice president, Primrose Schools Franchising Co., Atlanta, GA; Tee Houston-Aldridge, vice president, Priority Management Systems, Inc., Bellevue, WA; Fortune Nichols, creative marketing manager, L'Arome (USA) Inc., Rock Hill, SC.

14-4. **Advancing Without a Promotion:** "Action Plan for Success," Ronni Sandroff, *Working Woman*, Oct. 1989; "Handling Career Plateaus," Hank Karp, *National Business Employment Weekly*, Oct. 23, 1988; "How to Handle the Career Plateau," Hank Karp, ODT Associates, Amherst, MA; "The Plateau Payoff," Audrey Edwards, *Working Woman*, Oct. 1989.

14-5. **Growing with a Mentor:** "A Mentor for All Reasons," Michael Zey, *Personnel Journal*, January, 1988; "Mentors and Protégés: Portraits of Success," Aimee Lee Ball, *Working Woman*, Oct. 1989.

14-6. **Asking for a Raise:** "Fifteen Ways to Earn More Money," Anita Gates, *Working Mother*, April 1991.

14-7. **Declining a Promotion:** Frank Reinow, consultant, Franklin B. Reinow & Associates, Albuquerque, NM.

14-8. **Building a Productive Network:** Jill Duval, owner, Duval Publications, Albuquerque, NM; "The Professional (and Personal) Profits of Networking," Frank Sonnenberg, *Training & Development*, Sept. 1990.

14-9. **Staying Current in Your Job:** "The Age Wave," Patricia Galagan, *Training & Development*, Feb. 1990; "How to Help an Over-50 Friend Find the Ideal Job," Lawrence Le Shan, *Bottom Line Personal* (newsletter), July 15, 1991; "The New Generation: Older Workers," J.W. Gilsdorf, *Training & Development*, March 1992.

14-10. **Choosing the Right Seminar:** Ellen Dowling, co-owner, The Professional Training Co., Albuquerque, NM; Rick Shaum, director, DeLaPorte & Associates, Inc., Albuquerque, NM; Patricia Potter, vice president, Keye Productivity Center, Kansas City, KS.

Chapter 15: Career Shifts

15-1. **Escaping a Career Pigeonhole:** Michael Rex, organizational effectiveness consultant, Sandia National Laboratories, Albuquerque, NM; "The Typecasting Trap," Lisa Mainiero, *Training & Development*, March 1990.

15-2. **Considering a Career Change:** Jonathan Hartshorne, president, Work Life Counseling, Albuquerque, NM; Phyllis Kaplan, career counselor and developer of "Career Renewal Strategy: A Process for Career Choice, Decision and Change," Albuquerque, NM.

15-3. **Finding a Good Career Counselor:** Prudence Davis, career counselor and outplacement consultant, The Career Center, Albuquerque, NM; Shoshona Blankman, career and creative change counselor, Albuquerque, NM; Howard Figler, career consultant, Sacramento, CA.

15-4. **Going Back to School:** Rebecca Henriksen, director of marketing, Cardinal Stritch College of Milwaukee, Minneapolis branch, MN; Kate Schaefers, coordinator, career transition program, University of Minnesota, Minneapolis, MN; Carolyn Howard, industrial organizational psychologist, Winfield, KS.

15-5. **Experience Through Internships:** Phyllis Kaplan, career counselor and developer of "Career Renewal Strategy: A Process for Career Choice, Decision and Change," Albuquerque, NM.

15-6. **Shifting to Part-Time Work:** "Pioneers of the New Balance," Alan Deutschman, *Fortune*, May 20, 1991.

15-7. **Job Sharing:** "Two for One: A Working Idea," Jane Easter Bahls, *Nation's Business*, June 1989.

15-8. **Slowing Down Your Career:** Gary Soule, management and training consultant, Priority Management Systems, Inc., Minneapolis, MN; "Making a Choice," Donna Jackson, *New Woman*, April 1992.

15-9. **Returning to Work:** Eileen Casey, Shelburne, VT; Yvette Oldendorf, president, Working Opportunities for Women, St. Paul, MN.

Chapter 16: Leaving Your Job

16-1. **Quitting:** Sue Wilson, president, Sue Wilson Express Services, Albuquerque, NM.

16-2. **Preparing for a Possible Layoff:** Robert Barner, vice president, Parry Consulting Services, Inc., Jupiter, FL.

16-3. **Coping with Job Loss:** "You're Fired!" Neil Chesanow, *Working Mother*, June 1987; Shirley Herndon, owner/president, The Agency, Albuquerque, NM.

16-4. **Reacting to an Unfair Dismissal:** Barbara Otto, 9 to 5 National Association of Working Women, Cleveland, OH.

16-5. **Planning Now for Early Retirement:** Curt Cardinal, pre-retirement services supervisor, 3M Company, St. Paul, MN; Roger Putnam, vice president and general manager, career management services division, Personnel Decisions, Inc., Minneapolis, MN; Robert Riskin, career management consultant and author, St. Paul, MN.

Bibliography

Albrecht, Karl. *The Creative Corporation*. Homewood, Ill.: Dow Jones-Irwin. 1987.

Anderson, Kristin. *Great Customer Service on the Telephone*. New York: AMACOM. 1992.

Arnold, John. *Make Up Your Mind*. New York: AMACOM. 1978.

Bardwick, Judith. *The Plateauing Trap: How to Avoid It in Your Career...and Your Life*. New York: AMACOM. 1986.

Baker, Kim, and Baker, Sunny. *Office on the Go: Tools, Tips, and Techniques for Every Business Traveler*. Englewood Cliffs, N.J.: Prentice Hall. 1993.

Barner, Robert. *Lifeboat Strategies: How to Keep Your Career Above Water During Tough Times or Any Time*. New York: AMACOM. 1994.

Beatty, Richard. *The Résumé Kit*. New York: John Wiley & Sons. 1995.

Benton, Debra. *Lions Don't Need to Roar*. New York: Warner. 1992.

Bernstein, Albert. *Dinosaur Brains: Dealing with All Those Impossible People at Work*. New York: John Wiley & Sons. 1989.

Berg, Howard Stephen. *Super Reading Secrets*. New York: Warner. 1992.

Berger, Lisa. *Feathering Your Nest: The Retirement Planner*. New York: Workman. 1993.

Besson, Taunee. *National Business Employment Weekly Résumés*. New York: John Wiley & Sons. 1996.

Bixler, Susan. *Professional Presence*. New York: Putnam's Sons. 1991.

Bjelland, Harley. *Business Writing the Modular Way*. New York: AMACOM. 1992.

Boe, Anne. *Is Your 'Net' Working? A Complete Guide to Building Contacts and Career Visibility*. New York: John Wiley & Sons. 1989.

Bogard, Morris R. *The Manager's Style Book*. Englewood Cliffs, N.J.: Prentice Hall. 1979.

Bolles, Richard N. *What Color Is Your Parachute? 1997*. Berkeley, Calif.: Ten Speed Press. 1997.

Booher, Dianna. *Clean Up Your Act: Effective Ways to Organize Paperwork and Get It Out of Your Life*. New York: Warner. 1992.

Booher, Dianna. *Send Me a Memo*. New York: Facts on File. 1984.

Branden, Nathaniel. *The Power of Self-Esteem*. Deerfield Beach, Fla.: Health Communications. 1992.

Branden. *How to Raise Your Self-Esteem*. New York: Bantam. 1988.

Bridges, William. *Surviving Transition*. New York: Doubleday. 1988.

Brownstone, David, and Franck, Irene M. *The Manager's Advisor*. New York: John Wiley & Sons. 1983.

Canape, Charlene. *The Part-Time Solution*. New York: Harper & Row, 1990.

Casey, Eileen. *Maternity Leave: The Working Woman's Practical Guide to Combining Pregnancy, Motherhood, and Career*. Shelburne, Vt.: Green Mountain Publishing. 1992.

Christensen, Kathleen. *Women and Home-Based Work*. New York: Henry Holt. 1988.

Collins, Eliza G.C. *The Executive Dilemma: Handling People Problems at Work*. New York: John Wiley & Sons. 1985.

Cotham, James. *Career Shock*. New York: Berkley. 1992.

Covey, Stephen. *The Seven Habits of Highly Effective People*. New York: Simon & Schuster. 1989.

Craig, Betty. *Don't Slurp Your Soup: A Basic Guide to Business Etiquette*. New Brighton, Minn.: Brighton Publications, Inc. 1991.

Crystal, John, and Bolles, Richard. *Where Do I Go from Here with My Life*. Berkeley, Calif.: Ten Speed Press. 1982.

Davidson, Jeffrey P. *Blow Your Own Horn*. New York: Berkley. 1991.

Davis, Brian. *The Successful Manager's Handbook: Development Suggestions for Today's Managers*. Minneapolis: Personnel Decisions. 1996.

Dawson, Roger. *The Confident Decision Maker: How to Make the Right Business and Personal Decisions Every Time*. New York: William Morrow. 1993.

Detz, Joan. *How to Write and Give a Speech*. New York: St. Martin's. 1992.

Devine, Thomas, Rasor, Dina, and Stewart, Julie. *Courage Without Martyrdom*. Washington, D.C.: Government Accountability Project.

Donkin, Scott. *Sitting on the Job*. Boston: Houghton Mifflin. 1986.

Douglass, Merrill, and Douglass, Donna. *Manage Your Time, Your Work, Yourself*. New York: AMACOM. 1993.

DuBrin, Andrew. *Your Own Worst Enemy: How to Overcome Career Self-Sabotage*. New York: AMACOM. 1992.

Dynerman, Susan, and Hayes, Lynn. *Best Jobs in America for Parents Who Want Careers and Time for Children Too*. New York: Ballantine. 1991.

Eisenberg, Abne M. *Job Talk: Communicating Effectively on the Job*. New York: Macmillan. 1979.

Elgin, Suzette. *More on the Gentle Art of Verbal Self-Defense*. Englewood Cliffs, N.J.: Prentice Hall. 1991.

Elgin, Suzette. *Success With the Gentle Art of Verbal Self-Defense*. Englewood Cliffs, N.J.: Prentice Hall. 1989.

Falke, Martha. *The First Four Seconds*. San Antonio, Texas: Falcon House Publishing. 1990.

Farr, J. Michael. *America's Top Resumes for America's Top Jobs.*™ Indianapolis: JIST Works, Inc. 1998.

Farr, J. Michael. *The Quick Interview & Salary Negotiation Book*. Indianapolis: JIST Works, Inc. 1995.

Farr, J. Michael. *The Quick Resumes & Cover Letter Book*. Indianapolis: JIST Works, Inc. 1994.

Farr, J. Michael. *The Right Job for You*. Indianapolis: JIST Works, Inc. 1997.

Farr, J. Michael. *The Very Quick Job Search*. Indianapolis: JIST Works, Inc. 1996.

Fassel, Diane. *Working Ourselves to Death: The High Cost of Workaholism and the Rewards of Recovery*. New York: HarperCollins. 1990.

Fast, Julius. *Subtext: Making Body Language Work in the Workplace*. New York: Viking. 1991.

Figler, Howard. *The Complete Job-Search Handbook*. New York: Henry Holt. 1988.

Fletcher, Winston. *Meetings, Meetings*. New York: William Morrow. 1984.

Freedman, Howard. *How to Get a Headhunter to Call*. New York: John Wiley & Sons. 1989.

Freund, James. *Smart Negotiating: How to Make Good Deals in the Real World*. New York: Simon & Schuster. 1992.

Fry, Ron. *101 Great Answers to Tough Interview Questions*. Hawthorne, N.J.: Career Press. 1994.

Garcia, Reloy, and Sitzman, Marion. *Successful Interviewing*. Lincolnwood, Ill.: National Textbook Co. 1981.

Gelinas, Paul. *Coping with Anger*. New York: Rosen Publishing Group. 1988.

Geiseking, Hal and Plawin, Paul. *30 Days to a Good Job*. New York: Simon & Schuster. 1994

Glazer, Myron, and Glazer, Penina. *The Whistleblowers: Exposing Corruption in Government and Industry*. New York: Basic Books. 1991.

Golant, Mitch, and Golant, Susan. *Finding Time for Fathering*. New York: Fawcett. 1992.

Gonyea, James. *The Online Job Search Companion*. New York: McGraw-Hill. 1994.

Gordon, Gil, and Kelly, Marcia. *Telecommuting: How to Make It Work for You and Your Company*. New York: Prentice Hall. 1986.

Half, Robert. *The Robert Half Way to Get Hired in Today's Job Market*. New York: Bantam. 1983.

Hamlin, Sonya. *How to Talk So People Listen: The Real Key to Business Success*. New York: HarperCollins. 1989.

Hardesty, Sarah, and Jacobs, Nehama. *Success and Betrayal*. New York: Franklin Watts. 1986.

Harragan, Betty Lehan. *Games Mother Never Taught You*. New York: Warner. 1989.

Heim, Pat, and Golant, Susan. *Hardball for Women: Winning at the Game of Business*. Los Angeles: Lowell House. 1992.

Hochheiser, Robert. *How to Work for a Jerk: Your Success Is the Best Revenge*. New York: Vintage. 1987.

Holtz, Herman. *Beyond the Résumé: How to Land the Job You Want*. New York: McGraw-Hill. 1984.

Jackson, Tom. *Guerrilla Tactics in the New Job Market*. New York: Bantam. 1993.

Jacobi, Ernst. *Writing at Work*. Berkeley, Calif.: Ten Speed Press. 1985.

Katz, Stan, and Liu, Aimee. *Success Trap*. New York: Dell. 1991.

Keil, John. *The Creativity Mystique*. New York: John Wiley & Sons. 1985.

Kennedy, Gavin. *Managing Negotiations*. Englewood Cliffs, N.J.: Prentice Hall. 1982.

Kennedy, Joyce Lain. *Electronic Job Search Revolution*. New York: John Wiley & Sons. 1994.

Kennedy. *Electronic Résumé Revolution*. New York: John Wiley & Sons. 1994.

Kieffer, George. *The Strategy of Meetings*. New York: Simon & Schuster. 1988.

King, Norman. *The First Five Minutes*. Englewood Cliffs, N.J.: Prentice Hall. 1987.

King, Patricia. *Never Work for a Jerk!* New York: Franklin Watts. 1987.

Koren, Leonard. *The Haggler's Handbook: One Hour to Negotiating Power*. New York: W.W. Norton. 1991.

Krannich, Ronald, and Banis, William. *High Impact Résumés and Letters*. Manassas Park, Va.: Impact Publications. 1992.

Krol, Ed. *The Whole Internet: User's Guide and Catalog*. Cambridge, Mass.: O'Reilly & Associates. 1992.

Kuselias, Chris. *The Career Coach*. North Haven, Conn.: Kuselias Enterprises.

Kushner, Malcolm. *The Light Touch: How to Use Humor for Business Success*. New York: Simon & Schuster. 1992.

Lacey, Dan. *Your Rights in the Workplace*. Berkeley, Calif.: Nolo Press. 1992.

Lacey, Julia. *How to Survive Your Computer Workstation*. Kerrville, Texas: CRT Services. 1997.

Levering, Robert. *A Great Place to Work*. New York: Random House. 1988.

Lorayne, Harry, and Lucas, Jerry. *The Memory Book*. New York: Ballantine. 1986.

Malburg, Chris. *How to Fire Your Boss*. New York: Berkley. 1991.

Magid, Renee Y. *When Mothers and Fathers Work*. New York: AMACOM. 1987.

Makay, John, and Fetzer, Ronald. *Business Communication Skills: Principles and Practice*. Englewood Cliffs, N.J.: Prentice Hall. 1984.

Marino, Kim. *The Résumé Guide for Women of the '90s*. Berkeley, Calif.: Ten Speed Press. 1992.

Martel, Myles. *The Persuasive Edge: The Executive's Guide to Speaking and Presenting*. New York: Fawcett. 1989.

Martin, Phyllis. *Martin's Magic Motivation Book: How to Become an Anointed One in Your Organization*. New York: St. Martin's Press. 1984.

Mattimore, Bryan. *99 Percent Inspiration: Tips, Tales, and Techniques for Liberating Your Business Creativity*. New York: AMACOM. 1993.

Mazzei, George. *The New Office Etiquette*. New York: Simon & Schuster/Poseidon. 1983.

McCormack, Mark H. *The 110 Percent Solution: Using Good Old American Know-How to Manage Your Time*. New York: Random House. 1991.

McCormack, Mark H. *What They Still Don't Teach You at Harvard Business School* (audiotape). New York: Bantam. 1989.

McGee-Cooper, Ann. *Time Management for Unmanageable People*. New York: Bantam. 1994.

McGee-Cooper, Ann. *You Don't Have to Go Home from Work Exhausted!* New York: Bantam. 1992.

Medley, H. Anthony. *Sweaty Palms*. Berkeley, Calif.: Ten Speed Press. 1992.

Metcalf, C.W., and Felible, Roma. *Lighten Up: Survival Skills for People Under Pressure*. Redding, Mass.: Addison-Wesley. 1993.

Miramontes, David. *How to Deal with Sexual Harassment*. San Diego: Network Communications. 1982.

Montgomery, Robert. *Effective Speaking for Managers* (audiotape program). Mt. Laurel, N.J.: Learn, Inc. 1984.

Morrison, Ann; White, Randall; Ven Velsor, Ellen; and the Center for Creative Leadership. *Breaking the Glass Ceiling: Can Women Reach the Top of America's Largest Corporations?* Redding, Mass.: Addison-Wesley. 1992.

National Society for Internships and Experiential Education. *The National Directory of Internships*. Raleigh, N.C.: National Society for Internships and Experiential Education. 1991.

O'Brien, Jack. *Kiplinger's Career Starter*. Washington, D.C.: Kiplinger. 1993.

Oechsli, Matt. *Winning the Inner Game of Selling*. Indianapolis: Rough Notes. 1991.

Olmsted, Barney, and Smith, Suzanne. *The Job Sharing Handbook*. Berkeley, Calif.: Ten Speed Press. 1985.

Parker, Yana. *The Damn Good Résumé Guide*. Berkeley, Calif.: Ten Speed Press. 1989.

Persons, Hal. *The How-To of Great Speaking: Stage Techniques to Tame Those Butterflies*. Austin, Texas: Black & Taylor. 1992.

Peter, Laurence, and Hull, Raymond. *The Peter Principle*. New York: Buccaneer. 1996.

Peter, Laurence. *The Peter Prescription*. New York: William Morrow. 1974.

Petty, Richard E., and Cacioppo, John T. *Attitudes and Persuasion: Classic and Contemporary Approaches*. Dubuque, Iowa: William C. Brown Communications. 1981.

Petty, Richard E., and Cacioppo, John T. *Communication and Persuasion*. New York: Springer-Verlag. 1986.

Petrocelli, William, and Repa, Barbara Kate. *Sexual Harassment on the Job*. Berkeley, Calif.: Nolo Press. 1992.

Powell, J. Robin. *The Working Woman's Guide to Managing Stress*. Englewood Cliffs, N.J.: Prentice Hall. 1994.

Quill Corp. *How to File and Find It*. Lincolnshire, Ill: Quill Corp.

Riskin, Robert. *Between Opportunities: A Survival Guide for Job Seekers and Career Changers*. St. Paul: Aar Dee Aar Publishing. 1992.

RoAne, Susan. *The Secrets of Savvy Networking: How to Make the Best Connections for Business and Personal Success*. New York: Warner. 1993.

Robbins, Harvey A. *How to Speak and Listen Effectively*. New York: AMACOM. 1992.

Rowan, Roy. *The Intuitive Manager*. New York: Berkley. 1991.

Saltzman, Amy. *Downshifting*. New York: HarperCollins. 1992.

Sarnoff, Dorothy. *Never Be Nervous Again: Time-Tested Techniques for the Foolproof Control*. New York: Ivy. 1989.

Scheele, Paul. *The PhotoReading Whole Mind System*. Wayzata, Minn.: Learning Strategies Corp. 1993.

Schmidt, Peggy. *Making It on Your First Job*. Princeton, N.J.: Peterson's Guides. 1991.

Schwartz, Lester and Brechner, Irv. *Career Tracks*. New York: Ballantine. 1985.

Sheehy, Gail. *Pathfinders*. New York: Bantam, 1997.

Sher, Barbara, and Gottlieb, Anne. *Wishcraft: How to Get What You Really Want*. New York: Ballantine. 1986.

Snyder, Elayne. *Persuasive Business Speaking*. New York: AMACOM. 1990.

Stanton, Timothy, and Ali, Kamil. *The Experienced Hand*. Cranston, R.I.: Carroll Press. 1987.

Stewart, Doug. *The Power of People Skills: A Manager's Guide to Assessing and Developing Your Organization's Greatest Resource*. Lanham, Md.: University Press of America. 1993.

Stuckey, Marty. *The Basics of Business Writing*. New York: AMACOM. 1992.

Sullivan, George. *Work Smart, Not Hard*. New York: Facts on File. 1987.

Sullivan, S. Adams. *The Father's Almanac*. New York: Doubleday. 1992.

Tannen, Deborah. *You Just Don't Understand: Women and Men in Conversation*. New York: Ballantine. 1991.

Tavris, Carol. *Anger: The Misunderstood Emotion*. New York: Simon & Schuster. 1989.

Thomsett, Michael. *The Little Black Book of Business Etiquette*. New York: AMACOM. 1991.

Tingley, Judith C. *Genderflex: Men and Women Speaking Each Other's Language at Work*. New York: AMACOM. 1994.

Tkac, Debora, ed. *Everyday Health Tips: 2,000 Practical Hints for Better Health and Happiness*. Emmaus, Penn.: Rodale. 1988.

Tracy, Brian. *The Psychology of Achievement* (audiotape program). Chicago: Nightingale Conant. 1987.

Urdang, Laurence. *The Dictionary of Confusable Words*. New York: Facts on File. 1988.

Von Oech, Roger. *A Whack on the Side of the Head*. New York: Warner. 1993.

Wagner, Ellen. *Sexual Harassment in the Workplace: How to Prevent, Investigate, and Resolve Problems in Your Organization*. New York: AMA-COM. 1992.

Weisberg, Anne, and Buckler, Carol. *Everything a Working Mother Needs to Know*. New York: Doubleday. 1994.

Weiss, Donald. *Conflict Resolution*. New York: AMACOM. 1993.

West, Ross. *How to Be Happier in the Job You Sometimes Can't Stand*. Nashville: Broadman and Holman. 1991.

Wilson, Susan. *Goal Setting*. New York: AMACOM. 1994.

Winston, Stephanie. *The Organized Executive*. New York: W.W. Norton. 1994.

Wisinski, Jerry. *Resolving Conflicts on the Job*. New York: AMACOM. 1993.

Wonder, Jacquelyn, and Donovan, Priscilla. *The Flexibility Factor*. New York: Ballantine. 1991.

Wurman, Richard. *Follow the Yellow Brick Road: Learning to Give, Take, and Use Instructions*. New York: Bantam. 1992.

Yate, Martin. *Knock 'Em Dead: The Ultimate Job Seekers' Handbook*. Holbrook, Mass.: Bob Adams. 1994.

Yate, Martin. *Résumés That Knock 'Em Dead*. Holbrook, Mass.: Bob Adams. 1988.

Yeomans, William. *1,000 Things You Never Learned in Business School: How to Manage Your Fast-Track Career*. New York: NAL-Dutton. 1990.

Index

About the Author

Paula Ancona specializes in helping people in all professions and at all levels improve their work lives.

She is vice president of Management Recruiters of Chanhassen, an executive search firm specializing in placing information systems and software development professionals.

Ancona also is a frequent speaker and workshop leader. She makes presentations on topics such as career management, time management, and balancing work and family before organizations such as Professional Secretaries International, Ceridian Corp., St. Paul Companies, and First Bank of Minneapolis.

From 1988 to 1996, Ancona researched hundreds of career and workplace topics for her popular and practical "Working Smarter" newspaper column. Scripps Howard News Service, Washington, D.C., distributed the column weekly to about 380 newspapers in 48 of the top 50 newspaper markets nationwide, including *The Arizona Republic, The San Jose Mercury News, The Cleveland Plain Dealer,* and *The New Haven Register.*Her column generated the most reprint requests of all Scripps Howard columns.

Ancona's work also has appeared in the Scripps Howard News magazine's, *Chicago Tribune,* and *Full-Time Dads: The Journal for Caring Fathers.* She is profiled in *Applied Human Relations: An Organizational Approach,* Fifth Edition, by Douglas A. Benton.

Previously she was a noted staff-development director and manager at *The Albuquerque Tribune (NM).* In 1990 she was awarded a Scripps Howard Total Quality award for her work conducting reader focus groups and helping *Tribune* staff members understand their readers better.

A Cleveland native, Ancona earned a bachelor of science degree from Bowling Green State University in Ohio. She and her husband have three children and live in Minneapolis.

Paula Ancona's "Working Smarter" column is distributed weekly by Scripps Howard News Service to about 380 newspapers in 48 of the top 50 markets. This is a partial list of the newspapers that publish or have published the column:

Birmingham Post-Herald, AL
Montgomery Advisor, AL
Anchorage Daily News, AK
Arizona Republic, Phoenix, AZ
Mesa Tribune, AZ
Daily Republic, Fairfield, CA
Daily Democrat, Woodland, CA
Highlander Weeklies, CA
News Chronicle, Thousand Oaks, CA
Outlook, Santa Monica, CA
Pasadena Star-News, CA
Press Telegram, Long Beach, CA
Redding Record Searchlight, CA
San Gabriel Valley Tribune, Covina, CA
San Jose Mercury News, CA
Valley News, Los Angeles, CA
Ventura County Star Free Press, CA
Whittier Daily News, CA
New Haven Register, CT
Waterbury Republican-American, CT
Naples Daily News, FL
St. Petersburg Times, FL
Stuart News, FL
Tallahassee Democrat, FL
Daily Sun, Warner Robins, GA
Marietta Daily Journal, GA
Valdosta Daily Times, GA
Post-Register, Idaho Falls, ID
Chicago Tribune, IL
Sauk Valley Sunday, Sterling, IL
Goshen News, IN
Kokomo Tribune, IN
South Bend Tribune, IN
Hutchinson News, KS
Middlesex News, Framingham, MA

Patriot Ledger, Quincy, MA
Carroll County Times, Westminster, MD
Journal Tribune, Biddeford, ME
The Detroit News, MI
Jackson Citizen Patriot, Jackson, MI
Mining Journal, Marquette, MI
Laurel Leader-Call, MS
Sun Herald, Biloxi, MS
Independence Examiner, MO
Jefferson, MO
Minneapolis Star Tribune, MN
Norfolk Daily News, NE
Las Vegas Sun, NV
Winston-Salem Journal, NC
Cincinnati Post, OH
Plain Dealer, Cleveland, OH
Lancaster Eagle Gazette, OH
Oklahoma City, OK
Bucks Co. Courier Times, Levittown, PA
Pittsburgh Post-Gazette, PA
Florence Morning News, SC
Desert News, Salt Lake City, UT
El Paso Herald Post, TX
San Antonio Express-News, TX
Sunday Facts, Clute, TX
Sun (Bremerton), WA
Capital Times, Madison, WI
Mason City Globe Gazette, WI
The Reporter, Fond Du Lac, WI
Sunday Post-Crescent (Appleton), WI
Ottawa Citizen, Ottawa, Canada
San Juan Morning Star, Puerto Rico

America's Top Resumes for America's Top Jobs™
381 Resumes for More Than 200 Jobs
By J. Michael Farr

The ONLY book with sample resumes for all major occupations covering 85 percent of the workforce!

Sample resumes for more than 200 major jobs! Nearly 400 of the best resumes submitted by members of the Professional Association of Resume Writers, grouped according to occupation and annotated by the author to highlight their best features—plus career planning and job search advice from Mike Farr.

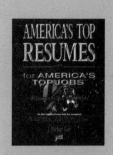

1-56370-288-6
$19.95

Tricks of the Trade
An Insider's Guide to Using a Stockbroker
By Mark Dempsey

How to Get the Best from Your Broker Without Your Broker Getting the Best of You

Millions of Americans who invest their money are at the mercy of full-service brokerage firms. What exactly are they paying for and how can they avoid costly mistakes? Our Wall Street insider presents the answers in a lively entertaining, informative style.

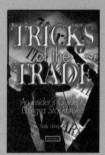

1-57112-084-X
$14.95

Be Your Own Business!
The Definitive Guide to Entrepreneurial Success
From the Editors of JIST Works, Inc.

Excellent descriptions of business alternatives for entrepreneurs—from franchises to consultants to independent contractors

Millions of Americans dream about starting their own businesses, but don't know where to begin. The information in *Be Your Own Business!* can help readers make all the right choices on their road to becoming successful entrepreneurs. A must for everyone considering starting a business!

1-57112-082-3
$16.95